The Consuming Geographies of Food

The consumption and distribution of food, as well as its production, has become a major policy issue over the past few decades; what we eat is no longer merely a private matter but carries significant externalities for wider society. Its increasing significance within the public arena implies a dissonance regarding the boundaries of food; where do we draw the line between food as private and food as public? What are the rights of society to impinge upon individual food consumption, and what conflicts will ensue when this boundary is disputed?

The Consuming Geographies of Food explores these multiple issues of food across different regions of the world from the consumer's perspective. It uniquely explicates the factors that lead customers towards certain typologies of consumption and towards certain types of retailing, offering a comprehensive review of the obesity problem, the phenomenon of food deserts and the issue of exclusion from a healthy diet. The book achieves this by firstly reviewing farming and associated innovations, technological and social. It then considers the effects of food on the consumer, the dynamic relationship between food and people and the issue of food exclusion before concluding with possible futures for food consumption, from low-technology projects to high-technology scenarios.

Based on original research into food access, ethics and consumption in both developed and less-developed countries this book will be of interest to students, researchers and academics in the fields of geography, economics, hospitality, health, marketing, nutrition and sociology.

Hillary J. Shaw is a Senior Research Fellow at the London School of Commerce and Managing Director of Shaw Food Solutions. His research interests include food security, sustainable development and food access. As well as leading a range of consultancy projects, he has been invited to speak at many international conferences and has published widely in the areas of food, health, diet and corporate social responsibility.

Routledge Studies of Gastronomy, Food and Drink
Series Editor: Michael Hall
University of Canterbury, New Zealand

This groundbreaking series focuses on cutting edge research on key topics and contemporary issues in the area of gastronomy, food and drink to reflect the growing interest in these as academic disciplines as well as food movements as part of economic and social development. The books in the series are interdisciplinary and international in scope, considering not only culture and history but also contemporary issues facing the food industry, such as security of supply chains. By doing so the series will appeal to researchers, academics and practitioners in the fields of gastronomy and food studies, as well as related disciplines such as tourism, hospitality, leisure, hotel management, cultural studies, anthropology, geography and marketing.

Published:

The Business of Champagne
A delicate balance
Steven Charters

Alternative Food Networks
David Goodman, Michael Goodman and Melanie DuPuis

Sustainable Culinary Systems
C. Michael Hall and Stefan Gossling

Wine and Identity
Edited by Matt Harvey, Warwick Frost and Leanne White

Social, Cultural and Economic Impacts of Wine in New Zealand
Peter Howland

The Consuming Geographies of Food
Diet, food deserts and obesity
Hillary J. Shaw

The Consuming Geographies of Food

Diet, food deserts and obesity

Hillary J. Shaw

Routledge
Taylor & Francis Group
LONDON AND NEW YORK

First published 2014
by Routledge
2 Park Square, Milton Park, Abingdon, Oxon OX14 4RN

and by Routledge
711 Third Avenue, New York, NY 10017

Routledge is an imprint of the Taylor & Francis Group, an informa business

British Library Cataloguing in Publication Data
A catalogue record for this book is available from the British Library

Library of Congress Cataloguing in Publication data
Shaw, Hillary J.
The consuming geographies of food: diet, food deserts and obesity / Hillary J. Shaw.
pages cm. – (Routledge studies of gastronomy, food and drink)
Includes bibliographical references and index.
1. Food consumption–Social aspects. 2. Food preferences–Social aspects. 3. Food habits–Social aspects. 4. Nutrition–Social aspects. 5. Diet–Social aspects. 6. Obesity–Social aspects. I. Title.
TX357.S46 2014
394.1′2–dc23
2013043560

ISBN: 978-0-415-81870-4 (hbk)
ISBN: 978-0-203-38780-1 (ebk)

Typeset in Times New Roman
by Out of House Publishing

MIX
Paper from responsible sources
FSC® C013604
www.fsc.org

Printed and bound by CPI Group (UK) Ltd, Croydon, CR0 4YY

For Julia, without whose desert safaris this book would not have been possible

Contents

Illustrations

Figure

Tables

Preface

We sometimes make strange choices when prioritizing our consumer spending. Ask people how they would choose an architect to design their home; would they choose the cheapest, or would they pick the best they could afford? Most will opt for the 'best' option; 'you are going to live in your home for years', as one respondent stated. Now consider food. The success story of the supermarkets, the abundance of cheap takeaways in every town centre and suburb, indicates we prioritize cheapness and ease of preparation over quality. Yet food is us, our bodies are made of food; 'you are what you eat' as the adage goes. You may live with a home extension for years, but you live with your body for a lifetime. We have become disengaged from our food, often seeing eating not as pleasurable but as a necessary refuelling routine. A consequence of this disengagement is the obesity epidemic in North America, Europe, the Middle East and Australasia, and even in developing countries such as Mexico, Brazil, India and China; countries once known more for famine than excess. This book explores the origins and reasons for our disengagement from food, from the beginning of farming to the morals of the modern consumer society. It examines why our biology and our psychology are ill-suited to convenience food, and concludes with a review of the options for a more sustainable diet; a diet that will maintain our individual health and an agri-food system that can feed not only the present world population of seven billion but the future anticipated population of ten billion.

The world faces two food crises, apparently opposite to one another but in fact closely related: the obesity epidemic and a crisis of sustainability of our food supplies. The Green Revolution of the 1960s achieved the unprecedented feat of making our food supplies grow faster than world population, even as global numbers of people were rising at the fastest rate in history. However, this cheap food has accentuated the obesity pandemic. Furthermore, the Green Revolution was predicated on cheap energy and abundant water; both these factors are becoming scarce and expensive. The concluding three chapters of *The Consuming Geographies of Food: diet, food deserts and obesity* explore how our diet can be made healthier and less obesogenic; these essential lifestyle changes will also contribute towards achieving a sustainable global food supply. The crucial questions are what changes are we prepared to make in our society and how big a role do we want technology to play in the food chain? As with food deserts and food access, the immediate issues of physical access and affordability are underpinned by deeper issues of economics, consumer psychology and lifestyle choices.

Abbreviations

ABC1	Wealthiest three classes in the UK's six-class social system
AOC	Appellation d'Origine Contrôlée
BMI	Body Mass Index
BSE	Bovine Spongiform Encephalitis
Cal	Calorie (1,000 calories)
CJD	Creutzfeld Jacob Disease
CSR	Corporate Social Responsibility
d	Old British penny, pre-1971 decimalization; 240d = £1
DDA	Disability Discrimination Act
DEFRA	Department for Environment, Food and Rural Affairs
EZ	Enterprise Zone
FFV	Fresh Fruit and Vegetables (not frozen or tinned)
FSA	Food Standards Agency
FV	Fruit and Vegetables (includes frozen and tinned)
GDA	Guideline Daily Allowance
GDP	Gross Domestic Product
GI	Glycaemic Index
GM	Genetically Modified
HFCS	High Fructose Corn Syrup
HFSS	High Fat Sugar Salt
HVO	Hydrogenated Vegetable Oil
KVI	Known Value Item
LIPT	Low Income Project Team
MJ	Megajoules
NHS	National Health Service. The national medical care provider in the UK
p	British penny (decimalized); 100p = £1
PDO	Product Designation of Origin
PRWORA	Personal Responsibility and Work Opportunity Reconciliation Act
RDA	Recommended Daily Amount
s	Old British shilling, pre-1971 decimalization, 20s = £1 (12d = 1s)

SES	Socio-Economic Status
SNAP	Supplemental Nutrition Assistance Program
UNESCO	United Nations Educational Scientific and Cultural Organization
USDA	United States Department of Agriculture
VAT	Value Added Tax. A form of sales tax in the UK
WHO	World Health Organization
WTO	World Trade Organization

1 Accelerate to impact

Man as innovator: from hunting to farming. *When tillage begins, other arts follow*

Homo sapiens has secured its place as the dominant species on Earth not by natural strength but by its ability to invent and make use of tools. This has enabled us to appropriate, according to Sundquist (2008), some 45 per cent of terrestrial biological net primary production (NPP) and a further 5–10 per cent of marine NPP, far more than any other species. NPP is defined as the total chemical energy captured by plants, principally by vascular plants on land and by algae in the oceans, minus the energy liberated by plant respiration. All our bodily energy comes directly or indirectly from plants; ultimately 'we are all grass'. Humans are not unique in using tools to enhance their food supply; primates and birds use sticks to dig for insects, rocks are widely used in the animal kingdom to break open food sources; and dolphins have been seen using conch shells to catch small fish. Learning to use new tools is also a trait not confined to humans. Elephants have been observed dropping large rocks onto electric fences to cut off the electricity (Poole, 1996). What distinguishes humans from other animals is the ability to improve tools over time; overcoming the limitations of mortality on such improvements, where acquired experience dies with the individual, by passing on the information gained from tool-use innovation, and ultimately to improve tool use to the point where tools can be used to produce other tools, a process known as technology. This process is accelerative because the more technology you have the more tools you can invent to advance technology yet further. Passing information, or technology, down the generations (across time) or down a river valley (across space) requires language; not just any language, and not even written language, but the capacity for abstract language. Many animals possess rudimentary language, to communicate and express warnings, attraction, dominance and other immediate needs; only humans have, so far as we know, the capacity for highly abstract thought. A bird can warn its companions of an intruding cat, but only so long as the offending feline is in sight of all birds. However, as Lorenz notes (1977: 160–1), if cats make no appearance for a whole generation of crows, there is no corvid form of the signifier 'k-a-t' to convey the concept of an absent yet existing soft furry four-legged animal with pointy ears, claws and sharp teeth that eats small birds. Only humans can pass abstract concepts such as 'otherwise', 'if' or 'probably' across time and space.

The point when man advanced from being a tool-user to a tool-innovator cannot be defined, but it probably was the transition from hunter-gathering to agriculture that began the process. Hunting requires a wide range of tools, from spears, blowpipes and nets to the construction of pits and fish traps, as well as a certain level of forward planning; driving animals into snares for example. However, agriculture, with its seasonal harvest times, its lumpy food outputs, demands a far more regulated and anticipated future and with it a more sophisticated programme of tool use to produce ever more specialized tools. Spears can be produced directly from stones or animal bones, and blowpipes from bamboo, but a horse-drawn iron plough requires several stages of production. Agriculture requires a high level of anticipatory abstract planning. Calendars are necessary to measure out and keep track of time, water storage and irrigation systems must be constructed in advance of any drought, and seed must be divided between that for consumption and that for saving and replanting for next year's harvest. Farmers can also accumulate possessions, whereas to hunter-gatherers excess baggage is an impediment to their mobility. Once material accumulation begins, luxuries are acquired, and an immobile lifestyle becomes virtually obligatory. The gauchos, cowboys of the Argentine pampas, eschew forks because if you use a fork then you need a plate, a table, a chair, then you are living in a house with a family; better to eat with your hands and remain mobile. The invention of cooking has also been argued to be crucial to mankind's progression. Cooking, demanding the taming of fire, breaks down molecules in the food to simpler, more easily digested forms. Cooking food makes digestion more efficient; without cooking, more nutrients are lost to gut bacteria and excretion. Cooking food means one can survive on less, or feed an energy-hungry brain; the brain accounts for over a quarter of the body's calorific requirements. Humans who cook their food can expand into food-poorer regions. Cooking sterilizes the food, killing parasites and reducing the disease burden. Cooking also softens the food; our brain judges the appeal of food not just on its taste but on its mouth-feel, its softness. With modern diets, replete with soft calorific processed foods, this feature has become a liability, encouraging us to eat unhealthily, although in prehistoric times it would have steered us towards juicy meat and away from chewy gristle. However, fire can be easily made and controlled; it demands little innovation, and even occurs naturally. Farming is what really set technology in progress.

Innovation: social and technological. *Build no more fortresses, build railways*

Accelerative innovation is social as well as technological. Hunter-gatherer communities tend towards a single dimensional division of society between men (hunters) and women (gatherers); in other respects the cooperation necessary to secure a successful kill produces a very egalitarian society. Farming, however, produces work specializations and class divisions. Trades such as plough-maker, guardsman, builder, fencer, woodcutter, accountant and administrator split off because specialists are more productive than generalists. Some farmers do better than others due to different skills and random weather events and social inequalities emerge. Specialization of trade requires an effective transport system, which links smaller communities into united regions, and roads transport armies just as they do goods, as the Roman Empire knew well. The famous Prussian field-marshal, Helmuth von Moltke, echoed this when he said 'Build no more fortresses, build railways.' Societies may resist this trend towards inequality: for example, the ancient Israelites had rules for avoiding concentration of land ownership. However, greed usually outweighs law and power elites are adept at changing norms and rules to legitimate any departure from ancestral customs. Roman law had the opposite effect to that of the ancient Israelites, tending towards concentration of land ownership. Under the Romans, abandoned land could be claimed by anyone (Seymour and Girardet, 1986: 59). Farms might be left untended because their proprietors died in war; only the Roman nobility possessed the resources to take up this land, using as labour the slaves garnered from these wars. Small family-owned farms were replaced by the *latifundia*; these ranged in size up to about 100 hectares, and were worked by landless labourers and slaves whose employment system laid the foundations for medieval serfdom.

Successful (or fortunate) farmers need employees; unlucky ones become landless labourers. Very good farmers control more of the food supply, perhaps ultimately the water supply through expanded land control and irrigation projects, and their eldest sons become absolute rulers of the valley kingdom. As with technology, social innovations beget more innovations; a standing army is raised to defend the granaries; the king acquires a coterie of courtiers; the rural shamans become priests and move in with the king to reinforce control of the peasants. The king's castle begets a walled town where traders gather, and urban life begins with all its luxuries and travails and complexities. Farming introduced profound social changes but mostly these changes were local or regional. Without fossil fuel-based bulk transport and away from the pre-industrial centres of civilization, communities largely practised subsistence agriculture. Surpluses from the peasants' labour enriched the local aristocracy until climate change, famine, pestilence or war with the next valley kingdom disrupted the archic order and reset to zero the agriculture-driven inequality mechanism. Even hunter-gatherer societies might develop a ruling elite and complex class system if the (uncultivated) food supply was plentiful. Ponting (1991: 31) describes a remarkably stratified non-farming society on the Pacific coast of North America where sea lions, otters and salmon supported a settled society. They lived in communities of around a thousand, with village chiefs, barter, food storage, even slaves. Their society endured until the arrival of an industrial people from a smaller continent far to the east. Even in the twenty-first century, hunter-gathering persists in the high Arctic, the remote African rain forests and a few isolated areas of Australia and India. Subsistence agriculture continues today in the less-developed regions of Africa. The key words are 'isolated' and 'less developed'; most of the world has been transformed from some imagined pristine garden into an interconnected agrisystem; transformed not merely biologically, but also societally and technologically. Farming also set us on the road to domesticating animals, not just keeping them as a food source but using them for other purposes too. Dogs would have been useful for herding cows as well as being living burglar alarms, and horses have many uses in warfare; cats were deified by the Egyptians because they preserved grain stocks from rats. Our millennia-old pet-keeping habit is less useful today when meat is becoming more expensive to produce.

Hunter-gatherer societies may have been (almost) rural, ruler-free and egalitarian but they were no Garden of Eden. Rising human populations forced many species into extinction, starting with the big slow-breeding lumberers and working down the size range (and up the breeding-speed range) leaving only those animals whose reproductive rates exceeded humanity's capabilities to catch them. The work hours necessary to acquire enough food rose steadily, and were increased further by the need to fend off raids from hungry neighbours. And that was alongside the change to a colder drier climate, the Younger Dryas period (estimated at around 12,000 years ago) that reduced the availability of both plant and animal biomass. Someone somewhere saw the need to cultivate and nurture a vegetable garden, to fence in and preserve some animals to ensure future supplies of food, milk and clothing, before the last gazelle was caught, the last rabbit snared and the last berry bush died in the drought; and so farming was born. Once farming began there was no turning back, because farming supports a far greater density of people than hunter-gathering. A maximum population density for hunter-gatherer populations is reckoned to be about one hunter per 26 km^2 (Simmons, 1996: 43), but as low as one hunter per 250 km^2 in the Australian desert. On that basis, Europe could support no more than 400,000 hunters, rather than the 40–60 million people who lived there during the Middle Ages. Farming, once established, continually erodes the possibility of hunter-gathering. Farmers, with their state and legally backed land claims, appropriate the most productive lands, pushing any remaining hunters on to marginal lands. Such land will only support a low population density, denying the accumulation of any wealth or power, and the way is opened to label hunter-gatherer societies as 'poor' and 'primitive'. Another mobile lifestyle feared and therefore despised by farmers is transhumance, the transfer of grazing animals between summer and winter pastures, as mobile animals may graze on fixed crops en route. The Turkish novel *The Legend of the Thousand Bulls* tells of the conflict between the Turcoman Yoruk tribe and the Ottoman government. The Yoruks, whose name may derive from 'yurumek', a Turkish word meaning 'to walk', traditionally transferred their grazing animals between the Cukurova Plains in winter and the Aladag Valley in summer; but the Ottomans developed the Cukurova as irrigated croplands. Settling the Yoruks also facilitated their registration for tax and military conscription. Ultimately this conflict between fixed and mobile lifestyles leads us to our modern urban architecture of fear, cities of little fortresses where the intervening spaces are rendered 'slippery', 'prickly' or 'jittery'; spaces rendered unusable by the new urban nobility in deliberate action against the loitering mobility, through inaccessibility, defence or surveillance (Bauman, 2011: 63). The immobile becomes increasingly frightened of the mobile and seeks to control it, to render it immobile, accountable, taxable.

Increasing size of farms worldwide. *O give me land lots of land under starry skies above, don't fence me in*

The size of the world's largest farms today would be as inconceivable to those first farmers in the Fertile Crescent, the Indus Valley or China as would the mechanized transport needed to operate them. The world's largest landholding in Australia, Anna Creek Station, totals 24,000 square kilometres; this equates to 1.15 times the size of Wales, or about one Vermont. In 1960 the World Census of Agriculture reported that agricultural holdings with over 500 acres (200 hectares) comprised less than 1 per cent of farms by number but occupied two-thirds of the world's farmland; agricultural holdings of under 12 acres (five hectares) accounted for 79 per cent of the world's farms but occupied just 7 per cent of the world's farmland (Buchanan, 1982: 56). The economies of scale gained by these large farms are in response to consumer pressure for lower food prices, irresistibly and tightly focused by the supermarket chains. Supermarkets compete primarily on price, and have become the biggest players in the food chain. Wal-Mart regularly features near the top of the world's largest corporations list, with giants like Tesco and Carrefour close behind. Not only has the share of consumer expenditure taken by food fallen markedly in the USA and other countries, from around 30 per cent in 1940 to 12 per cent in 1990, but over this same period the share of that food expenditure actually reaching the farmer has fallen from 38 per cent to 17 per cent (Lappe et al., 1998: 73). In other words, farmers in 1940 received 11.4 per cent of US consumer spending; in 1990 they got 2 per cent, and the farmer of 1990 spent more on equipment, chemicals and loans than his or her 1940 counterpart. The issue of consumers reducing their expenditure on food is discussed further in Chapter 6. The effects of this pressure on the agricultural sector have been dramatic. Agricultural employment has plummeted as big farms have become more mechanized. The falling price of food, relative to inputs such as tractors, oil and wages, means that small fragmented holdings can no longer support a family. Buchanan (1982: 36) reports that in 1960 three tons of bananas would buy a tractor; in 1970 it took 11 tons. The minimum profitable size for an agricultural holding rises relentlessly. However, large farms may be less productive per hectare,

Table 1.1 Percentage of workforce employed in agriculture, 1800–2000, for France, UK and USA

Year	*France*	*UK*	*USA*
1800	55	38	83
1850	49	20	52
1900	42	10	35
1950	25	7	13
2000	4	1	2

Sources: *The Statesman's Yearbook*, various years.

because they focus on productivity per worker, whereas smaller ones look at productivity per hectare. Large farms are more likely to own significant tracts of idle unproductive farmland; in Brazil, 42.6 per cent of all agricultural land lies uncultivated, but this rises to 88.7 per cent of land forming part of the largest landholdings, of 1,000 hectares or more (Lappe et al., 1998: 47). In Africa, by 1970 2.69 million hectares of Kenya's best agricultural land was occupied by just 3,175 farms of an average farm size of 8.5 km^2, leaving just 2.65 million hectares of agricultural land for Kenya's 777,000 smallholders (an average size of 0.34 km^2) (Harrison, 1990: 75). In Brazil the smallest 30.4 per cent of farms, of size 10 hectares or less, occupy just 1.5 per cent of Brazil's agricultural land; meanwhile the country's largest farms, of size 1,000 hectares of more, account for just 1.6 per cent of all farms but account for 53.2 per cent of Brazil's agricultural land (Langevin and Rosset, 1999: 326). Perhaps the ultimate land concentration process has been reached in the Dominican Republic, where 0.07 per cent of the population owns 45 per cent of the arable land, and over 10 per cent of rural families have no land at all (George, 1999: 215). The global North has also seen major concentration of farm ownership and declining agricultural employment; Table 1.1 shows the declining percentage of the workforce employed in agriculture for three developed countries, 1800 to 2000.

From 1871 the share of UK GDP originating from agriculture fell from 20 per cent to 6.8 per cent in 1931 and to 1.3 per cent today (Self and Storing, 1971: 17). The number of full-time farmers in the UK fell from 500,000 in 1939 to just 152,000 in 2009, while the average size of their farms rose from 63 acres (25 hectares) in 1908 to 140 acres (57 hectares) in 2009 (Madeley, 2002: 15). By 2000 the largest 14 per cent of UK farms, of size 250 acres (100 hectares) or over, accounted for 65 per cent of the agricultural area of Britain. Even France, with its strong peasant agricultural tradition, has seen a trend towards fewer larger farms. Between 1970 and 2020 the number of French farms fell from 1,600,000 to 490,000, the average size of those farms increasing from 19 to 42 hectares. Similar trends have occurred in the USA and Canada, with farm numbers in America falling from 7 million in the 1930s to under 3 million in the 1980s. Statistics for American and Canadian farms are given in Table 1.2.

Table 1.2 Farm data for the USA and Canada

Year	*No. of farms (USA)*	*Average size (acres) (USA)*	*No. of farms (Canada)*	*Average size (acres) (Canada)*
1900	6,000,000	150		
1930	6,800,000	170	700,000	200
1950	5,600,000	210	600,000	250
1970	2,900,000	370	420,000	400
1990	2,100,000	460	229,000	728
2010	2,200,000	440	205,730	780

(1 hectare = 2.47 acres)

Sources: Lang and Heasman (2004: 150); Seitz and Hite (2012: 86).

Farming has become more efficient, more mechanized, more productive, but in the process we have lost a crucial connection between ourselves and our food and the land that it grows from. We have become severed from our almost-literal roots. Relph (1986: 32) cites the persistence of a Vietnamese woman maintaining her farm in the middle of a war zone; she said 'This is the land of my ancestors, so I couldn't leave.' In the more developed world, by contrast, we have become divorced from the means of production of our food, as Marx (almost) said. In many industrialized countries, less than one worker in 50 is now employed in agriculture. We can distinguish four stages by which Western society has divorced itself from its most basic requirement, the need to feed itself. These can be categorized as:

1. Industrialization
   Stage 1 was the separation of our employment from the land. The Industrial Revolution, which began in the UK just before 1800 and rapidly spread to the rest of Europe and North America, took workers off the land and into cities. Here, as shown in Chapter 4, they were left subject to all manner of hideous food abuses and adulterations; and many of these bad food practices persist today.
2. Globalization
   Stage 2 was the separation by distance from our food; late nineteenth-century innovations such as refrigerated ships and the spread of railways worldwide allowed Europeans and North Americans to source their meat from Argentina, their rice from Asia, their sugar from the Caribbean and their fruit from Africa. The foods we ate were no longer restricted by, and therefore unrelated to, the region or season we found ourselves inhabiting; our food might as well come from another planet.
3. Supermarketization
   Stage 3 was the separation of the consumer from the local food chain, as car ownership became widespread in the twentieth century, first in America and then in Europe. This facilitated the development of out-of-town

malls and supermarkets, and in our relentless quest for cheapness through bulk, we traded away the accountability of the food chain that often came with small local grocers and butchers.

4. Dromology
   Stage 4 has been the separation of the consumer from the recognizability of the food they actually consume. Fast lifestyles, 'deskfasting', microwave meals, eating 'on the hoof', snacking, convenience foods; we now have a dromology of food that has left us fuelling up on fare that our grandparents would scarcely have recognized as edible, on fodder whose ingredients cannot be accurately guessed even by the most expert chef, although an industrial chemist might have a fair chance of understanding them.

Now, like a lonely divorcee, we miss the companionship of food we can actually relate to, and, partly by choice, partly by force, we may yet return to a more accountable, more recognizable food system. We need to ensure that this is also a healthy, equitable and sustainable food system.

The shift to agriculture gave us cities, and the political and military systems associated with them; the limitations of agriculture can destroy these cities. Geometry dictates that a pre-industrial city whose population doubles will on average have to increase its food miles by 41 per cent. In practice the distance this city needs to transport food will increase by more. Cities tend to be founded in fertile areas; as the crops are harvested further out, more infertile land will be encountered. Meanwhile peri-urban development tends towards lower densities, so doubling the population increases the urban radius by over 41 per cent. Over time, the fertility of the longest-exploited farmland, close to the city, declines, thus exacerbating the transport problem. Cities flush the fertility of their farmland down their sewers and into the sea. Food transit times increase as even pre-industrial cities suffered traffic congestion, and animal-powered transport consumes more food in transit. Rome, with its 1 million inhabitants, came to rely on grain harvested from North Africa and from Europe far beyond the Alps. The Romans needed ever more military protection for their lengthening food chains, a mercenary-based protection that was doomed to failure. A key point in the Roman Empire's decline was the loss of North Africa's fertile wheat fields and olive groves to the Vandals in AD 429. North Africa had supplied two-thirds of the 750,000 tons of grain annually consumed by Rome in 100 AD (Seymour and Girardet, 1986: 58). The economic effect on Rome was similar to how the West would have fared if, in 1991, Saddam Hussein had seized the oilfields not just of Kuwait but of Saudi Arabia too. Our intensive farming, reliant on oil and other non-renewable inputs, has not yet endured as long as the Roman Empire. Although we are efficient at extracting ever more cheap Calories from our farmland, the food we now produce may be less healthy than the underclass of Rome enjoyed from their North African fields.

Agricultural innovations. *O for a horse with wings*

Agriculture has come a long way since the first wild grains were harvested and stored, which according to the archaeologists was around 9000 BC. By 3000 BC the Nile waters were dammed and regulated, a process that reinforced social inequalities in ancient Egypt, empowering the engineers, the priests and the ruling landowning elite. The horse collar, invented in China, became widespread in Europe by around 900 AD, and by making the transmission of horsepower much more efficient, facilitated the ploughing of heavy wet clay lands. In Europe, the food supply was augmented by the potato, imported from South America in the 1600s. The 1700s saw the Agricultural Revolution in England, preceding the better-known Industrial Revolution. In 1701 Jethro Tull pioneered the seed drill, and new ploughing techniques along with the adoption of crop rotation further enhanced agricultural productivity. The 1800s saw an increase in artificial chemical inputs to agriculture, starting with imports of nitrates for fertilizer from South America, which provoked a war between Chile, Peru and Bolivia. In 1910 the Haber-Bosch method of producing ammonium nitrate was discovered by two German chemists, raising the limits of plant productivity. The Haber-Bosch process went into commercial production in 1913, just in time for the military to use it to produce the megatons of explosives to be used during World War One. Use of nitrogen fertilizer rose rapidly, reaching 2 million tons worldwide in 1940 and 75 million tons in 1995, and consuming considerable quantities of fossil fuels in its production and transport. Fossil-fuel inputs to agriculture began with the steam-powered plough in the 1860s, and the petrol-powered plough, used in the USA from 1892. Farm mechanization proceeded rapidly with the tractor population of the USA growing from 250,000 in 1920 to 600,000 in 1927, 2.3 million in 1945 and 4.8 million in 1958 (Evans, 1989: 117). Over this period the number of horses on US farms fell from 27 million to 3 million. The combine harvester appeared in the USA in the 1920s, but Denmark had no combine harvesters until after 1945; by 1969 it had over 40,000 of them. Cows were not immune to mechanization; whereas in 1945 only 3 per cent of European cows had been milked by machine, in the 1980s only 3 per cent were not milked by machine (Ponting, 1991: 246). Meanwhile the mechanization of agriculture reached the poorer parts of the world, with India's tractor population rising from 66,000 in 1967 to 215,000 in 1975 and Pakistan's similarly rising from 12,500 to 38,000 over this period (Harrison, 1990: 99). Today (2013) India has over 4 million tractors, Pakistan 320,000.

The biologists had their input too, with Gregor Mendel's experiments in plant breeding during the 1850s paving the way for the discovery of DNA in 1953 by Watson and Crick. This led on to the 1960s Green Revolution, when biologists joined with chemists and engineers to vastly increase world food output. Selective breeding gave us lodge-resistant dwarf grain where more nutrients went to make edible seeds, not stalk. By the 1980s selective breeding had gone as far as it could with the genes nature provided, but from the 1990s onwards the genes themselves could be altered, a controversial technique known as Genetic Modification. There are environmental concerns over non-renewable resources such as fossil fuels and ground water. However, despite global population growing at an unprecedented rate of 1 billion more people every 13 years, food output per capita actually rose. The world received a wake-up call in 2008 when crude oil prices soared to US$100 per barrel, having been (in 2008 prices) at US$20 or less from 1880 through to 1970, and again in 2000. Food prices also sharply increased, driven upwards by droughts in major grain-producing areas, food commodity speculation, and diversion of land into biofuel production. Longer-term threats to the global food supply included the shift from grain to meat-based diets in developing countries like China, climate change, shortages of oil and water and the loss of farmland to urbanization. The Green Revolution had given the world as a whole an assured food supply, albeit not always equitably distributed, but 40 years on, questions were again being asked as to whether a global population of 7 billion now, 10 billion in the future, could feed itself. This issue is further explored in Chapter 8 of this book.

More food in the world, but not where it's needed. *Feed me, I'm fat*

Global food production in 2013 uses technologies that would have been inconceivable to farmers even in 1900. The primary result has been a significant increase in per capita food availability, despite an unprecedented growth in world population since 1900. At the start of the twentieth century there were 1.6 billion people on Earth; it had taken 150 years to double our population from 0.8 billion in 1750. The next doubling, to 3.2 billion, took a little over six decades, and the next doubling after that, to 6.4 billion, took just over 40 years, to 2005. The 7 billion mark was reached in 2011, as humanity grew in numbers by 1 billion every 13 years. Population growth is now slowing, due to a rapid fall in the fertility rate. In Iran the fertility rate fell from 7.0 in the late 1960s to 1.8 in 2011. The replacement rate is reckoned as 2.1, and many countries now have fertility rates below the crucial 2.1 figure, including parts of South America, the Caribbean and Southern Asia, where birth rates have been historically high. The global fertility rate has fallen from 5.0 in the 1950s to 2.5 in 2010. Population growth will increasingly be driven by longer life expectancies rather than high fertility rates. Thomas Malthus (1766–1834) would have been as astonished at this development as he would have been at the technology now used to produce our food. Malthus expected population growth at an exponential rate, outstripping increases in agricultural output, producing famines and taking the human population back below the maximum sustainable capacity; exponential growth would then resume and the cycle would endlessly repeat. Malthus did not foresee the 'demographic transition' that occurs as countries become more prosperous. As GDP rises, as female literacy rises and well-paid urban careers beckon, as life expectancies rise but pensions replace large families as the principal means to avoid destitution in old age, women choose to have fewer children, as few as one or less on average in many nations today. Most demographers now expect world population to peak at around 10 billion in 2050 and then slowly fall.

Malthus also did not foresee the great increase in global food production from the 1950s. Global annual cereal production rose from 900 million tons in 1960 to 2,250 million tons in 2005; over this period global population rose from 3.03 billion to 6.70 billion, meaning that per capita grain production rose 13 per cent. For all foodstuffs, per capita availability reportedly rose by 20 per cent over this time span (Dryzek and Schlosberg, 2003: 56). Morris et al. (2003: 163) cite a global per capita food production increase of 27 per cent between 1961 and 2000. In terms of Calories, world agriculture produced 17 per cent more Calories per capita in 1998 than in 1965. The prices of staple foods fell by 55 per cent over those 33 years (Food Ethics Council, 2010: 35). In India, a country whose population has grown from 435 million in 1960 to 1,100 million in 2006, the gains in per capita food production are even more striking. Between 1960 and 2006 annual Indian rice production rose from 10 million tons to 73 million tons, a per capita gain of 190 per cent. India's wheat production rose, over the same period, from 50 million tons to 125 million tons. India in 2011 consumed 220 million tons of grain, but produced 245 million tons of it; China, another country whose population has risen sharply since the 1960s, also produces more grain than it needs. Yet in 2012, 1 billion people, a seventh of the world's population, are malnourished; they consume enough Calories daily for survival but lack sufficient micronutrients for long-term health. A further 900 million are even worse off; they are undernourished, lacking even the daily Calories they need. Those 1.9 billion underfed people share the planet with 1.6 billion people who are overweight, and a further 0.4 billion who are obese. However, the numbers at risk of starvation are falling; the numbers of obese are growing. In the 1950s there were fewer than 100 million overweight or obese people, but by 1995 that had doubled to 200 million obese adults worldwide. By 2015 the World Health Organization predicts there may be 0.7 billion who are obese, alongside 1.6 billion overweight (Paarlberg, 2010: 81). In 2010, the annual global death toll from starvation fell below 1 million, but 3 million died from obesity in that year (Horton, 2012).

In the USA, average daily calorie consumption rose from an already-excessive 3,100 in 1970 to 3,900 in 2000, contributing to that nation's current adult obesity rates of 35 per cent. Globally, enough food is being produced but much of it rots, or even more obscenely is discarded in an edible state, before it reaches any consumer. And what is consumed is being eaten by the wrong people, by people already overfed rather than the hungry. Malthusian food shortage has mutated into Sen's economic famine. Amartya Sen, an Indian economist, notes that 'available' does not mean 'affordable', and the poor can starve in the face of plenty if they lack the money to buy this food. The 1845 Irish potato famine provides an example of this; in 1845 Ireland

Table 1.3 Comparison of global growth in food production and food trade, 1968–98

Commodity	*% increase in production*	*% increase in international trade*
Cereals	76.9	155.6
Vegetables	148.9	337.9
Vegetable oil	244.8	621.6
Fruit	92.5	272.9
Meat	134.6	310.7
Milk	43.0	172.4

Source: Adapted from Madeley (2002).

was exporting maize to Britain where consumers had greater buying power (Madeley 2002: 12). The demand for meat, dairy products, wool and grain by urban dwellers of North America, the UK, continental Europe, created what have been termed 'empires of grass' in the prairies of North and South America, Australasia and later in Russia (Pawson, 2008: 229), while the indigenous peoples of those areas often became impoverished and hungry. The global flow of food from poor-hungry to wealthy-satiated was greatly facilitated by major falls in transport costs as marine technology improved. The cost of shipping wheat from New York to Liverpool, was 4s 17½d (24p) per quarter ton in 1860s but fell to 11½d (5p) in 1902 (Collingham, 2011: 19). Today containerization has cut transport costs even further; loading loose cargo onto a ship at a US port cost US$5.86 per ton in 1956; in 2006 it cost 16 cents per ton (Davies, 2006: 6). With the largest container ships able to transport 16,000 standard 20-foot containers, and one container able to hold 48,000 bananas, one ship can now transport 768 million bananas; enough to give one banana to every person in Europe. Food is abundant when you can afford it and transport is cheap.

The world faces a crisis, not of food production but of food security. The World Food Summit, 1996, defined food security as 'when all people, at all times, have physical and economic access to sufficient, safe and nutritious food to meet their dietary needs and food preferences for an active and healthy life'. When transport is cheap those producing food in poverty-stricken famine areas will always prefer to sell that food in distant prosperous regions. Madeley (2002: 116) notes that, between 1968 and 1998, world population rose by 64 per cent but that production of six basic agricultural commodities has (excepting milk) risen by in excess of that amount (Table 1.3). However, the increase in quantity traded of these six commodities has without exception exceeded the increase in production; these commodities have become far more mobile than they were in 1968. The increased mobility of world goods, including basic foodstuffs, is likely to exacerbate the centripetal tendency of such goods towards the world's well-fed and wealthy.

The world's adequately fed, and overfed, may feel insulated from the diseases of food shortages, the swollen belly of kwashiorkor, the bowed legs of rickets, the dulled eyes and retarded development of famine. The 120 million children in Africa and Southern Asia at risk of blindness from vitamin A deficiency seem to be on a different planet to the bustling aisles of Wal-Mart or Waitrose. However, the rise of obesity and its concomitant diseases, from diabetes to depression, threatens to overwhelm health budgets across the developed world and beyond. The next section explicates the transition the wealthy world has made, or been persuaded to make, between diseases of food shortage, or 'food-production' diseases, and diseases of overeating, or 'food-consumption' diseases.

Food is faster, cheaper, but not better. *If you buy cheap meat you will smell what you have saved when it boils*

Since the Green Revolution of the 1960s, food has become more abundant, especially for the wealthier global North, and in accord with the laws of supply and demand, food has also become cheaper in real (inflation-adjusted) terms. In the USA the price of wheat has fallen by around 50 per cent against the consumer price index, and by an astonishing 96 per cent against wages, over the past 200 years (Dryzek and Schlosberg, 2003: 57). In the UK the real price of food fell by 31 per cent between 1975 and 2000 (London Development Agency, 2005: 32). This decline in food price has given the world's urban classes, and especially the urban elite in the developed world, not just a food surplus but new foods; faster, easier, softer, tastier, more sugary, brighter-coloured, foods. These new foods, however, are often poor in terms of health benefits. The more processed and easier to handle, cook and eat our food is, the less good it seems to be for our bodies. In nutrition terms we face a dilemma similar to that faced by NASA, the space exploration agency of the USA. In the 1990s NASA was preparing for the Pathfinder Mission to Mars, and NASA's chief engineer, Rob Manning, was interviewed by Doug Cohen of ASK (Academy Sharing Knowledge). An extract of this interview is reproduced below (Cohen, 2007):

MANNING: 'In late '92 or early '93, Brian Muirhead, the flight systems spacecraft manager of Mars Pathfinder, said, "I need a chief engineer who can deal with the software and electronics of this mission, because we're doing new things." Brian and Tony Spear, the Pathfinder project manager, were able to pull together a very young and energetic team peppered with old, wise people. Mars Pathfinder was among the first of the faster, better, cheaper missions. We modified the old way of doing business, trying to streamline it to make it faster and cheaper.'

COHEN: 'It's hard to do more than two of "faster, better, cheaper".'

MANNING: 'The trouble is, you need all three.'

To paraphrase Rob Manning, food can be faster (i.e. more convenient), cheaper, better (i.e. healthier); you can have any two of these, but you need all three.

Societies shifting from hunter-gathering to farming traded high mortality, low morbidity and low numbers for lower mortality but higher morbidity and hugely increased numbers. Farmers were shorter, sicker and more worn out that their hunter-gatherer ancestors had been; shifting to farming caused the average height of people to shrink by 15 centimetres. New diseases were caught from animals: smallpox, tuberculosis and measles from cattle, flu from birds and pigs, leprosy from water buffalo and worms from manure spread as fertilizer. Muscle and skeleton were worn down by constant hard labour, and teeth eroded by chewing on grain rather than meat; repetitive tasks such as grinding corn caused arthritis. Calorie production rose to meet the energy needs of a growing population, but the proportion of protein and vitamins in the diet fell. In a hunter-gatherer society, you were fit, or you died; farming meant you survived, but lower mortality coexisted with increased morbidity. The ailments mankind acquired through his transition to farming, such as measles, worms and rickets, include both communicable and non-communicable diseases. These illnesses may be termed 'food-production' diseases because they are associated with the way we produce food; although some are caught through consuming food (measles and worms for example), no one sets out to consume food in a way that will give them such medical problems. However, many eagerly consume food with too much fat, sugar or salt, despite being aware of the health risks. This food, unlike worm-ridden meat, is unhealthy only if consumed in excessive amounts. Therefore one may term the non-communicable diseases associated with the modern, Western, highly processed, obesogenic diet, such as diabetes, coronary vascular diseases and many kinds of cancers, diseases of food consumption. We no longer wear our teeth down on gritty grains, but we suffer dental caries from excessive sugar. The grinding stomach pangs of hunger have been replaced by intestinal cancers, while lack of fibre and inactive lifestyles predispose us to piles and colon cancer. Our bones no longer buckle under rickets, but our joints labour under arthritis exacerbated by obesity. Vitamin deficiencies no longer plague our bodies, but type 2 diabetes attacks our limbs and eyes while fat clogs our circulatory systems. The old food-consumption diseases were often killers; the new ones are more likely to be cripplers, demanding long-term costly medical interventions, leading to concerns about how we will fund rising health costs in those countries fortunate enough to have well-developed healthcare systems.

We produce more food, more cheaply, but often the nutritional quality of that food is lower. An early example of this in England is provided by the enclosure process, whereby common land was appropriated by landowners and converted into hedged fields where animals could be privately reared for sale. The enclosure process in England arguably began with the Statute of Merton in 1235 and gathered pace during the eighteenth century. Cows could then be fed a high-energy grain diet and because they got less exercise they put on weight and therefore sold for more at market; however, this meat was fattier. Fat enhances the taste so the beef from these 'enclosed' cows was tastier, but it was scarcely healthier for the consumer. A similar change has occurred in chicken farming. In 1940 the UK government's food composition tables listed chicken as 10.3 g fat and 26.2 g protein, a ratio of Calories from fat and from protein of 92.7 to 104.8 (Crawford, 2005: 28). In 2005 the Food Standards Agency listed chicken as containing 23 g fat and 16 g protein; giving a ratio of 64 Calories from protein to 207 from fat. Dr Crawford, at the Institute of Brain Chemistry and Human Nutrition, analysed chicken thighs from a local organic farm shop and found 154 Calories from fat to 74 from protein. Consumers may perceive chicken as a lean, healthy meat; but compared to 1940 people must consume two or three times the amount of fat to get the same amount of protein. Chickens are often reared in high-density environments, and like the cattle grazing in the enclosed fields of the 1700s, they get little opportunity for exercise and the chickens are similarly fed high-energy foods to promote weight gain. As we have become disengaged from our food we also disconnect this food from its animal origins. We see the cuddliness and cuteness of farm animals on children's farms as almost pet-like on the one hand; on the other hand we almost deny that such animals exist as living beings on food-producing farms, transforming them into inanimate machines or commodities, to be efficiently processed for human consumption at the lowest cost.

Not only has meat become fattier, but the level of essential micronutrients, vitamins and minerals in our food has declined. One estimate is that the levels of these nutrients have fallen 'by up to 76 per cent' (London Development Agency, 2005: 20). Intensive farming methods aim to convert sunlight, water, carbon dioxide, and nitrogen into edible Calories as quickly and efficiently as possible, without regard for the minerals these foods are also supposed to contain. Milk, for example, contains fewer micronutrients because today's cows yield milk at five or six times the level of their 1940s counterparts; the cows eat less wild clover and grass, but more cereal and soya that was itself intensively produced. Table 1.4 shows the change in mineral levels in various foods (Heaton, 2001).

Changing the diet of cows from grass to grain and soya raises another human nutrition issue; this shift raises the Omega-6 levels relative to Omega-3 levels in beef. Grass-fed cows have more Omega-3. Omega-3 and -6 are fatty acids with opposite effects on the human immune system. Omega-3 suppresses inflammation whereas Omega-6 excites the immune system. Enhancement of inflammation, an immune response, is implicated in promoting cancer and asthma. Many European and North American children live in hyper-clean homes where there is little risk of infection, an environment that may be to blame for auto-immune diseases such as asthma, because the juvenile immune system needs some pathogens to act against to develop properly. The higher risk of auto-immune diseases

Table 1.4 Decline in mineral levels per food item, 1940–2000

Food	*Magnesium*	*Calcium*	*Iron*
Parmesan	–70%		–90%
Stilton	–45%	–10%	–57%
Cheddar	–38%	–9%	–47%
Milk	–21%	–2%	–62%
Beef rump steak	–7%	–4%	–55%
Streaky bacon	–16%	–87%	–78%
Turkey	–4%	–71%	–79%

Source: Adapted from Heaton (2001).

means we need more immune-/inflammation-suppressing Omega-3, not the immune-stimulating Omega-6. A further source of nutrient loss is lengthening food chains, combined with poor storage and handling of food. Cut vegetables may be left for hours exposed to air and sunlight, or stored at the wrong temperature, and vitamin levels decline. Our obsession with cheap food means we have outsourced the growing, cutting and packing of vegetables to cheaper-labour countries, and the food has a longer journey to the UK consumer. Data from the Consumers' Association (2004), given in Table 1.5, shows a considerable drop in vitamin C levels in supermarket vegetables that have travelled long distances, compared with the 'textbook figure' for freshly harvested vegetables. However, in some cases vitamin C levels have been artificially raised due to the use of chemically similar citric acid as a preservative.

If the quality of our meat and the micronutrient content of our fruit and vegetables has declined, there is one food that was never very good for our health, but has become almost ubiquitous in our diet. This food, once known as 'white gold' because of its rarity and therefore costliness, is now much more common and much cheaper, and has played a major role in our society and economy. We now look at the history of that 'white gold': sugar.

The rise in sugar consumption. *Sugar and spice and all things nasty*

Sugar is obtained from several sources: the sap of maple trees in the Americas, sugar cane from India, sugar beet which was the traditional source of sugar in Europe, and from bees as honey. Hindu literature refers to sugar cane in 500 BC; in 300 BC one of Alexander's generals, Nearchus, wrote while visiting India of reeds that produced sugar, but without bees (Johnstone, 1976: 58). The sugar cane industry reached the Mediterranean in 600 AD, brought by the Arabs; the Mediterranean sugar trade was monopolized by Venice in the fifteenth century. European explorers such as Christopher Columbus took sugar cane to the Caribbean and Australia. The Caribbean was ideal for sugar cane production, using African slave labour. With cheap land for

Table 1.5 Textbook and actual levels of vitamin C in selected foods

Food	*Textbook level*	*Actual level*	*% of textbook*
Asda runner beans	18	2	11
Asda kiwi in tropical fruit salad	59	36	62
M&S fresh mango	37	16	42
M&S brussels sprouts	115	56	48
Safeway broccoli florets	87	47	55
Safeway melon slices	26	11	42
Sainsbury's apple bites	6	49	816
Sainsbury's sliced melon	26	20	76
Somerfield swede	31	26	85
Somerfield orange	54	41	75
Waitrose pineapple pieces	12	19	156
Tesco pineapple	12	53	441
Tesco cauliflower	43	39	91

Source: Consumers' Association (2004).

plantations and even cheaper labour, the price of sugar fell and 'white gold' became available to the working classes of Europe. The Napoleonic Wars (1803–15) temporarily cut off Britain's access to Caribbean sugar cane, increasing sugar cane prices and stimulating the development of the sugar beet industry. Initially, sugar beet yielded less sugar than cane, but the yield has been raised by selective breeding. A further sugar price rise came about when slavery was abolished in the nineteenth century; plantation owners substituted cheap labour from India and China, changing the demography of some countries and laying the foundation for many ethnic conflicts today. Meanwhile improvements in transport technology kept the inflation-adjusted price of sugar falling, as Table 1.6 shows.

Sugar was crucial to the British economy of the 1700s and 1800s. The factory jobs created by the Industrial Revolution were arduous, especially before machinery was developed to do more of the work. Building the canals and railways was also very labour-intensive. The sugar plantations of the Caribbean were an early form of biofuel; whereas today we drive machines with sugar cane-derived fuel to do useful work, then we fuelled humans with sugar cane-derived energy. However, people develop a liking for foods, such as sweet sugar, that aren't healthy. People seldom eat pure sugar, but add it to other foods: tea, cakes, flour, biscuits, jam. There is an amusing episode in John Logie Baird's life, the inventor of television; before he experimented with this new medium he tried building jam factories in the Caribbean. The fruit was produced there, as was the sugar, so why ship fruit with its high water content to the UK when you could boil off the water and just ship the jam? So in 1919 Mr Baird built his jam plant in Port of Spain, Trinidad, only to find that boiling the jam created so much heat in the already-humid Caribbean climate that the workers opened all the windows, and the abundant insect life of the region was attracted into the jam vats by the smell of the sugar. Jam with

Table 1.6 Sugar consumption per capita and real sugar price in the UK, 1700–2010

Year	*Kg sugar consumed per capita, UK*	*Retail price of sugar per kg (adjusted to 2010 prices)*
1300		£354
1450		£304
1550		£85
1650		£55
1700	1.8	
1725	3.5	
1750	3.5	£28.30
1775	4.9	
1800	8.5	
1825	8.0	
1850	13.0	£7.10
1875	26.6	
1900	35.0	
1925	39.0	£4.05
1950	44.2	£3.44
1965	48.5	£1.30
1983	44.5*	
2010	53.0	90p

* Of which 13.5 kg was sugar added by the consumer, and 31 kg was sugar 'hidden' in foodstuffs (Cannon, 1987: 111).

Sources: Adapted from Ferguson (1971: 66); Mathias (1976: 453); Johnstone (1976: 60); Ponting (1991: 237).

added insect protein didn't sell too well in Britain so he returned to the UK in 1920 and invented television.

Sugar performs several functions in food besides sweetening it (Davis, 1984: 23). Sugar softens the gluten in flour, making bread lighter; it acts as an anti-coagulant in custard; sugar retains moisture in cakes, and gives an appetizing brown colour to biscuits; sugar activates yeast, promoting fermentation in alcoholic drinks. Sugar is also anti-bacterial, prolonging the shelf-life of foods, important for food manufacturers and retailers. Sugar becomes embedded in the food chain, and remains there when most work is no longer heavy manual labour. Today much of the sugar we consume is so-called 'hidden sugar', in foods as diverse as tomato soup, cereal bars and ketchup. Hidden sugar rises, as consumers become accustomed to sweeter tastes. A popular cereal brand contained 9.6 g sugar per 100 g in 1978 but 17 g sugar in 2007. Cream of tomato soup that contained 2.6 g of sugar in 1978 had 6.4 g in 2007. The volume of sugar used by the UK breakfast cereals industry rose by 80 per cent between 1966 and 1990, exceeded by the increase in sugar usage within the soft drinks industry, up 260 per cent over the same period. Teenagers in Scotland now consume 287 cans of carbonated sugary drinks a year (*The Observer*, 2013), each can containing eight spoonfuls of sugar, a sugar intake of almost a kilogram a month from these drinks alone. Worryingly, soft drinks do not produce satiety (a feeling of fullness deterring further eating), however much sugar they contain, because they are absorbed rapidly in the stomach (Hallam and Midmore, 1995: 119).

High fructose corn syrup (HFCS) is a form of sugar developed by Japanese scientists in the 1970s; it was cheaper than cane sugar because it could be made from corn. It lengthened the shelf-life of food products, and made biscuits look an appetizing shade of brown, as if freshly baked. Unfortunately it is not so good for human metabolism because fructose is metabolized differently from other sugars, being more easily turned into glycogen and fat (see Chapter 2) rather than burned as energy (Critser, 2003: 11). Trans fats, also known as hydrogenated vegetable oils (HVOs), are another additive that stabilizes food; they have a higher melting point than unsaturated fats, and give the food a soft mouthfeel. However, HVOs can create fatty deposits in the arteries, leading to high blood pressure and stroke. HVOs are another artificial product; the technique of hydrogenation of natural (unsaturated) vegetable oils was developed in 1911, and marketed as a kitchen lard called Crisco (Critser, 2003: 15). The difference between saturated and unsaturated fats is that the former have the maximum number of hydrogen atoms attached to the carbon chain of the fatty acid; unsaturated fats have double bonds between some carbon atoms; a double carbon bond can be replaced with a single bond and two hydrogen atoms. The stability of saturated fats means they are slower to oxidize, a process that makes the food taste rank and unappetizing. As usual with food there is a political element (further explored in Chapter 4); palm oil is one of the few naturally occurring saturated fats and was castigated by nutritionists as 'tree lard' or 'rat oil'. Malaysia produces considerable quantities of palm oil, and Malaysia was a vital South-East Asian ally of the USA during the 1970s when many other countries in the region were pro-Communist. Hence Malaysia found a ready trading partner for its palm oil, which is now found in a range of foods, from French fries and margarine to cookies and pies. A combination of chemistry, food industry economics, consumer preferences and politics has conspired to make much of our food unhealthier, more calorific and obesogenic, than it might otherwise have been. We should also note here the rise of another unhealthy but appetizing food preservative: salt. Salt does not promote obesity but excess consumption will cause high blood pressure, strokes and heart attacks. The recommended daily amount (RDA) of salt, sodium chloride, is 6 g. Like sugar, salt is a preservative and enhances flavour; therefore food manufacturers may raise salt levels in their products. Some food labels may attempt to mislead consumers by stating sodium levels; because sodium is the lighter partner in sodium chloride, the RDA for sodium is not 3 g but 2.4 g. As with sugar, sodium levels in some foods have risen since the 1970s. While salt has been reduced in bread and dairy products, it has risen

Table 1.7 Daily energy intake and food energy availability in the US per capita (age-adjusted), 1971–2000

Year	*Female energy intake kcal*	*Male energy intake kcal*	*Food availability kcal*	*US adult obesity rate*
1971	1542	2450	3240	13%
1980	1522	2439	3240	15%
1990	1798	2668	3620	23%
2000	1877	2618	3720	31%

Source: Adapted from Harnack and Schmitz (2005: 22, 25).

in ready meals, sauces and cereals, and in crisps salt has nearly doubled from 0.54 g per 100 g in 1978 to 1.05 g per 100 g in 2003.

Table 1.7 shows how the energy within the food bought in the USA, and the food actually eaten, has risen since 1971, and how the US obesity rate has risen in tandem over this period.

As Harnack and Schmitz (2005) note, the energy intake data (from the USA's National Health and Nutrition Examination Survey – NHANES) do not correlate as well with the rise in US obesity as do the food availability figures (Food Supply Series). This is odd because the former is supposed to measure what people actually eat; the latter includes food fed to pets, thrown away by households, or wasted at other stages of the food chain. Perhaps the accuracy of the NHANES figures, which in the absence of a spy at every US dinner table depend on self-reporting, has changed. Were consumers less diligent in 2000 than in 1970 at reporting sugary snacks, items easily forgotten while keeping a food diary? A second explanation is more likely; the nature of the food thrown away (the difference between 'availability' and 'intake') has changed between 1971 and 2000. Busier lifestyles can mean less propensity to cook vegetables and meat, even if these items were bought by health-seeking consumers. Instead, it is much easier now than in 1971 to buy as a back-up, and then consume, sugary ready meals in lieu of time-consuming (to prepare) traditional meats and vegetables, which then go bad and are discarded. So it is not just the total Calories we consume that promotes obesity but also the change in type of foods we obtain those Calories from, that now makes our diet less healthy.

Who's eating all the pies? *There is hardly anything in the world which some man cannot make a little worse and sell a little cheaper, and the people who buy on price only are this man's lawful prey*

Since the Green Revolution agriculture has achieved something Malthus would have thought impossible; it has increased food supply per capita in the face of a global population that has more than doubled from the 3 billion people on

Earth in 1960. In fact the world even now produces enough food not just for today's 7 billion but for the expected peak population of 10 billion in 2050; as we shall see in Chapter 8, some 40 per cent of the food we now produce is wasted at some stage between transport from the farm and the consumer's home. If all this food actually went to feed people we could today sustain a population of over 11 billion. Our concerns today are over food quality, not quantity; sustainability is also a major concern, with increasing use of non-renewable inputs, coupled with shifts towards a less-sustainable meat-based diet in many countries. We have a market demand-driven food system; theoretically this means that food quality, food choices, are consumer-driven. In practice consumer food choices are heavily modified by the marketing messages emanating from the most powerful actors in the food chain, the producers and supermarket retailers. Even without advertising, consumer choices are greatly influenced by time poverty, hedonism, changing family structures and a range of other socio-economic and demographic factors. The issues concerning consumer choices, food marketing and social factors are covered in Chapters 3 through to 6 of this book; Chapters 7 and 8 discuss how we might address concerns about food quality, obesity and sustainability our food system has created. Meanwhile in Chapter 2 we explore the specific biological, social and economic issues of the global obesity epidemic.

2 You are what you eat

The biology of food and fat. *The fat controller*

Our bodies are well equipped to enable us to cope with insufficient food supplies; they are adapted for long periods of food scarcity with occasional periods of feast. What we are not as well adapted for is the period of continuous feast or food surplus we now have in the developed world, and increasingly in the global South too. We require a range of both micro- and macronutrients for repair and reproduction. Micronutrients include vitamins and a range of 20 or more elements from iron to iodine for essential metabolic functions. However, most of the human body is composed of just four elements: oxygen (65 per cent), carbon (18 per cent), hydrogen (10 per cent) and nitrogen (3 per cent). These elements, along with a small amount of sulphur, make up the three macronutrients we require, carbohydrates, fat and protein. Food entering the mouth is broken down physically (by chewing) and chemically (by saliva). Saliva breaks down starch, found in bread, into sugar, so bread tastes sweeter when chewed. The mouth also gives important sensory information about the food we have eaten. We detect the mouthfeel or texture of food, preferring smooth to rough or abrasive food. We do not want to swallow sharp objects like bone fragments that might damage the lining of our digestive tract. We also detect chemicals released as we physically break up the food, as taste or, primarily, smell. Sweetness is important, since poisonous food is generally bitter, but no sweet foods found in nature are poisonous. In the stomach further mechanical and chemical breakdown takes place, and some water is absorbed. However, the main absorption takes place from the small intestine. What is not absorbed passes to the large intestine, essentially a storage area for faeces until elimination is convenient. Although there are a number of smaller organs such as the gall bladder and appendix that assist digestion, these are the principal components of our food absorption system. One might also add the liver to this list, since the liver is the first port of call for all nutrients absorbed from the small intestine. The liver detoxifies the chemicals coming from the gut, processing them into a form the body can use.

Sugar is vital for body functions, but can do considerable damage if it reaches excess levels. The Islets of Langerhans within the pancreas produce insulin when they detect raised sugar levels in the bloodstream. When individuals cannot make insulin, the result is type 1 diabetes. Sugar remains in the bloodstream, where it causes the platelets to become sticky and clump together; this blocks small capillaries, so blood no longer flows efficiently in the extremities of the body, the fingers and toes and the small delicate blood vessels in the eyes. Delicate blood vessels in the retina may bleed into the eyeball, clouding it; along with damage to the retina itself, causing visual loss. This is why diabetes can cause limb extremity gangrene and amputations, and also blindness. Small blood vessels in the kidneys are also damaged, leading to dialysis. Excess blood sugar may damage the nerve endings on the extremities, causing tingling and numbness, an early symptom of type 2 diabetes. This type of diabetes was once called adult-onset diabetes, but has been renamed as so many obese children have contracted the disease. The nerve damage causes injuries to the feet to go unnoticed, and these injuries heal slowly due to capillary damage; infection can easily set in unnoticed, another route to amputation. Excess blood glucose also impairs the immune system, by displacing vitamin C (to which it is similar in molecular shape) from the phagocytic white blood cells. This may promote cancer because the phagocytic cells devour rogue cancerous cells as well as bacteria and viruses. Blood glucose may also promote cancer by facilitating the tumour's process of anaerobic respiration, converting glucose into lactic acid; lactic acid in turn acidifies the blood, causing inflammation and further damage to delicate capillaries.

When the body is functioning normally, insulin produced in response to blood sugar stimulates cells across the body to take up this sugar, which is then used for energy. Insulin also stimulates the liver to remove blood sugar and store it as glycogen, in the muscles where it can be quickly converted into glucose for energy; glycogen is also stored in the liver itself. The body has only a limited capacity for glycogen storage; once this is full the body stores excess sugar with fat as triglycerides in adipose tissue, which is commonly referred to as 'fat', or 'fatty tissue'. Adipose tissue is far from simply an inert 'fat store'; despite its rather negative image in current Western body image fashion adipose tissue performs a number of vital biological functions, and is an active part of the body's hormonal regulatory systems. Besides its role as a store of energy and lipids (themselves essential for biochemical functions), adipose tissue physically cushions vital organs and provides thermal insulation. Fat is actually stored as droplets within cells called adipocytes found within the adipose tissue. Insulin suppresses glucagon, a hormone which stimulates the conversion of glycogen back into glucose, and the breakdown of tryglycerides into fatty acids and glucose (via lipase). So higher insulin levels cause the body to store fat in its adipocytes. After some hours without ingesting food, glycogen levels are low and blood glucose is also falling. At this point the hypothalamus sends a message to the brain that we perceive as hunger. Low blood sugar, hypoglycaemia, causes a feeling of restlessness (the body is saying, 'go and find food NOW'). The stomach feels empty and aching, and the urge to eat becomes irresistible. The problem is that all this occurs before the body has begun to burn its fat reserves. In pre-industrial days, this biological feedback system served us well. The limited amount of sugars we ate were mostly complex sugars, large sugar molecules absorbed more slowly by the gut. Blood sugar rose only gradually after a meal, so insulin levels also rose slowly. However, today's diet of processed food contains a higher proportion of simple sugars, smaller sugar molecules that cause a rapid spike in blood sugar levels. In response to this sugar spike, the Islets of Langerhans produce a surge of insulin. The initial problem is that excess insulin desensitizes the body cells to its message to take up glucose; the body therefore remains short of energy, causing tiredness, the kidneys heroically try and remove the excess glucose in urine, causing excessive thirst and sweet urine (a telltale sign of diabetes), and the body suffers the ill-effects of high blood sugar described earlier. To distinguish this acquired form of diabetes (where the body does not recognize the insulin it already has) from the congenital kind (where insulin was never produced) we call this acquired type of the disease diabetes 2. Initially, the body may try and compensate for incipient insulin resistance by raising insulin production, until the Islets of Langerhans give up under the pressure. In the meantime, insulin catalyses a substance called catecholamine, which acts to constrict the blood vessels. Blood pressure therefore rises, and since unhealthy foods, high in facts and sugars, are also often high in salt, blood pressure may already be high. Hypertension, high blood pressure, then raises the risk of strokes and heart attacks. The body also has a complex hormonal system to regulate fat storage and fat burning. While lipids are essential for many biological functions (vitamins A, D, E and K are lipids), excess lipids cause fatty deposits in the arteries, resulting in strokes and heart attacks. Fatty deposits in the liver may predispose to cirrhosis. Raised consumption of sugary drinks, especially these containing HFCS or high levels of sucrose, may cause non-alcoholic fatty liver disease (NAFLD). Besides the hormones insulin and glucagon mentioned earlier, there is a hormone, leptin, produced in response to excess lipids in the blood. Leptin suppresses the appetite and promotes the burning of lipids for energy. If the body is not physically active so there is less demand for this energy, another hormone, adiponectin, is produced; this encourages the adipocytes within the adipose (fatty) tissue to store lipids as triglycerides. As body fat stores rise, less adiponectin is produced but leptin levels remain high to encourage fat burning rather than more food intake. Under normal biological conditions, and a pre-industrial diet without sugary fatty processed foods, insulin, glucagon, leptin and adiponectin form a negative feedback system that keeps body weight and body fat stores at healthy levels.

Five problems can arise with this feedback system, associated with our modern food system.

- Hunger, as noted above, can drive us to eat before we begin burning fat stores. With pre-industrial food this would entail consumption of fruit and vegetables with complex low-GI (Glycaemic Index) sugars and the occasional meaty fatty feast if a large animal was killed; nowadays we are likely to consume a high sugar, high-GI snack, predisposing us to insulin spikes, insulin insensitivity and type 2 diabetes.

- Hedonic hunger, literally 'pleasure-induced hunger'; the situation we are all familiar with whereby we feel fully sated but can always find room for that extra sweet chocolatey snack; another situation not generally encountered in pre-industrial days. Then, only the king would have regularly encountered sugary confections prepared with costly 'white gold' from the Orient. In pre-industrial famine–feast times hedonic hunger was a useful adaptation; by encouraging us to eat beyond satisfaction, our energy stores were maximized for that next long food shortage. Today that famine never comes. Hedonic hunger is exacerbated by the release of dopamine in the brain that is induced by sugary foods; dopamine gives a feeling of pleasure, and its release is significant in forming addictions.
- 'Asymmetry of appetite'; our appetite can easily exceed immediate calorific requirements, but seldom falls below those requirements, unless we are suffering from some appetite-suppressing disease such as some cancers, when the appetite is reduced by cytokine release.
- The body is not simply an energy-in energy-out machine, so that cutting back on calorie intake would result in weight loss or at least reduced weight gain. The body will reduce its calorie consumption in response to less food eaten. Adipose tissue, as we saw above, is not just 'inert fat' but is metabolically active and reducing adipose tissue will mean fewer Calories burnt. After an extended period of Calorie deficit the body will bring in a number of mechanisms to further conserve on energy use; proteins in the muscles will be digested, hair growth ceases, the functioning of the immune system is curtailed, body temperature reduces slightly, even respiration rates may fall (Harcombe 2010: 43). All this means that dieting produces an initial weight loss but to keep shedding weight the dieter must further reduce food intake. However, our psychology leads us to reward ourselves after successful weight loss.
- We may become desensitized to leptin after extended periods of high levels of this hormone, in the same was as insulin sensitivity can greatly reduce after extended high levels. Leptin suppresses the appetite in response to high body fat levels, so leptin suppression means no feeling of satiety, rather a continued hunger, after a large food intake. Essentially you could be on the way to obesity, but still want to eat more. Worse, insulin suppresses the effect of leptin; as the body clears sugar from the blood (the job of insulin), the body then requires more food (sugar). So an insulin-resistant person may have high levels of insulin in the blood, setting up a vicious circle where leptin fails to suppress the appetite, leading to further eating, further (ineffective) insulin production, further leptin suppression and further stimulation of appetite.

Further psychological and biological problems are caused by the increased levels of fructose and the introduction of HFCS to our diet (fructose occurs naturally in fruit, but we eat far more of it now in processed food). Besides the preservative and appearance enhancing properties of HFCS mentioned in Chapter 1, fructose tastes sweeter than other sugars. Our biologically determined liking for sweet foods makes us crave foods containing fructose, as the food processing industry knows well. Fructose can subvert the biological energy feedback mechanisms described above. Unlike other sugars, fructose enters the bloodstream rapidly (it is a monosaccharide) and is then easily converted into triglycerides, which are stored in the adipocyte cells as fat reserves, rather than being burnt for energy. Fructose then promotes the release of fatty acids into the bloodstream and therefore counters the action of insulin; this may cause higher levels of insulin to be produced, leading to type 2 diabetes (Critser, 2003: 136). Fructose itself can enter body cells by a process that does not require insulin, and fructose does not stimulate leptin (appetite suppressant) production, so fructose intake fails to produce satiety, therefore a diet rich in fructose will promote obesity more than a diet high in other sugars (Power and Schulkin, 2009: 118).

Diseases attributable to obesity. *The opera(tion) isn't over till the fat lady sings*

Obesity, an excess presence of adipose tissue in the body, causes a wide range of diseases or malfunctions in bodily systems; it also has deleterious psychological effects. We have already described the effects of type 2 diabetes on the body, and how type 2 diabetes is linked to excess sugar intake. The UK has (2011) 2.9 million people diagnosed with type 2 diabetes, and an estimated 850,000 who have the disease but have not yet been diagnosed (Young, 2012). A further 7 million people are at high risk of contracting type 2 diabetes, and some 3–4 million of these will actually develop it before dying of other causes. The USA has (2011) 18.8 million diagnosed diabetics, and an estimated 7.0 million who have diabetes but have not yet been diagnosed, plus a further 79.0 million in a pre-diabetic state. Diabetes cases are rising fast; the UK had just 1.4 million diabetics in 1996, but expects to have 5 million by 2025. Globally, diabetes cases have risen from 30 million in 1985 to 135 million in 1995, 177 million in 2000, and to 366 million in 2011; a total of 552 million cases are expected by 2025. Almost all the increase is from type 2 diabetes. Those with a BMI of over 35 are 20 times more likely to develop type 2 diabetes than those with a BMI of 18–25. Type 2 diabetes was rare in children in the USA in 1992, with American paediatric diabetes centres then reporting around 3 per cent of their diabetes patients as type 2. However, by 1999 these children's diabetic centres were reporting up to 45 per cent of their new cases as type 2 (Lowell, 2004).

The other primary effect of obesity is increased body weight, and increased loading on the joints, especially the knees and ankles, leading to arthritis.

Eating an obesogenic diet is also associated with poor micronutrient intake, so the bones of overweight people face a double jeopardy of excess loading and low calcium levels, leading to osteoporosis and fractures. Weight loading on the abdomen may lead to stress incontinence. Increased adipose tissue in the chest and neck area may interfere with breathing at night leading to obstructive sleep apnoea, a condition where the sufferer temporarily stops breathing in their sleep. This wakes them up, and breathing resumes; chronic tiredness during the day ensues, heightening the risk of accidents when driving or working. Sleep apnoea in children leads to learning difficulties and poor memory, exacerbated by irritability, which can adversely affect the learning environment of an entire class at school. Weakened lungs are more prone to asthma attacks, and obesity also raises the risk of pre-eclampsia in pregnant women. Gallstones and gout have also been linked to obesity, as have cancers of the breast and colon, and fertility problems in females. A tenth of all UK cancer deaths amongst non-smokers are attributed to obesity, as are a seventh of male cancer deaths and a fifth of female cancer deaths in the USA. Overall, in 2007, obesity was blamed for the loss of some 18 million days off work due to illness in the UK. A significant effect of excess adipose tissue is to lengthen the circulatory system (adipose tissue needs nourishment too) which promotes heart attacks. The risk of cardiovascular disease rises by a factor of 3.6 for each unit rise in BMI, and 85 per cent of the UK's hypertension incidence is associated with patients of BMI over 25. Overall the multiple morbidities caused by obesity 'age' a person's body so that a 40-year-old may have the body of a 55-year-old from an earlier, less obese generation (Hulsegge et al., 2013).

Psychological disorders include low self-esteem, body dysmorphia and eating disorders such as bulimia and anorexia; obese people may be prone to yo-yo dieting with large swings in body weight down and up again. Obese people have reduced chances of finding a marriage mate or job, reinforcing low self-esteem and possibly leading to further eating disorders. Obese children are prone to teasing at school, reducing their learning capabilities. In a society that elevates slimness to a virtue, overweight people are labelled as lazy, self-indulgent and lacking mental discipline. Many of our insults are linked to fatness, such as 'fathead', 'thickhead', 'lardass'; the Fat Controller is portrayed as a pompous, inflexible, old-fashioned character. We link mental acuity, sharpness and nimbleness with the equivalent physical characteristics of slimness and agility. Unfortunately, as with physical eating disorders, there is a pernicious positive feedback mechanism whereby taunted fat people may resort to comfort eating, escalating the problem. Although obesity can lead to depression, there is little conclusive evidence that obese people are more likely to commit suicide (Klinitzke et al., 2013). Morbidly obese people may face difficulties with certain suicide methods, for example their body mass means overdosing on pills has less effect, and physical suicide methods such as hanging or drowning are harder to accomplish. However, being obese raises the chances of an early death; in 2002 some 30,000 deaths annually were attributable to obesity (Lowell, 2004); in Spain the 2002 figure was 18,000 and in the USA, 300,000 deaths a year (Costa-Font and Gil, 2008). Britons who are obese are likely to die 11 years earlier than if they had a normal BMI; 13 years early if severely obese in their 20s. However, the main societal issue with obesity is that the ailments it causes are cripplers, not killers; patients can survive for years with cancer, strokes, arthritis, amputations and blindness, but require expensive long-term care. Obesity is a costly luxury that few governments can afford to ignore.

Financial costs of obesity. *The profligacy of fat*

Obesity causes costs to society in several ways. Not only are there direct medical costs, both private and government health service costs, but productivity is lost due to days off work. In 2001 the UK's National Audit Office estimated the costs of obesity to the British government as £0.5 billion annually, and costs to the wider UK economy as £2 billion a year. The larger figure did not include informal care costs; it only included sick leave where a doctor's note was obtained. Butland et al. (2007: 39) put the annual costs of obesity to the UK as nearly £7 billion, of which £1 billion was direct medical costs to the National Health Service (NHS), around 2.5 per cent of total NHS spending. Raynor and Scarborough (2005) estimated the costs of obesity to the NHS at £6 billion. Lost earnings, according to Butland et al., amounted to some £3 billion or 45,000 lost working years. In 2011 the British Prime Minister, David Cameron, put the cost of obesity to the UK as £4 billion to the NHS, 4 per cent of total NHS spending, and total costs are calculated as between £15 and £20 billion a year when accounting for lost productivity and welfare payments such as Sickness Benefit. With a UK adult obesity rate estimated at 23 per cent, or 11.5 million adults, the cost of each obese person is around £350 (US$550) a year to the NHS and a total of £1,500 to the entire UK economy. Obesity also accounts for a considerable fraction of health spending in other countries. Producing a meaningful comparison of obesity rates and the resultant healthcare costs for a given country in a given year is difficult. The obesity rates themselves may be based on self-reporting surveys or a sample of patients presenting at primary healthcare providers and are not always totally accurate. The medical costs of obesity can vary depending on the healthcare system in place in that country. A poorer country with less public healthcare availability will appear to spend less on obesity-related illnesses, and a country where much healthcare is privatized, like the USA, tends to inflate medical costs. Some sample figures are presented in Table 2.1. The significance of increased fruit and vegetable consumption is illustrated by a 2001 report from the Australian Fruit and Vegetable Coalition that consuming just one serve (portion) a day would result in direct savings to the Australian healthcare system of AU$513 million a year (Kirchhoff et al., 2011: 1032).

Table 2.1 Obesity rates and healthcare costs, selected countries

Country	*Year*	*Healthcare costs due to obesity*	*Adult obesity rate*	*Cost of a 1% obesity rate*	*Implied annual cost per obese person (US$)*
Netherlands	1995	4% of total	6.5%	0.61%	–
France	1995	2% of total	7.5%	0.27%	–
France	2002	2 billion euros	10.0%	200 million euros	440
Portugal	1996	3.5% of total	14.0%	0.25%	–
Spain	2002	7% of total	14.0%	0.5%	–
Australia	1989	AU$395 million, 2% of total	8.0%	0.25% or AU$49.4 million	310
Australia	2000	AU$1,690c million, 3% of total	21.0%	0.14% or AU$80.5 million	420
New Zealand	1991	2.5% of total	11.0%	0.23%	–
Canada	1997	CAN$1.8 billion, 2.4% of total	16.0%	0.15% or CAN$112.5 million	345
Canada	2001	CAN$4.3 billion, 2.2% of total	17.0%	0.13% or CAN$253 million	700
USA	1986	US$39.9 billion, 5.5% of total	20%	0.28% or US$2 billion	1,087
USA	1990	US$45.8 billion, 6.0% of total	22.5%	0.27%, or US$2 billion	1,254
USA	1998	US$75 billion, 6.5% of total	29.0%	0.22%, or US$2.6 billion	1,206
USA	2008	US$200 billion, 9.1% of total	35.0%	0.26%, or US$5.7 billion	2,326
Col. 1	Col. 2	Col. 3	Col. 4	Col. 5	Col. 6

Notes on calculations: Column (5) assumes a linear relationship between the obesity rate (4) and the healthcare costs (3). In practice there will be 'economies of scale' such that an extra 1 per cent obese will result in a less than proportionate rise in costs, e.g. hospital facilities already in place. Column (6) has been calculated by taking the adult obesity rate x population aged 16 and over, and dividing into total obesity costs. While some of the obesity costs will be childhood obesity, the greater proportion of obesity-related healthcare costs will be from adult obesity.

Sources: Belanger-Ducharme and Tremblay (2005); Butland et al. (2007); Carter and Moodie (2005: 169); Costa-Font and Gil (2008); *Food Magazine* (2004a: 11); Fry and Finley (2005); Lake (2006); London Development Agency (2005: 38); Patel (2008: 63).

An approximate 1 per cent rise in obesity causes a 0.25–0.3 per cent rise in healthcare costs, and each extra obese person costs their national healthcare system around US$500 annually, outside the USA. This can be set against costs of anti-obesity initiatives, remembering this figure does not include non-healthcare costs such as lost work days and informal care. When obesity becomes widespread other costs emerge. In the UK, hospital beds and ambulances require modification to accommodate obese patients. Airlines burn more fuel and non-obese passengers may complain if seated next to an obese passenger. The extra aviation fuel burnt by US airlines alone due to rising passenger weight was estimated at 350 million gallons a year in 2005 (*The Times*, 2005: 39). Obese employees may pay more for health insurance. A poor standard of hospital food has also been blamed for delayed recovery time among patients, causing increased bed usage; many modern hospitals have been built without kitchens; food is prepared centrally and is often of low nutritional quality. If this food arrives in the ward cold and unappetizing, patients may undereat, retarding their recovery. In prisons and young offender institutions, poor food, high in additives and low in nutritional quality, raises the incidence of anti-social behaviour (London Development Agency, 2005: 39). In 2011 some young offender institutions spend just £2.50 per day per inmate on food, and very little on fresh fruit or vegetables, leading to inmates bullying each other for extra fruit.

Analysing obesity: causes and effects. *If you can't tell a spoon from a ladle then you're fat*

Obesity is commonly defined by a person's Body Mass Index or BMI. The BMI is defined as weight in kilograms divided by height in metres, squared. A person with BMI of under 18.5 is categorized as underweight, whilst 18.5–25 is normal weight, 25–30 is overweight, 30–40 is obese and over 40 is morbidly obese. This is easy to calculate, but there are several drawbacks to BMI as a measure of obesity. First, the England rugby team is obese! Muscle is about 18 per cent denser than fat and the BMI does not differentiate between muscular and fat people of the same height. Second, the human body is not two- but three-dimensional; taller people may have larger horizontal body cross-sections than short people. The BMI was originally known as the Quetelet Index, developed by the Belgian scientist Adolphe Quetelet in 1842. Quetelet himself stated that the proper power for the height was three for babies (who are more spherical), 2 for teenagers who are more like beanpoles and 2.5 for adults; the American dietician Ancel Keys popularized this obesity measure as the BMI in the 1970s. In 2013 Nick Trefethen, Professor of Mathematics at Oxford University, proposed changes in BMI as (height to power 1.3) divided into (weight to power 2.5). A person of 80 kg, 1.8 m tall, would now have a BMI of 26.1, similar to the old measure. But shorter people's BMI rises under the new measure; a 55 kg person of height 1.50 metres had an old BMI of 24.4 but under Trefethen's measure it is 26.0. A tall person, weight 100 kg, height 2.00 metres, finds their BMI has changed from 25.0 to a new figure of 24.4. Third, the BMI makes no allowance for different racial characteristics; Asian people have different patterns of body fat from Europeans, and it has been proposed that their boundary between normal weight and overweight should be not 25.0 but 23.5. Alternative metrics of excess weight include waist measurement; a maximum of 100 cm or 40 inches for men and 88 cm or 35 inches for women. Other metrics include the waist to hip ratio, which should be no more than 1:1 for men and 0.9:1 for women, or skinfold measurement (the thicker the skinfold the more subcutaneous fat is present), or body density (fat has a density of 0.9 g / cm^3, whereas lean tissue is 1.1, so the less dense the body, the more fat is present). However, it is not easy to get the waist measurement right, and it can vary throughout the day; waist circumference is smallest in the morning and increases through till dinner time. Hip measurement is increased by muscle mass as well as fat deposits. Body density is hard to measure, and skinfold thickness depends on taking at least four representative measurements and averaging. Therefore the old measure of BMI looks likely to be in use for some time yet, and historical data of obesity rates are almost always based upon the simplified Quetelet measure.

The modern processed food many of us eat, rich in harmful sugars and saturated fats, makes us more prone to obesity. However, some of us were more prone to obesity even before we were born, due to genetics; more precisely, epigenetics. Epigenetics describes how our genes may be changed by environmental factors after we are born, and such changes can be inherited by our children, if the epigenetic changes affect the mother's unfertilized eggs or the father's sperm. Our DNA is fixed at the moment of conception, but the expression of the genes can be altered, for example by the addition or removal of chemical groups like methyl from our DNA. A foetus can detect if it is to be born into a food-rich or food-poor world, from the level of nutrition received across the placenta, and if it detects a food-poor world it switches its metabolism to 'energy saving mode'; a useful adaptation if its biological prediction comes true. This switch is known as the 'thrifty gene hypothesis'. No one told Dutch foetuses in their first trimester during the winter of 1944–5 that famines could be artificially created by temporary political developments; in this case the Nazi occupation of Holland in the last months World War Two. This time was known to the Dutch as the 'hunger winter'; Nazi forces severely restricted food supplies to Dutch civilians to punish them for failing to support the Nazi war effort. Famine deaths reached 22,000 as daily calorie intake fell to 580 by February 1945. Dutch babies born in late spring and summer 1945 were, unsurprisingly, smaller than average, as stunting growth is one way to save Calories. What was unexpected was that the offspring of these children, too, were below average weight. An epigenetic switch had been irreversibly thrown into 'hoard body fat' mode, in this case within the father's sperm or mother's egg pre-conception. These 1945-born children grew up more prone to obesity, diabetes and cardiovascular disease, as did their children. The foetuses of mothers in countries like Brazil, Mexico, India and China face a not dissimilar situation to those Dutch mothers nearly 70 years ago; in these rapidly developing countries, it has been possible to go in a few years from food shortage to food abundance – especially the wrong sort of food, such as an abundance of burgers from chains like McDonald's.

China's per capita GDP was about 2 per cent of the USA's in the 1970s; it is now over 10 per cent of current US per capita GDP, over 15 per cent at purchasing power parity. In the rapidly growing east coast cities, per capita Chinese income has risen even faster. Between 1958 and 1961 China suffered a severe famine. Therefore Chinese children born before 1970, and especially those born between 1959 and 1962, have metabolisms geared to hoarding Calories as fat, yet now inhabit a Calorie-rich environment.

A similar switching mechanism can be seen in undernourished children in Africa; they either develop marasmus, extreme emaciation or kwashiorkor, a belly swollen by fluid accumulation. Those with kwashiorkor have a higher mortality rate from starvation, and die with some fuel stores still in their body; whereas marasmus children have utilized all their energy reserves before they die. The children with marasmus had lower birth weights than those with kwashiorkor; so lower birth weight correlates with having a metabolism that is more effective at utilizing fat reserves in times of famine (Gluckman and Hanson, 2012: 144). Kwashiorkor derives from a West African term meaning 'the sickness a child gets when another is born'; children are prone to kwashiorkor when weaned from the breast (because of another birth), and the older child shifts to a protein-poor, starch-rich diet. The starchy foods are bulky relative to their calorie content, making it hard for a child to consume an adequate energy intake. Should these famine-hit African countries industrialize rapidly, an obesity epidemic may develop there some 20 years afterwards. The rapid but uneven economic development in some formerly poorer countries has resulted in an unprecedented combination of simultaneous undernourishment, malnourishment (adequate or more calorie intake but deficient in micronutrients) and overnourishment. Egypt, whose agricultural output and wealth rose rapidly at the end of the 1990s, has both malnutrition and obesity in its population. James Neel, who proposed the thrifty gene hypothesis in 1962, suggests this mechanism gave an advantage to communities facing famine, especially when mankind shifted from hunter-gathering to farming. Hunter-gatherers have less need of a thrifty gene because populations are low and game is plentiful; if you fail to catch enough food it is probably because you are no longer fit enough to chase it. Farming, however, allowed human populations to rise to unprecedented levels where a bad harvest or three could seriously threaten the entire community. The thrifty gene hypothesis has even been invoked to explain why obesity is high in the Anglophone countries of USA, Canada, Ireland, Australia and New Zealand. The Irish endured a major famine in 1845, and many emigrated, enduring months-long voyages in harsh conditions. Did those with thrifty genes have a selective advantage on these voyages, raising the prevalence of such genes in the Anglophone population today? On the other hand this theory does not explain why the UK itself is also one of the more obese nations, although it might contribute to explaining the higher rate of obesity in Scotland which suffered deprivations under the Highland clearances of the eighteenth and nineteenth centuries.

A range of demographic, social and economic changes, apparently unconnected with nutrition, has also raised obesity rates worldwide. The world's falling birth rate may be exacerbating the problems of obesity and diabetes (Gluckman and Hanson, 2012: 155). First-born children are more prone to thrifty gene-induced obesity because a woman's first foetus has a less-developed placental blood supply compared to any subsequent children, so this first foetus is more likely to perceive a nutrition-poor environment, and adjust its physiology accordingly. As the global fertility rate declines, a greater proportion of children will be first-borns. Moreover, the first-born is more likely to have a younger mother, perhaps still in her teens, and younger mothers also provide poorer foetal nutrition. Global declines in birth rates have been linked to greater wealth and a delay in childbearing by women choosing to delay childbirth in order to develop a career first, and mothers aged over 35 also provide poorer nutrition to their embryos. The birth rate has fallen fast in China, lowered by the One Child Policy, resulting in families with only one child and four grandparents competing to show her love, a love often manifested by feeding because these grandparents grew up in an era of food scarcity in the 1960s; a belief that children who are 'heavy' at a young age are well-nourished and will become tall and healthy adults persists today among Chinese grandparents (Goh, 2013: 366). This makes it imperative that healthy eating is encouraged especially among children. We also have the 'obesogenic environment': a combination of lifestyle and built-environment factors that promotes weight gain. As small local food stores have closed, many consumers drive to supermarkets; consumers without cars subsist on foods from the remaining local convenience stores and takeaways; stores often lacking fresh produce but selling food heavy in fat and sugar. These issues are discussed in greater detail in Chapters 5 and 6 of this book. Obesity can be promoted by the entire urban environment, not just the food retail environment; in Utah, USA, Zick et al. (2009) found that obesity rates are negatively correlated with the age of the suburb you live in. Older suburbs have tree-shaded sidewalks amenable for walking, they have facilities such as shops within walking distance, they have narrower streets that slow the traffic and make walking more pleasant, and they have a street pattern that has greater connectivity, offering direct walking routes. Older neighbourhoods have mixed land uses, meaning that the workplace, the school, the shop, are all close to each other. Fear of street crime also shifts transport mode away from walking, into buses, taxis and cars; dangerous busy roads deter cycling. We also have much labour-saving technology; the car itself and household appliances, the work environment and computers all reduce physical activity. Emails are obesogenic because we no longer walk to colleagues; a 65 kg person uses 3.9 Calories a minute walking, versus 1.8 sitting down. Once our employer paid us to work off Calories, now we pay gyms to get exercise. Shopping at a supermarket consumes 272 Calories an hour against 390 an hour for High Street shopping, because the latter entails more walking, without a trolley to carry the goods. So a person who used to walk 15 minutes to the high street every week, for a one-hour shop, but now drives to the supermarket for a weekly one-hour shop will consume, over a year, 12,500 Calories less; equivalent to 1.6 kg of fat. If on the way home we buy a small portion of fish and chips it will take us one hour of boxing, or 2 hours 20 minutes of walking, or 8 hours 30 minutes of watching TV, to burn off the 685 Calories in that food. Television is obesogenic, because we spend so many hours passively watching it, because low-level activity such as fidgeting lessens when watching TV, and because people often snack whilst watching TV, and then do not remember what they have eaten. Stroebele and de Castro (2004) found that an average of 3.53 meals per person per day were consumed when the TV was on, as against 2.76 on TV-less days. The TV-led meals were smaller, but calorie consumption was higher overall. Many parents use the TV as a handy way of keeping children occupied; again fear of crime leads parents to sit their children in front of the screen rather than sending them out to play. Between 2000 and 2005 the average amount of time a British child spent in front of a TV or computer screen rose from 4.7 to 5.3 hours a week, while in the USA, time spent in front of the TV rose from 10.4 hours a week in 1965 to 15.1 hours a week in 1985 (Schlosser, 2002: 46); a quarter of US children aged 2–5 years had a TV in their bedroom, encouraging consumption of convenience foods instead of healthier meals with the rest of the family.

The geography of obesity. *Lardy lands*

Many wealthy countries saw a rapid rise in obesity during the 1980s and 1990s; obesity rates have levelled off since 2000, but shown little sign of falling. In many developing countries, obesity rates started rising in the 1990s and continue to climb today. In the UK the average adult BMI has risen from 25.5 in 1992 to 26.7 in 2002 and to 27.0 in 2004. This implies an average adult weight gain of around 5 kg, from 75 to 80 kg; with an adult population of 50 million, the UK has therefore acquired a virtual extra population of some 3 million people, since adipose tissue also has nutritional requirements. As the UK runs a trade deficit in food, this is not good for the British economy. In the UK, 7 per cent of adults were obese in 1980, but 24 per cent were in 2005. Finland saw its average adult BMI rise from 25.9 in 1972 to 27.2 in 2002, a development linked to the decline in heavy manual jobs (Bockermann et al., 2008). The USA has seen its adult obesity rate climb from 15 per cent in 1976 to 32 per cent in 2000 (Butland et al., 2007: 24) and now has one of the world's highest national obesity rates. (More data on changing national obesity rates over time are available at www.fooddeserts.org/images/obesityInternational.htm.) Obesity is negatively correlated with income in wealthy countries; the poor are more obese in Taiwan (Pan et al., 2008), and Italian children are more likely to be obese if their parents lack a university education or if they live in the poorer regions of Italy, the south or the Italian islands (Albertini et al., 2008). In Canada the picture is less clear; the provinces with the highest obesity rates – Yukon, North West Territories, Nunavut and Saskatchewan – have

Table 2.2 UK obesity rates by social class, 1993–2009

Year	*Social class 1 (wealthy)*	*Social class 5 (poor)*	*Class differential*
1993 – women	9%	11%	2%
1993 – men	11%	13%	2%
2004 – women	22%	30%	8%
2004 – men	18%	24%	6%
2009 – women	16%	30%	14%
2009 – men	20%	26%	6%

Sources: Cross-Government Obesity Unit (2008); National Obesity Observatory (2013).

a higher than average GDP per capita, while the other provinces with high obesity rates, Newfoundland and Nova Scotia, have below-average incomes. In the UK the Cross-Government Obesity Unit, (2008: 2) reported on a widening of class–obesity differentials between 1993 and 2004, as shown in Table 2.2. More recent figures from the National Obesity Observatory (2013) suggest continued widening to 2009, especially among women.

Obesity trends in Brazil illustrate how obesity has shifted from being a privilege of the rich to a burden on the poor. In 1975 low-income Brazilian women were four times as likely to be underweight as obese. In 1997 these women were 40 per cent more likely to be obese than underweight. In 1975 the poorest quartile of Brazilian women were half as likely to be obese as the wealthiest quartile; in 1997 the poorest quartile were 10 per cent more likely to be obese than the wealthiest quartile. Some time around 1990 the burden of obesity ceased being mainly associated with wealth and became associated with poverty (Power and Schulkin, 2009: 129–30). The association of obesity with poverty is mirrored in the UK's type 2 diabetes figures, where in 2011 the prevalence rate of this ailment among the poorest decile was 2.5 times the national average. The developing nations where obesity is rising are also on the verge of a major health epidemic of obesity-related diseases. In India in 2011, 5 per cent of the population, 60 million people, were classified as morbidly obese (BMI in excess of 40). India had, in 2011, 50 million with diabetes 2 (80 per cent of them obese) and the Indian toll from diabetes 2 is expected to rise to 100 million by 2025. China has a diabetes type 2 epidemic with 92 million sufferers in 2011, while Chinese urban child obesity rates have risen from 1.5 per cent in 1989 to 12.6 per cent in 1997. Mexico had a diabetes 2 prevalence of 14 per cent in 2011; diabetes 2 rates on Nauru reached 33 per cent in 2011. Mexico in 2008 saw 70,000 deaths from diabetes, and the disease cost the Mexican economy some 67 billion pesos or US$6 billion, a figure expected to double by 2017. This rise in obesity and diabetes is partly caused by the rapid shift from food scarcity to (cheap) food abundance and the effects of the 'thrifty gene' described above, but the developing-world obesity epidemic is also driven by socio-economic changes. These are the same changes already seen in the global North, but in the South they are occurring at a far greater pace. In India, Africa and South America the population has urbanized rapidly, moving away from walking to mechanized transport, from manual work to office work (Abubakari et al., 2008; Rguibi and Belahsen, 2007; Filozof et al., 2001). In Pacific Islands such as Kiribati and Nauru, rising urbanization has conspired with poverty and scarcity of agricultural land to create a society reliant on overseas remittances and dependent on cheap fatty meat and processed foods imported from New Zealand (Locke, 2009). In some sub-Saharan African countries, obesity is seen as a positive quality, indicative of health and fertility, for women of marriageable age (Van de Merwe and Pepper, 2006). In rural areas of Mauritania and Uganda young women may be effectively force-fed huge amounts of Calories, a practice known as leblouh or gavage, to give them the desired obese look (Gluckman and Hanson, 2012: 40). This association of fatness with health is not confined to Africa. In Greece a plump physique is associated with well-being and prosperity, while in Punjab a traditional greeting goes 'you look fresh and fat today' (Williams et al., 1998: 271).

We can now briefly describe the geographies of obesity. On a global scale there are five regions of obesity, with different underlying causes of obesity in each region. These are:

1. North America, Europe, Australasia
   The poor, those without personal transport, eat less fresh produce and more locally retailed and takeaway food, richer in fat and sugar. Also some people may be genetically predisposed to obesity through past migration selecting for the 'thrifty gene'.
2. Rapidly developing countries, e.g. Mexico, China, India
   Recent fast increase in food availability is promoting obesity among those starved as children or foetuses. Also rapidly falling birth rates may cause only children to be overfed by older relatives as a mark of love.
3. South-West Asia
   Social occasions are often marked by large meals, for example in Kuwait (Al-Kandari, 2006) and the United Arab Emirates (Malik and Bakir, 2007), and a hot climate may deter walking, especially by those whose wealth allows for car ownership (car travel rather than walking can be a signifier of financial success).
4. Sub-Saharan Africa
   Obesity is still seen as a sign of wealth, and for women as a sign of marriage eligibility; not dissimilar to how obesity was perceived in Europe a few centuries ago. In some remote rural communities forced feeding of women still occurs to prepare them for marriage.
5. Pacific Islands
   As in North America and Europe, low purchasing power leads to the consumption of inferior meat that would not find a market in more affluent countries, only here the poverty is on a national, not individual, scale.

> Flap meat, fatty meat eaten in Fiji, Kiribati and Nauru that originates in New Zealand, is an example of cheap food promoting obesity in the Pacific Islands region. Many of these Pacific Islands have economies that have been impoverished by resource extraction or colonial exploitation and their populations are now mainly on low incomes.

Obesity, therefore, has a range of multiple causes. Some causative factors are biological: overeating, eating the wrong foods, having a physiological makeup that predisposes towards obesity. Many other causes are economic, social and cultural. As we saw in Chapter 1, our attitude towards food is a major factor in whether we choose to make an effort to eat healthily, or just see eating as a refuelling exercise, to be got over with as quickly and conveniently as possible so we can move on with life. Do we engage with our food, or just scoff it? Chapters 3 and 4 explore our psychological and cultural attitudes to food, while Chapter 5 will review the economic and social changes to the food chain, the way consumers buy food.

3 Minding our diet

Sanitizing our food. *The more you eat, the less flavour; the less you eat, the more flavour*

In Chapter 1 we saw how consumers have become disengaged from the food we eat, and how this has led us to see food as merely 'fuel', a necessity to be eaten as quickly and cheaply as possible. We want food sanitized, plastic wrapped, not just for hygiene but so that we do not get messy while handling it. The slab of lamb in a Styrofoam modified-atmosphere carton is conveniently remote from the cuddly, woolly little animal gambolling in a field, that we take our children to see after Sunday roast. Supermarkets that give us strawberries in December have severed any link between food and seasons, and British food shoppers prioritize convenience and price over quality of food. If these consumers acquire extra spending power they will likely spend it on non-food products (Harrington, 1989: 202). In 2000, 42 per cent of British grocery shoppers gave 'convenience of doing all the shopping under one roof' as the main factor in choice of food retailer, 70 per cent saying this was 'important'. The factor 'price' was rated as the main determinant of retailer by 18 per cent, with 68 per cent saying price was 'important' (Reynolds, 2004: 13). Food is supposed to be messy, sticky and above all smelly. 'Was it an accident that modernity declared war on smells?' asks Bauman (1993: 23). He answers, smells are ungovernable, defiant, inextinguishable; they do not respect borders, and they are dirty. Smells, the smells of nature, are atavistic; they signify primitive decadence, and can only partially be masked by the artificial sophisticated scents of manufactured modernity. The natural, decayed, uncontrolled, unmanicured state of things is to smell, whereas cultured modern life should be odour-free. Food stains clothes and makes them smelly and greasy, something we cannot permit in today's neatly tailored primped world. Above all, says Bauman, smells remind us of death and we hide death away in hospitals and care homes; death is sanitized by elaborate rituals of departure. Likewise, modern food must not die but remain forever fresh, to be consumed sometime at our convenience. The 'civilizing process' as described by the German sociologist Norbert Elias in his 1939 seminal work *Über den Prozeß der Zivilisation* is observable in the way we sanitize food. Elias' civilizing process may be seen as an extension of shame or disgust; what was once acceptable, such as farting or belching, becomes disgusting, unacceptable. Elias did not claim that we became nicer to each other, merely more circumspect about our personal actions in each other's presence. Hence, our food must become ever more disguised, ever more remote, from its carnal bloody raw origins. In the 1300s Guillaume Tirel, chef to the French King Charles V, wrote a cookbook, *Le Viandier*, which included 'a recipe for a swan that has been skinned and roasted before the skin is put back on the cooked bird' (Trubek, 2008). Contrast today's sanitized treatment of animal protein, where no trace of eyes or hoofs or claws or fur or feathers can remain associated with our meat, which rather must be ready packed in plastic as inanimate slabs of protein, their origin undetectable except by the supermarket label. In contrast, Halal butchers sell meat with the offal (heart, kidneys, liver) still attached, because offal spoils quickly; if the offal smells fresh, the meat must be good.

The sandwich, named after the eighteenth-century John Montagu, fourth Earl of Sandwich, says much about our attitude to food; he ordered his meat between two slices of bread, to allow him to play card games without getting his hands greasy. Using bread as a 'plate' goes back to medieval times or earlier; gravy-soaked meat was placed upon 'trenchers', slabs of stale bread, and the meat consumed with a knife and spoon. The gravy-soaked trencher was given to the dogs or the poor by wealthy diners, or eaten by the less affluent. Similarly, the Cornish pasty, consisting of a meat mince inside a pastry casing in a D shape, with a thicker crimped edge along the curve, enabled Cornish miners to eat the contents without touching them; the crimped edge was discarded. This was important when miners' fingers might pick up arsenic contamination (Cornish Pasty Association, 2013). What Montagu invented was the closed sandwich that became popular in the nineteenth century with factory labourers who needed a form of fast food they could eat at work. Other societies still maintain a tactile relationship with their food; the Chinese chew chicken legs and bones in public, because of the intense meaty taste of the bone marrow and fat. It is no coincidence that the Chinese like their food very fresh, so fresh that the Tesco supermarket in central Beijing has a tank from which customers select the fish they want killed and sold to them. Jewish Kosher restaurant chefs in New York also value the texture of meat; it should be so tender it falls apart unless cut carefully by hand. We may distance ourselves from food but at a deeper subconscious level we are influenced by the sensory attributes of the objects around us, their colours, shapes, sizes and other physical properties. Some of these influences are instinctive, inborn, they had survival value in guiding us towards nutritious plants and away from poisonous ones; our preference for sweet tastes, for example, because no toxic plant tastes sweet. Other influences are more artificial, the product of the culture we grow up in. All of these stimuli have a powerful effect upon our dietary choices.

The five senses and food. *Scents and sense-ibilities*

Despite our disengagement from food smells, the odour of food has a powerful positive effect on our desire for it, as many shopkeepers know well. It is no accident that, while supermarket lamb chops are sanitized in plastic wrapping, roast chickens can still be seen turning on a spit in many supermarkets; the smell of roast chicken is a powerful hunger stimulant, and connects to the happy emotions we associate with family Sunday dinners. The in-store bakery does the same with the smell of baked bread, as does the store café with its aroma of coffee. However, our first impression of any object is its colour, size and shape, because 90 per cent of our sensory information comes through our eyes. There is a powerful language of colour associated with food; the greens, yellows, oranges and reds we first see on entering the fresh fruit and vegetable (FFV) section of a supermarket reminds us of freshness and healthiness, which is why many supermarkets place these items near the door where it is the first display the customer sees. Red is the colour of many fruits and we still associate red with sweetness, so that red foods can have reduced sugar and still taste as sweet as sugared non-red foods. Red is the colour of excitement, danger, blood, fire, warmth and so many retailers put special offers in red type; it is also why Communist revolutionaries adopted red as their symbolic colour. Red is also linked with good fortune in East Asia, and red rice in this region of the world commands a higher price than ordinary rice because of its association with good luck (Juliano, 1985). If red is associated with action, green symbolizes calm, nature, original, fresh. Green packaging is taken to mean eco-friendly, and a particular shade of white-green invokes the fresh clean taste of peppermint. Blue is an anti-food colour because so few foods are truly blue; it signified poison to the Victorian British, and many toxic substances came in blue glass bottles. Blue suppresses appetite, so dieters are advised to eat from blue plates. The importance of food colour was illustrated by an experiment in which diners were given a meal of blue-tinted steak and green chips, but served under a light which made the food look normal. When the light was changed to white and the abnormal colours became apparent, some diners were physically sick. Purple, the colour of luxury in Europe, generally has more positive connotations in the world of food; it is associated with summer berry fruits. A recent cultural modification has been the association of purple with antioxidants in foods such as blueberries, and this colour code has been extended to the humble potato. Purple Majesty potatoes have been sold by Sainsbury since 2011, marketed as containing healthy anthocyanins, a type of antioxidant also present in purple broccoli. Because anthocyanins are not easily absorbed by the gut they survive to the lower intestine where they protect against bowel cancer. However, in 2013 scientific concerns began to emerge that antioxidants might not have health benefits; in fact overconsumption of them might actually promote cancer. This story has yet to play out, to develop into a new food scare, to reduce the sales of antioxidant foods, or be retracted and die down. Black is a colour that had psychologically negative connotations with food but has been culturally modified into a more positive role. Black once signified rotten or mouldy food but European and North American consumers are becoming accustomed to black foods through exposure to truffles, olives and liquorice. Garlic can be converted from white to black through heating in humid conditions, a process that gives it a long shelf-life; when people eat black garlic they often perceive a non-existent trace of liquorice, whereas in fact the garlic tastes sweeter.

One factor we are not good at evaluating is the absolute size of things; rather, we respond to relative changes in shape. We consume drinks more quickly in short wide glasses than in tall narrow ones, because when drinking from the latter the level of the drink falls faster with each sip. We eat more when the food is on a larger plate, or when eating with larger cutlery, a phenomenon known as 'unit bias'. We accept the portion size offered as the appropriate size to consume, so if yoghurt is sold in larger pots we eat more of it. This has led to a disturbing trend known as 'supersizing' whereby food retailers, food producers and fast food restaurants compete by increasing portion sizes; a trend facilitated by declines in the real prices of food and transport, so that most of what the customer pays is for service elements such as premises, salaries and advertising. As portion sizes creep up, we eat more and feel more satisfied; we do not connect our expanding waistlines with any individual 'supersized' serving. There is a similar process in the clothing industry with garment sizes being relabelled upwards because clothing manufacturers do not want to alienate customers by reminding them of their inability to fit into smaller sizes (Critser, 2003: 58). Small-sized clothes became as big as former medium-sized clothes, removing an incentive to stay slim. Examples of increasing portion size, and calorie count, in UK ready meals include Marks & Spencer's spaghetti bolognese, 283 g in 1990 and 400 g in 2005. Iceland's beef stew and dumplings weighed 285 g in the 1990s but 500 g in 2005. A typical child's ready meal in UK shops today weighs 300 g, an adult portion size in the 1990s. Between 1960 and 1996 the energy content of a McDonald's portion of fries rose from 200 to 610 Calories; a typical McDonald's meal rose from 590 to 1,550 Calories. Even bread slices have grown; a segment of a Warburton's medium sliced loaf weighed 36.4 g in the 1990s, but 40.5 g in 2000 (Lowell 2004). Since 2007 this trend towards increasing portion size has now reversed in many cases, with food manufacturers imposing hidden food inflation by reducing pack sizes, while maintaining or even increasing prices. This reversal, discussed in Chapter 6, may not however reduce the trend towards obesity. People who gained weight now have higher Calorie requirements, so their appetite is greater. Shrinking portion sizes may simply push consumers towards cheaper foods in an attempt to balance the budget while satisfying the stomach, and cheaper foods tend to be more obesogenic.

Description and branding of food. *Eating the brand*

If portion size can fool us, so can the brand name. Critser (2003: 48) reports on a school in Los Angeles, USA, where the children preferred Pizza Hut branded pizzas to the more nutritionally balanced ones made according to United States Department of Agriculture (USDA) guidelines. The USDA pizzas contained 375 Calories; the Pizza Hut ones had almost twice that. In the 1990s the school repackaged USDA pizzas in Pizza Hut packaging and the schoolchildren did not notice any difference; they were essentially 'eating the brand'. Bell and Valentine (1997: 83) noted a domestic example of this, where a low-income mother would feed her children economy-brand cereal from a Frosties packet. Robinson et al. (2007) give examples of pre-school children in Maryland preferring McDonald's food in McDonald's packaging to the same food in unbranded containers; the same children preferred branded carrots over unbranded. Even at ages three to five, these children were very brand-aware. Eurofood (2007) also reported that children rated food as tasting better if it came in McDonald's packaging; this applied to food both from McDonald's and from other burger manufacturers. Adults are also susceptible to this type of suggestion, in both positive and negative directions. Breakfast bars are believed to taste worse if the packaging says they contain soy, even if they do not, while 'Black Forest Double Chocolate Cake' tastes nicer than identical cake simply labelled 'Chocolate Cake'. Labelling a food product as 'organic' enhances its perceived taste and reduces the Calories it is estimated to contain (*Cornell Chronicle*, 2013). Putting the image of a person or a face on food packaging also enhances the attractiveness of the brand. In 1870 the USA passed the Federal Trademarks law, enabling manufacturers to protect images and symbols connected with their brand. This visual device was quickly taken up by food manufacturers to reassure customers of the wholesomeness of industrially produced food (Carolan, 2012: 135). An early example was the Quaker Oats Man, from 1877, and in 1906 W. H. Kellogg printed his signature on each box of cornflakes, and his face on each pack from 1907. The image need not even be real; the Jolly Green Giant image on canned vegetables, used from 1926, also forged an emotional connection with consumers. The perceived emotions of other people also affect our food preferences; Barthomeuf et al. (2009) found that preferences against disliked foods, and preferences for liked foods, could both be minimized by the association of these foods with, respectively, faces showing pleasure and disgust. So putting a smiley face on your product may not attract those who already like your brand, but it may reduce antipathy to it by those who do not (J. J. A. Shaw, 2012: 88).

Cultures of food. *After a good dinner one can forgive anybody, even one's own relatives*

For people and families displaced from their homeland region, traditional food and food consumption habits are maintained as a link to their cultural traditions. Food is 'noisy' (Smith and Jehlika, 2007: 397): it speaks volumes both to and about its consumer; about where they come from, what religion and social class they originate from, their ethics and personal preferences.

Sometimes migrants face a conflict between traditional country-of-origin food traditions and those of the host country, leading to undesirable health outcomes. People of Pakistani origin in the UK may keep to the Pakistani meal custom of eating a large midday *salan* (curry), which is seen as wholesome and filling (Jamal, 1998); they see the British habit of three lighter daily meals as unsatisfying. They eat one large *handi*, or family meal, daily, symbolizing family unity. In Pakistani households that have migrated to Europe, food is perceived by the children as reflecting 'maternal love', whereas these children see Western food as reflecting 'independence, convenience and adventure'. So when Pakistani teenagers socialize with Europeans they eat the family *handi* and the customary three Western meals, leading to obesity. Migrants tend to be poorer, on lower wages, than people born in the host country and this can lead these migrants to eat a poorer diet than they would have consumed in their country of origin because host-country food prices are higher. Migrants may also perceive Western foods as being of higher status, although often such archetypal 'Western' foods as the beef burger are less healthy (Winham, 2009). However, there are also powerful economic incentives to cater for migrant food cultures; sometimes such incentives come from unexpected sources. The University of Manchester, UK, located near Manchester city centre, attracts many Muslim students from residential areas a few miles to the south of the campus; because of strong family and religious ties, many Muslim students choose a university within daily commuting distance of home. However, Manchester University canteen did not serve Halal food, and it was not possible for students to go home for lunch and be back in time for 2 p.m. lectures. This had a deterrent effect on student recruitment that became financially significant for the university when tuition fees were introduced in England in 1998, incentivizing Manchester University to provide Halal food items.

On an individual level, people cling to their food traditions, but societies as a whole have generally embraced food cultures from across the world, as migration and holiday travel have broadened people's experience of other countries. The colonial empires built by Britain, France and other European countries have created a legacy of links, economic, linguistic and cultural, between the former colonies and the colonizers, and these links are replicated in the food cultures of different nations. Indian restaurants in the UK began with the Hindostanee Coffee House in George Street, London, which opened in 1809. The first modern-style curry house restaurant in Britain was the Salut-e-Hind in Holborn, London, opened in 1911, followed by The Shafi in Gerrard Street, London. These establishments, staffed by Lascars, sailors from East Bengal (now Bangladesh), were mainly patronized by other Indians; the first Indian restaurant popular with British customers was the Veeraswamy, opened in 1927 in Regent Street, London; this restaurant still operates today. The UK has ethnic minority communities from many countries, creating a demand for a wide range of ethnic foods, and holidays abroad by Britons have also widened the demand for exotic foods. The recent fashion for safari holidays has created demand for exotic meats such as ostrich, eland, impala, wildebeest, zebra and even python. These meats are perceived as healthier as they are lean and chemical-free. However, UK supermarkets have been wary of giving shelf space to these meats in place of faster selling, conventional higher profit meat lines.

Other European countries have also witnessed an internationalization of their food cuisine. Sweden is Europe's biggest per capita consumer of Mexican food while the Netherlands has a large market for Chinese, Italian and Mexican food. In Denmark a cultural food clash occurred because Denmark has a strong culture of pork consumption; pig-rearing is a major industry there. However pork is *haram* (forbidden) in Islam. The mayor of a Copenhagen suburb, in the 1990s, even banned all Halal-slaughtered meat from public institutions within his jurisdiction (Haldrup et al., 2006) while some early Muslim migrants to Denmark abandoned their cultural mores to drink alcohol, eat pork and even change their names from Islamic to Danish-sounding ones. Until migrants have built up sufficient numbers to maintain a viable food retail system, religious institutions, schools, etc., they frequently subsume their culture to the host one; early Muslims arriving in the UK would buy food from Kosher shops, because Kosher dietary laws are similar to Halal rules. Jews arriving in the UK in the 1890s, fleeing Russian pogroms, would adopt English names, and Indians arriving in south Wales in the 1970s were advised by the local council how to cook less odorous foods so as not to annoy the locals. Today, of course, we live in more enlightened culturally aware times. France, with its strong former-colonial links to North and West Africa and the Middle East, has couscous as its favourite dish, and is a strong market for Halal food. France has been subjected to similar socio-economic trends that in the UK have shifted food consumption away from traditional family meals and towards convenience fast food, and in 2011 the French government succeeded in having UNESCO declare the 'French dinner table' a part of world cultural heritage. The former French kings would be drooling in their graves, but there were concerns among the living that this move implied that traditional French cuisine is an 'endangered species'. Judging by the changing behaviour of French consumers, traditional French cuisine might well be 'endangered'. French children are following their British counterparts in preferring chips, chocolate and ice cream (Cooke and Wardle, 2005) while their parents are eschewing the traditional French four-course dinner for easier-to-prepare foods such as couscous or choosing takeaway meals like burgers and pizzas. Most French aim to spend no more than 20 minutes cooking an evening meal, and 55 per cent of them now eat this meal in front of the TV rather than at a dinner table; Spain too is abandoning its healthy Mediterranean diet (*The Guardian*, 2004: 17). German households retain a strong preference for cheap dried foods that can be stored for long periods, a hangover from the privations of World War Two; this reduces their propensity to consume fresh fruit and vegetables. Dutch housewives are reported to be among the most price conscious in Europe (Seth and Randall,

1999: 132) so like the British they prioritize cheapness over food quality. In Norway, as in France, convenience fast food, or 'one hand food', has taken hold (Nasjonalforeningen for folkehelse, 1998: 1) while the consumption of fast food, desserts, chocolate and crisps has risen sharply in Poland since 1990 (Rudawska, 2001). This prioritization of cheapness over quality can be traced back to US shoppers in the 1950s and probably originated with the privations of the Great Depression of the 1930s and then World War Two (Logemann, 2012: 93).

The newly-affluent Asian nations are also shifting to a less healthy diet. South Korea has progressed from a per capita GDP of just 5 per cent of the USA's in 1970 to almost 50 per cent today; in 1970 the South Korean diet was mainly unrefined cereals and vegetables but today the national diet has shifted towards milk, meat, eggs and fish. Taiwan has experienced a similar income trajectory to South Korea, and animal fats have increased in the diet (Kim et al., 2005), with obesity rising in both countries. China too is succumbing to the global advance of convenience food; between 1989 and 1997 the more affluent Chinese reduced their per capita grain consumption by 15 per cent while meat consumption rose by 50 per cent (*The Economist*, 2003: 4). Worryingly for nutritionists, between 1980 and 2003, China's per capita poultry trebled, with beef up 120 per cent, but vegetable consumption fell by a fifth (grain fell 40 per cent, but fruit rose by 40 per cent) (Gould and Villarreal, 2006). A global fast food industry is emerging, with the same broad varieties of takeaway food – Chinese, Indian, Italian, Mexican, Thai – familiar on any British High Street, also selling well in the fast-growing Asian economies. India, which has hosted a significant Chinese community since the 1700s, has developed a blend of Chinese and Indian food, Chindian, Chinese food plus Indian spices. Italian pizzas sell well in China, but with a deeper bread base. The Japanese have also taken to Chinese food, despite a long history of hostility between those two countries. Even Iran now hosts 20 different American-style fast food chains (Momtaz et al., 2013: 606).

Food as fear. *Chew your food well, or it may chew you*

Not all modern developments in the modern food chain are universally welcomed by consumers; a culture of fear has developed around some foods. The spectre of obesity hovers behind all food treats; some foods excite more acute fears. Red meat is associated with cardiovascular disease and cancer as well as obesity (Steinfeld et al., 2006) while the technological advances in agriculture, discussed in Chapter 1, caused some consumers to worry about the wholesomeness of the food on their plates. Genetically Modified (GM) foods have spawned an entire literature of food fear, with reports that some animals instinctively avoid GM crops and concerns that GM DNA will irreversibly escape into wild plant populations. There are also socio-ethical issues such as the Terminator Gene in crops sold to Indian farmers, forcing them to buy new seed from the agri-corporations every year rather than following traditional farming practice and saving some seed to sow for next year's harvest. Should large seed corporations such as Monsanto have such commercial power over small farmers? What political power do these multinationals exert over the Indian government? And is this akin to neo-colonization? Truth is the first casualty of the food wars, with the anti-GM faction denying any report exonerating the new technologies. GM is the successor food fear to additives and E-numbers, a concern with a strong class element. In the UK, fear of additives was lowest in Scotland and highest in the affluent south-east and especially London where 85 per cent of women said they would pay more for additive-free food. The ABC1 social classes feared additives more than the C2DE classes, and younger consumers had greater fears than the old (Grant, 1989: 282). Milk raised special fears, perhaps because it is a pure white food given to vulnerable children; antibiotics, bovine growth hormone and mastitis in cows raised concerns. The commercialization of the growth hormone Recombinant Bovine Somatropin in the USA in 1994 sparked fears among European consumers about the content and health implications of their milk. We fear that which cannot be seen, tasted or smelt, so contamination of food by unseen pollutants that might stealthily poison us over many years worry us more than obesity or food poverty. If the disease produces horrific images, such as those of burning cow carcasses resulting from the UK's foot and mouth outbreak of 2001, we fear it more.

Minimata disease was an early case of mass slow poisoning of a food product; mercury compounds had been released into the sea at Minimata, Japan, from 1932; by the 1960s several thousand people had been crippled by a range of symptoms acquired from eating poisoned shellfish. Radioactive contamination of food, from lamb in Cumbria affected by the Chernobyl disaster to Japanese beef polluted by radiation leaking from the stricken Fukushima power station, is one of the modern plagues alarming consumers. Spain suffered its own Minimata-type disaster when, in the early 1980s, 1,000 people began dying of a strange wasting neurological disorder. The authorities were quick to blame the disaster on contaminated cooking oil, but other evidence points to the true cause as being misuse of pesticide causing excessive levels of organophosphates in tomatoes (Woffinden, 2001). The official line that inferior cooking oils contaminated with aniline had undercut genuine Spanish olive oil was far less damaging to the Spanish agricultural economy than the notion that illiterate workers had misread instructions for pesticide use on southern Spanish tomato farms and used too much. Food, politics, technology and economics formed another toxic brew in the mid-1980s when British cows began behaving strangely. In 1986 farmers noticed cows becoming aggressive, hypersensitive to sound and touch, walking erratically, falling down and unable to get up again. Mad Cow Disease, as the affliction was to become known, peaked in 1992 with 37,280 cows struck down in that year (*New Scientist*, 2011a). A total of 180,000 cows were affected in the UK alone; 4.4 million cattle had to be slaughtered, costing the UK economy £4 billion. Affected cows were found to have spongy brains, riddled with holes, hence the official name of the disease, Bovine Spongiform Encephalitis (BSE). It was an oddly transmitted disease, spread not by bacteria or viruses but by prions, misshapen sections of protein that could cause healthy protein they came into contact with to also become misshapen and dysfunctional. From 1962, cattle, vegetarian by nature, had been fed the remains of other dead cattle to produce beef faster and more cheaply; the prions from dead cattle brains and spinal cord entered new cows, survived the digestion process, and infected their brains, perpetuating the disease. In 1989 cattle remains were banned from UK cattle feed. BSE appeared in other countries; by end-2000 Belgium, Denmark, France, Germany, Ireland, Italy, Netherlands, Portugal, Spain and Switzerland had seen cases, followed by Canada, Japan and the USA. The UN Food and Agriculture Organization expressed concern that BSE could appear in less-developed nations, lacking resources to detect and contain the disease, but so far this has not occurred. Other animals have their versions of BSE; scrapie is found in sheep, and cats, mink and ostriches are prone to similar disorders. Humans too have been diagnosed with this brain disease; Creutzfeld-Jacob Disease (CJD) has been known in the Fore people of Papua New Guinea, whose food culture once included eating brains of dead relatives, to acquire their wisdom. The Papuan version of CJD was known as Kuru. Cases of CJD, virtually unknown in Britain before 1984, rose to a relatively modest peak of 27 in 2000. The first death from CJD was in 1995, and a definitive link between BSE and CJD was proved in 1996. UK cattle exports were banned worldwide in 1996 (the ban was lifted in 2006). BSE caused British beef production to fall from 1,000,000 tons annually in the 1990s to just over 600,000 tons in the early 2000s. Further scares originated from the news that CJD could be transmitted in blood transfusions. In an attempt to reassure the British public, John Gummer, UK Minister of Agriculture, fed his daughter a beef burger live on TV in May 1990. The feared mass epidemic of CJD never materialized; total deaths by 2009 had amounted to 166 in the UK and a further 44 elsewhere, including France, Ireland, Japan and the USA. The disease in cattle appeared to have died out too, with just ten cases of BSE recorded worldwide in 2010.

The question is where did BSE come from; why did it suddenly erupt in 1986? A common theory is that prions from scrapie-infected sheep killed in the same slaughterhouse as cattle transferred to cattle feed; prions can cross species boundaries, or no Britons would have contracted CJD. But despite most people having been exposed to these prions – the truly dangerous aspect of our modern mechanized food system is that it is an excellent mechanism for transmitting food diseases widely and rapidly – only a very small percentage of those exposed actually got CJD. Perhaps bovine prions do not easily subvert human brain protein. There was also a genetic theory; all the victims of CJD had a prion gene called MM, which has a prevalence of 37 per cent in the general population; other versions, MV or VV, may have a longer incubation period, so we may not be out of the woods yet, although each passing year must make that scenario less likely. With Kuru, those with genetic makeup MV took longer to develop the disease. A less-publicized theory links manganese and chicken feed. Propensity to develop CJD may be raised by a high ratio of manganese in the soil relative to copper (Humphrys, 2001: 252). Manganese miners in Chile are prone to 'manganese madness', a disease similar to CJD; manganese generates damaging free radicals in the brain, especially if copper levels are low, and free radicals can deform proteins. The organophosphates in sheep dips, whose development is closely linked with military research into nerve gases, are known to deplete copper and activate manganese in sheep. The 'mad cows' had also been fed chicken meal, and chicken meal is fortified with manganese because manganese deficiency in chickens can cause skin-shelled eggs that crack easily or even deformed chicks (*Merck Veterinary Manual*, 2012). Thankfully there were too few victims of CJD in the 1990s to ascertain whether eating chicken could render humans more prone to that horrific disease, but the chicken industry had a narrow escape from the negative publicity it would have suffered had the manganese connection been widely reported.

There have been so many food health scares in the past few decades that the public may be overwhelmed with food advice and food scares and ignore sound advice, especially if successive food messages contradict each other. People have been told not to eat too much tuna, because of metal pollution, and to eat oily fish such as tuna. In the UK, Edwina Curry warned about salmonella in eggs in 1988, severely denting egg consumption (the public overreacted to a small localized issue) but eggs have been promoted as a healthy breakfast food. There is a dissonance between how experts analyse hazard from risk and how the public perceives danger. For the expert, hazard = magnitude x probability. The hazard from meteorite strike on London that might kill 1 million people but has a 0.001 per cent chance of happening in a given year presents the same hazard as a major fire at a crowded shopping centre that might kill 1,000 people and has a 1 per cent chance of occurring in any one year. Both disasters have, in maths-speak, a chance of killing 10 people a year although of course such events do not spread their casualties evenly over many years. For the public, however, there is a further calculation of risk = hazard x outrage. In other words, the public agonizes more over disasters that it finds unacceptable than other disasters with the same risk that are more acceptable. In the example above, we can probably do little to avert a meteorite that has London's name on it, but a disaster at a shopping mall due to human negligence or error – that must be dealt with, now. If the meteorite's target was Tokyo, with a possible 2 million deaths or 20 per year, the public would still demand the shopping centre risk be dealt with first.

Public outrage is higher if the hazard is:

1. Coerced, not voluntary; many have little choice, for example, but to travel by train.
2. Industrial, not natural; someone has created this hazard, not nature.

3. Unfamiliar, not familiar; it is caused by some strange chemical, not water.
4. Memorable, rather than not memorable; the hazard has created ghastly media images, such as the burning cattle carcasses affected by foot and mouth disease.
5. Dreaded, rather than not dreaded; we dread the idea of our brains dissolving into a spongy mess with CJD, but we do not dread obesity, which has a vastly higher death toll than CJD.
6. Catastrophic, not chronic; if 100 people die at once in a flood that occurs every 1,000 years (= 0.1 deaths per year), there is more concern than if one person dies on a rickety river bridge every five years.
7. Unknowable, not knowable; we did not fully understand the mechanism whereby some people got CJD, and many did not, but we feel we know more about what causes obesity.
8. Controlled by others, not controlled by self; we fear a plane crash more than a car crash, because we feel more in control in a car, even though far more people die in road accidents than in plane accidents. We feel in control of what obesogenic foods we eat, but fear unknown E-numbers, even though many E-numbers are natural and harmless.
9. Unfair, not fair; food chain practices that are perceived as raising corporate profits are less acceptable than dangerous food consumption practices that give us pleasure, such as eating sugary foods.
10. Moral concerns, not morally irrelevant; we are more concerned if the hazard causes suffering to animals, or social inequality.
11. Sources of information are not trusted, rather than trustworthy; if public information is disseminated by a source perceived as having a vested interest, or by an organization recently reviled, such as the banks during the credit crunch, the public becomes more concerned about the hazard.
12. Process unresponsive to public concerns, not responsive; hazards created by remote global corporations give rise to more public concern than hazards created by familiar local UK-based companies that we feel are accountable and listen to public opinion.

We can summarize these factors in Table 3.1. Analysing some risks Western society currently faces and scoring the degree of fear each factor invokes gives an almost perfectly inverse relationship between the numbers affected and the magnitude of the risk in the public eye.

Unknown = Can the risk be there **now** without us perceiving it, is there a **present worry**?
Lack of control = Do we feel we cannot avoid or control this risk?
Unacceptable = Do we feel the **benefits** are not worth the **risk**?
Dread = Fear of **future** escalation of damage.
Numbers = Are **large** numbers of people affected (economic loss, health damage or death)?

Table 3.1 Society fear score, selected risks (Low = 0, Medium = 1, High = 2)

Risk	*Unknown (present)*	*Lack control*	*Unacceptable (balance)*	*Dread (future)*	*Numbers (affected)*	*Voice (clout)*	*Score /12*
Nuclear power	High	High	Medium	Medium	Low	Low	6
Climate change	Medium	High	High	High	Medium	High[(a)]	10
Violent crime	Medium	High	High	Medium	Low	Low	6
Traffic deaths	Low	Low	Low	Low	High	Low	2
Plane or train crash	High	High	Medium	Medium	Low	High	8
Obesity	Low	Low	Low	Medium	High	Low	3
Famine	Low	High	Medium[(b)]	Medium	High	Low	6
Cancer, AIDS	High	Medium	High	High	Medium[(c)]	High	10
BSE	High	High	High	High	Low	High	10
Food additives, GMO	High	High	High	High	Low	High	10

(a) Although deaths attributable to climate change are mainly in the poor global South, the issue has a high profile in Western media.
(b) Although the face of famine – starving children, bellies swollen with kwashiorkor, is unacceptable, in practice we accept the global food economic system that produced famine in economically deprived regions.
(c) Less than 15 per cent of deaths globally are from cancer, though this may rise with increasing longevity.

Voice = Do those **actually affected** have influence (clout), politically, or are they mainly the **voiceless poor**?

This analysis suggests why obesity, or 'globesity', the global epidemic of obesity, raises perhaps fewer concerns than it should. Obesity is popularly associated with self-indulgence; actually it is often linked with poverty, the inability to afford healthy food. Obesity is seen as something we can control; yet losing weight is very hard for most people. Obesity is seen as the result of choosing to eat certain foods; in fact our food choices and the nutrition content of our food are less under our control than we like to think. Obesity is seen as imposing a low level of costs; because much healthcare is free at the point of consumption, having been paid for by taxes or insurance, we underestimate its costs. Obesity is seen as killing few people; in fact it kills more people each year than die of under-nutrition.

We have examined some factors that have created a culture of fear in our food consumption. Although obesity has a lower profile than perhaps it should, the food fears we do recognize are affecting our propensity towards obesity. The rest of this chapter examines the impact this culture of fear is having on our food choices, as mediated by our underlying psychological preferences for certain foods.

Food neophobia. *Out with the new and in with the old*

Food neophobia, literally the fear or dislike of new foods, varies at different ages. New-born children have simple taste preferences for sweet foods; human milk and even human amniotic fluid is sweet. As we have seen, this preference for sweet is biologically useful for keeping us from consuming poisonous plants which are bitter, never sweet. The flavour of the mother's amniotic fluid and milk is also affected by her diet; if she eats vegetables the baby too will detect these sulphury, earthy flavours and form a preference for them. If she eats spicy foods the baby will taste these. This too is a useful biological feature as it ensures that children like the foods customarily eaten by the family they are born into, and so eat well and thrive. Therefore breastfeeding babies can, if the mother eats plenty of vegetables, raise a child who also likes these foods. Preferences for fatty foods are not inborn but learnt in the first two or three years of life (Miljkovik et al., 2008), and the foods a baby smells also helps form its tastes. Unfortunately many baby foods are highly sweetened, because the manufacturers want the mother to perceive that the infant really likes their brand of food, and this sets up the child for a lifetime bias towards sweet foodstuffs. Babies will, as any parent will testify, put almost anything in their mouth but food neophobia begins at around age four. Again this is useful because babies need to acquire certain bacteria; they need to prime their immune system so it knows what to fight. Food neophobia kicks in at about the same time the emotion of 'disgust' appears, when the child starts to avoid things like excrement. By now the child's body should have its requisite cargo of bacteria and a functioning immune system. We may not wish to reflect too much on the fact that nine-tenths of the cells making up a human adult are bacteria; the only reason we look human is that our cells are much larger than bacterial ones.

Studies of food neophobia in childhood may give conflicting results depending on whether 'consumption' or 'preferences' are being researched, what social and ethnic group the children are from, and whether boys or girls are being studied. Boys tend to dislike vegetables more than girls. Food neophobia increases among the less-affluent. After puberty, food neophobia declines again, as the child prepares for independence and eating new foods beyond the family setting. However, if the child has a dislike of vegetable tastes this may persist through adulthood. Most of what we 'taste' from food is actually perceived through smell which is closely linked to the limbic system, the part of our brain that deals with emotion. Adults prefer the foods they liked as children, useful for reinforcing family ties. Emotion, seemingly irrational, is a vital mechanism for speedily avoiding danger; imagine the plight of an unemotional person, being rapidly approached by a hungry lion, who relied on pure logical calculation to decide whether to climb a tree or run. Damasio (1996) describes a patient whose prefrontal cortex (logical thinking area) and limbic area (emotion) were severed to alleviate seizures. The patient, states Damasio, would become stuck in a loop, perpetually deliberating, unable to reach a conclusion without the benefit of an 'emotional nudge'. Likewise, we benefit from the emotional response of rapid ejection from the mouth of foods of dubious taste, without deliberation as to whether the food might actually be beneficial not harmful.

Culture is significant because what foods different cultures find acceptable or not is often rather arbitrary. There is a scientific foundation for the Kosher/Halal food rules; pork is prone to harbouring parasites if not properly cooked, and shellfish can easily become contaminated as they are bottom-feeders. Rabbit meat (low in cholesterol and fat) is popular in Spain, but has almost vanished from British plates since the myxomatosis epidemic of the 1950s onwards. However, why do Britons accept frogs' legs from France but do not eat dogs' legs? Why not fish-, or meat-flavoured ice cream? Why is yoghurt fruit-flavoured but not vegetable-flavoured? The frontiers of what foods are culturally acceptable can shift, just as other activities can shift in or out of cultural acceptability. Smoking has become taboo; gay marriage has become tolerated. Rabbit and pigeon are out of fashion as foods, while we now buy chocolate flavoured with chilli, sea salt and Marmite; we do not (yet) have broccoli-flavoured yoghurt but we do have bacon-flavoured jam, from a company called Eat 17, in Walthamstow, London, postcode E17. Bacon-flavoured soda is sold by a US company called Lester's Fixins. Heston Blumenthal, who might be described as an 'anarchist chef' for his experimental dishes such as snail porridge, produced savoury, mustard-flavoured ice cream for sale by Waitrose in 2013 (demand was low). Blumenthal has also pioneered, or rather reinvented, dormice as a food; Heston's dormice lollipops echo the time when this rodent was a Roman delicacy. Walkers Crisps had a competition in 2008 to find new flavours (finalists' entries included Cajun Squirrel, Chilli Chocolate and Fish and Chips), and spreadable cheese now comes in a chocolate flavour. The middle classes attempt to be different, experiment with new tastes and flavour combinations, whereas less-affluent classes are more conservative in their food tastes (Bugge and Almås, 2006). In a hedonistic society, a 'morality of fun' emerges, whose only imperative is enjoyment, because the consumer is 'haunted', as Baudrillard puts it, by 'fears of missing out' (Poster, 2001: 51–2). However, just as consumers are becoming more adventurous with new tastes, or new taste combinations, they may also be becoming more cautious and old-fashioned in their food preferences.

Food nostalgia. *Eating your childhood*

Food technophobia, allied with a general discontent with modernity, is causing some formerly old-fashioned foods to make a comeback. Smash was an early convenience food: a yellow powder simply requiring water to convert into something resembling mashed potato, for time-pressed mums too busy to peel and mash the real thing. It was promoted by an iconic advertisement featuring Martian robots who mocked Earthlings for preparing mashed potato the old-fashioned way, 'They peel them with their metal knives … They are clearly a most primitive people' intoned the spacefaring robots, followed by a metallic laugh, in the 1974 TV advert. Of course we would all soon be following the Apollo astronauts to our Moonbase home and eating little pills for food, so nobody would need knives or any other kitchen utensils in a spaceworld home without kitchens (we did get hospitals and schools without kitchens). The Smash brand was bought by Premier Foods and revived in 2004. The 1974 advert seems almost deliberately naive, unsophisticated, sinisterly quaintly non-PC in the way it refers to 'primitive people'. It harks back to a world where Robertson Jam used a golliwog as its logo, a world faintly echoed in the 'Man from Del Monte' adverts of the 1980s. In these, a Caucasian man visits tropical plantations staffed by Hispanics and Africans, who wait expectantly for the avuncular White's commendation of 'He say YES'.

Desires for a 'simpler' world combined with higher food prices from 2007 onwards to revive the demand among Britons for old-fashioned foods such as pigs' trotters; these returned to the shelves of the upmarket supermarket chain Waitrose in 2008, at £1.99 kg. In 2008 Waitrose also began selling Bath Chaps, or pigs' cheeks; at £2.99 kg, they were significantly cheaper than prime pork at £5.99 kg. Oxo Cubes, Angel Delight, Spam, corned beef, turnips, Chicken Kiev, Twiglets, Arctic Roll and Angel Delight are among other revived foods that had departed from mainstream British cuisine by the 1990s. The celebrity chef Heston Blumenthal has revived the 1970s classic prawn cocktail. Turnips, a staple English food in the Middle Ages, are cheaper than parsnips and good for bulking out stews and casseroles, and can be added to mashed potatoes; real ones or Smash. The childhood nostalgia element is most visible in the revival of old-fashioned sweet shops where luridly coloured boiled sweets whose hues once derived from coal tar dyes sit in huge jars, to be sold by the quarter-pound. The unit weight has changed and the colours no longer come from coal tar, but such shops now sell childhood memories such as aniseed balls, lemon bonbons, sherbet and liquorice. Drinks like Tizer, the bright red fizzy liquid sold as an 'appetizer' in 1924, made a comeback in 2007; parents see it as a better alternative to Cola or Pepsi. At least it is British, they may reason, not foreign-American. For childhood-nostalgic adults, Dandelion Burdock and Cloudy Lemonade are back, and they come in returnable bottles, more environmentally friendly and another memory of decades ago revived. Such food nostalgia may explain the success of Polish food in Britain. Polish food is like old-fashioned British food, with meat, cabbage, beetroot and apple pie. *The Grocer* (2007: 34) reported that two-fifths of customers at the Polish Deli, Trowbridge, a small town in southern England, were English, coming for the Polish sausages, dumplings and smoked mackerel. Meanwhile horsemeat is enjoying a revival in France, after the specialist *boucheries chevalines* almost died out in the 1990s. Then, horsemeat was only a fallback meat, for eating on Mondays when beef butchers traditionally shut; now horsemeat is eaten any day of the week, and is seen as upmarket, healthy, low in fat and high in iron. Horsemeat represents a quintessentially French resistance to the inroads of fast American food; in Chapter 4 we see why horsemeat is acceptable in some countries but rejected in others.

The growth of nutraceuticals. *Hippocrital food*

Concerns about the health of our food have revived the notion of food as a medicine. As far back as the fifth century BC Hippocrates said 'Let food be your medicine, and medicine be your food.' There is a long history of food as medicine, present also in traditional Chinese medicine and 2,000-year-old Indian Ayurvedic practice. In Europe, rhubarb and prunes have for centuries been used as laxatives, while fruit and vegetables are known to cure acne. Sage was believed to cure cuts and sores, its name deriving from the Latin *salvare*, to cure or save. The Romans believed that watercress would invigorate you, clear up a range of ailments and even sharpen the intellect; in medieval times this plant was eaten to 'clear the blood' after a winter diet of root vegetables. In fact watercress is a good source of iron, calcium and vitamin C, and it helps eradicate free radicals, so may protect against cancer. While the biology of nutrition and disease was unknown, traditional food cures often had a basis in empirical observations. The idea of food as medicine gained commercial influence in the 1980s with the emergence of terms such as nutraceuticals (a combination of pharmaceutical and nutrition), superfoods and functional foods. The idea began in Japan, and a key difference from traditional food folk remedies was the presence of technology; health ingredients such as vitamins or extra fibre had been added. In some jurisdictions these terms have no legal meaning and can therefore be used loosely as marketing aids; the European Union has, from 2007, prohibited the term superfood unless the health claim is backed by scientific research. Exotic berries such as gojiberries, blueberries, chokeberries or cranberries, sold at high profit margins, are frequently credited with 'nutraceutical' properties, whereas more mundane fruits such as apples or blackberries are not. Various yoghurts and probiotic drinks are also credited with everything from protecting from cancer to reducing cholesterol, eliminating wrinkles and enhancing memory; the key feature being that these foods do not occur in nature and can only be obtained from a certain manufacturer, a certain food retailer. Some foods can switch genes on or off, which blurs the boundary between 'food' and 'drug'; foods accredited with medical benefits have to go through a far less rigorous testing process before reaching the market than new drugs. For example the prevalence of type 2 diabetes has created a demand for drugs such as Acarbose, miglitol and metformin, which inhibit α-amlylase and α-glucosidase; however, these drugs have undesirable side effects including flatulence and diarrhoea (Vadivel and Biesalski, 2013: 1026). Therefore foods such as Purple Camel's Foot seeds, sourced from tropical regions and having similar inhibitory effects, have been marketed as a 'nutraceutical' remedy for type 2 diabetes.

Carotenoids are an example of a beneficial food substance that, because they are in commonplace fruits, like blackberries, and vegetables, are relatively unsung by the food industry. Carotenoids are a group of red/orange/yellow pigments with antioxidant properties that are found in a wide range of fruit and vegetables; these pigments include lycopene that colours tomatoes red, carotene that makes carrots orange, and lutein that makes peppers yellow (Perrett et al., 2013). Many green vegetables also contain carotenoids, the red/yellow colour masked by chlorophyll. As antioxidants, carotenoids neutralize harmful chemicals produced when white cells fight infection; this action destroys the carotenoids. When an individual has an abundance of carotenoids, their skin has a 'healthy glow' that, in controlled colour tests, has been deemed more attractive to the opposite sex than a suntanned skin, or pale skin, and this applies equally across all skin colours, European, Asian or African. A carotenoid-based skin glow may therefore serve the same role as bright colours do in a range of animals, from yellow tits to peacocks to the red bellies of stickleback fish. The bright colouration signals that the individual is disease-free and strong, and therefore a healthy mate who can fight off threats. Since sex and attracting a mate is as powerful a driver in humans as it is in other animals, the promotion of carotenoids could be a means of raising fruit and vegetable consumption. But there is less profit here for the food industry, so such promotion will more likely be funded by government health agencies.

Future nutraceutical opportunities will arise to tackle the endemic diseases of the twenty-first century: Alzheimer's disease (as we all live longer) and type 2 diabetes. More advantageously, we might develop foods that avert obesity altogether while retaining the pleasurable fullness of food, foods that promote satiety yet are low in Calories. High fibre foods might be made as tasty as sugary puddings, and guar gum in yoghurts may do the same job; foods that slow the rate of stomach-emptying would also deter excess consumption (Butland et al., 2007: 63). However, the nutraceuticals that will actually get developed are likely to be those offering greatest commercial gain, not the larger societal or health gains. In Chapter 8 we explore the routes to a healthier and more sustainable food system. But first we examine the deeper psychologies and cultures of our food in Chapter 4.

4 Philosophies of food

Food, religion and festivals. *Eating for Edesia*

Food and religion are intimately linked. We start this chapter with food and religion because both concepts take us back to our origins. The word 'religion' derives from the Latin 're-ligio', meaning 'to tie back', to link to our beginnings. On a personal level, food is our mother's first gift to us (Falk, 1994: 14); it enables us to progress from our origins to adulthood. Food comes from the hearth, the heart of the house, it symbolizes a deep connection between kitchen, eating and maternal love, family union (Moisio et al., 2004). We see an underfed child and instantly assume parental neglect; we are far less likely to presume such neglect when we see an overfed, obese child. Yet if food is so closely linked to the mother, the family table, eating together around the hearth, then surely a child eating an obesogenic ready meal alone upstairs in front of their computer is a manifestation of 'love-less' food. Perhaps cooking is seen as drudgery in Western secularized society not because we have no love of cooking but because we have no love for cooking, whereas in rural Sri Lanka, for example, preparing family food is a highly valued role, a 'critical function … entrusted to women' (Harrigan, 2013). In traditional Sri Lankan society, the woman of every household is royal queen and priestess, 'She rules the household whilst her husband only reigns.' Ultimately, all food comes from the soil, from the earth, our 'created home'; the earth is where we return at death, perhaps for rebirth, so food links us to our perpetual earthly origins. Religious festivals often coincide with the passing of the shortest day (end of winter, renewal of the sun and life), spring sowing time or autumn harvest time. Note the association of Easter eggs with the renewed fertility of spring, while the chocolate they are made of is believed to have aphrodisiac qualities. Holly sprigs are associated with Christmas cakes; the holly representing life that has not died back during Winter. The roundness of the cake symbolizes the cycle of life, death and rebirth, also the cycles of the heavens, the shape of the Sun and Moon. The agricultural apparatus used may itself be sanctified, as in the 'Blessing of the Plough', a Christian ritual with medieval-pagan origins celebrated at the beginning of the agricultural year in January. Mother's Day originates from the ancient Greeks' homage to Rhea,

Mother of the Gods; at dawn she was offered sacrifices of honey, cakes, wine and flowers. Most religions impose dietary restrictions upon their adherents. Early Christianity had few such dictates, but its followers were commanded to 'abstain from things sacrificed to idols, from blood, and from things strangled' (because such animals would still contain their blood) (Acts 15:29). The command against eating blood was an inheritance from Judaism, with its more elaborate Kosher laws, and these laws were also adopted and adapted by Islam to specify which foods are Halal (permissible) and which are Haram (forbidden). Catholicism later added dietary rules such as eating only fish, not meat, on Fridays, leading to the introduction in 1962 of the Filet-o-Fish onto the McDonald's menu because business at their Cincinnati restaurant, in a predominantly Catholic area, declined on Fridays (Villarrubia, 2010). The fish symbol was an important means for early Christians to recognize each other during persecution under the Roman Empire. The significance of this symbol derives from the acronym, in Greek, for 'Jesus Christ God's Son, Saviour' being 'Iesous Christos Theou Yios Soter', or ICThYS, the Greek word for 'fish'; the idea also linked to Christian dogma such as 'Fishers of Men', Peter as fisherman, and the story of Jesus drawing a coin from the mouth of a fish. Today, Seventh Day Adventists are often vegetarian in recognition of God's gift of life and the dietary laws of the Book of Leviticus.

Rituals of food and diet are important for distinguishing 'us' from 'them'; meal-sharing reinforces community, it divides invited from uninvited. Food consumed at feasts is likewise divided from food unconsumed; such leftover food has somehow become debased, even though perfectly edible, it is halfway towards rubbish, refuse. The same principle applies to the (somehow always uneaten) food left on altars as sacrifices, even if unburnt, it is now refuse, contaminated, not for dignified consumption, any more than one would relish a wrapped sandwich retrieved from a bin. Such altar-discarded food may, however, be given to humans of lower status; under the Hindu custom of Prasad, former God-food is given to the poor. Jesus reinforced the faith of his disciples with the Last Supper; beforehand he had dismissed the betrayer Judas, who was therefore excluded from this meal (John 13:21–30). Transgressing such dietary laws can bring dire consequences. In 1972 US Presidential candidate George McGovern fatally damaged his campaign when he went into a New York Jewish delicatessen and ordered 'a kosher hot dog and a glass of milk', contravening Jewish Kosher laws on mixing meat and dairy. His rival, Richard Nixon, easily won New York with its large Jewish population. More secular meal events also perpetuate social links. The US Thanksgiving meal is an important means of transmitting shared norms and customs, along with recipes, down through time (Wallendorf and Arnould, 1991), and important family and social occasions, such as birthday parties, would be unimaginable without food. Inviting chosen guests to dinner parties reinforces friendships through both the invite list and the food provided, and prompts subsequent reciprocation at an invitee's house. More darkly, the tradition of providing a 'last meal' for a condemned prisoner, of greatly superior quality to normal prison fare, originated in the belief that such a meal would placate the soul of the executed, and prevent it returning to haunt the executioner. If food can affect the emotions, then food must link to the emotions of the eater, be a window upon their personality. Viewing a stranger's meal can then make this person 'known' to us; Amnesty International, in recent years, has campaigned for abolition of the death penalty by running adverts showing the last meals of executed prisoners who were later discovered to be innocent. Unsurprisingly the meals these condemned prisoners chose were generally comfort beige foods, fatty meat, chips, potatoes, ice cream, bread and sausages.

For the religious, embedded within food is love for community and love from God. Consuming food, particularly at special feasts, is recognizing and respecting God's love for Man, as Provider of Life. The Aztec religion took this to an extreme, believing that because the gods provided food, when you ate you actually ate a part of the gods; a belief not too dissimilar to the Catholic dogma that the Communion bread and wine are divinely transubstantiated into the actual flesh and blood of Jesus. So under Aztec theology it was essential that the gods were fed, and the food they liked was human blood, necessitating a steady supply of sacrificial victims from prisoners of war. The Geneva Convention had yet to reach South America. The opposite of feasting is of course fasting, and fasting expressed the opposite direction of love, Man's love for God. Fasting brings one closer to God, onto a higher spiritual plane of self-denial, in contrast to the self-indulgence of fatness. Fasting humbles the mind and weakens the body, brings one a little nearer death and therefore union with God. The Muslim fast of Ramadan, when food is not eaten between dawn and dusk, brings spiritual reflection, and in Punjab an extended fast of two days is undertaken when petitioning God for special favours (Bell and Valentine, 1997: 41).

Food as love. *If food be the music of love, eat on*

Food has much in common with sex. Both food and sex are intimate, internal; both can arouse strong emotions, both are closely linked to love and affection. Food is warm, soft, sensual, sweet; so too is the mouth, the portal by which food enters the body, and of course the mouth is also strongly sexual. The Australian Aboriginal phrase 'Utna ilkukubaka' may mean either 'Have you eaten?' or 'Have you had sexual intercourse?'; food along with procreation are the two basic necessities of life. In Western culture slang food-related words, especially those related to meat, are used to describe women in a casual sexual sense, for example 'bit of meat', a 'meat market' for a place to meet prostitutes, a 'chick' (Belasco, 2008: 36, 49). Meat is carnal in its literal sense of 'flesh'; carnal also means pleasures of the flesh, including sexual pleasures, and the idea of violence, conquest, is captured in the word 'carnivorous', or 'flesh eater', since sex is closely linked to concepts of conquest, rape, violence and submission.

Many foods are believed to be aphrodisiacs; tenth-century Arabs thought whale bile increased sexual arousal while Livia, wife of the Roman Emperor

Augustus Caesar, used dried Spanish flies for the same purpose (one can only wonder at the taste). Certain foods were believed to have aphrodisiac properties from their shape, resembling either the male or female sex organs, or from other associations with the reproductive process. Filipinos attributed aphrodisiac properties to duck embryos, while the Chinese relied on snake sperm and iguanas were used for this purpose in Nicaragua. Phallic-shaped aphrodisiac foods include bananas and asparagus, while avocados were believed to be aphrodisiac by the Aztecs because their shape resembles the male testicle; the word 'avocado' derives from the Aztec word for testicle, *ahuacuatl*. The ancient Egyptians attributed aphrodisiac powers to lettuce because it grew straight and tall. The Spanish Catholic priests banned the consumption of avocados, and tomatoes because these 'pommes d'amour' were also thought to increase sexual desire. Open figs were said to resemble the female genitalia, and the fruit was also attributed aphrodisiac properties because of the Bible account in Genesis 3 where Adam and Eve used fig leaves to cover their private parts. Another food believed by the Aztecs to have aphrodisiac properties was chocolate; they forbade women to eat it, and in 1624 the Austrian Professor John Franciscus Rauch banned monks from eating chocolate because it 'inflamed the passions'. There may be some scientific basis for this, because chocolate enhances endorphin and serotonin levels, so may reduce inhibitions while raising the sex drive. Today chocolate is often given to a loved one on Valentine's Day, the spring fertility festival or modern dating festival. Supermarket shelves laden with chocolate Easter bunnies nicely encapsulate the blend of commercialism, love, lust and pagan ritual that Valentine's Day now comprises. Almonds, said by the nineteenth-century French writer Alexandre Dumas to be an aphrodisiac, contain potassium and vitamins E and B6, which reduce stress and lower inhibitions; they also contain folic acid, which boosts histamine levels and so heightens orgasm. Garlic is used as an aphrodisiac by some, and it contains allicin which raises blood flow, assisting male orgasm; however, one might want to avoid this food in more romantic, sensual liaisons. The close link between smell and emotions means highly odorous foods like garlic and onions, foods that might create wind or bad breath, are avoided for intimate meal occasions (Rozin and Fallon, 1987), as are messy, drippy, sticky foods like spaghetti that might spoil one's physical appearance. However, once one has secured a partner then appearance becomes less important; Averett et al. (2008) note that entering marriage is associated with weight gain, and leaving it with weight loss. There is a similar but less pronounced weight effect with cohabitation. Our food creates our appearance, and appearance is important for dating, but food also creates pleasure and the pleasure aspect dominates once a partner is gained.

Food as pride. *Posh nosh*

We associate food with far more than just nutrition; animals 'eat' but only people 'dine'. In Baudrillardian terms food has a 'symbolic value' beyond its 'use value' (nutrition) and its 'exchange value' (market price). Food, the provision of excessively large amounts of food at banquets, far more than could possibly ever be eaten even by the large number of guests present, has long been used as a signal of wealth and power. The Roman emperors, and before them the Babylonians, were infamous for their hyperfeasts of conspicuous consumption; at least the Romans could claim they were doing it in honour of their god of feasting, Edesia. King Henry VIII of England had at Hampton Court Palace 55 kitchen rooms staffed by 200 employees who served 600 meals a day. The annual consumption of food at Hampton Court ran to 1,200 oxen, 8,200 sheep, 2,300 deer and 1,900 pigs. A century later King Louis XIV of France, the opulent and ostentations 'Sun King', would impress guests with banquets of 20 or more dishes that lasted for hours. These feasts served a political purpose; King Louis XIV centralized the feudal French state, taking power in from the regional nobility who formerly enjoyed considerable autonomy. In the Middle Ages the European monarchs were often 'dimly perceived, politically ineffective figures' (Poggi, 2004: 26); Louis XIV compelled many members of the French nobility to move from the regions to live at the Palace of Versailles, close to Paris. France, with its large territory extending from the North Sea to the Mediterranean, could provide a wide range of foods for the delectation of the French court. The food habits of the ruling elite of Britain and France slowly made their way down the social scale, helped along by the French Revolution in the last decade of the eighteenth century, when many chefs formerly employed by the French aristocracy fled across the Channel to the safety of Britain. Auguste Kettner, once chef to Emperor Napoleon III, moved to London and opened Kettners restaurant in 1867. The genteel tearooms of Victorian Britain were seen as an extension and continuation of the eighteenth-century dining rooms of the aristocratic mansions, where staff wore black and white uniforms reminiscent of butlers' dress. This style of waitering can still be experienced today at the Bettys chain of cafés in Yorkshire, England, a chain founded by Frederick Belmont, a Swiss confectioner who came to England in 1907.

Tea originated in China and came to Europe in the seventeenth century; it was then affordable only by the wealthy, but became cheaper after the British East India Company began cultivating tea in Assam in the 1820s. This paved the way for the Victorian British meal institution of 'afternoon tea', with cakes and pastries. At venues like The Ritz in London, afternoon tea became an occasion where couples could date without a chaperone, a meal culture that lasted until World War Two when the fashion for female slimness arrived, Britain acquired the coffee habit from America, and society became less formal. Mid-afternoon, or mid-morning, tea is now seen by many as a cheaper treat than a full restaurant meal, and is useful to restaurants to fill a slack time between lunch and dinner. The emergence in Victorian Britain of large urban hotels, largely due to the railway industry, allowed the middle classes to gentrify the process of eating out. In the eighteenth century eating at taverns and inn, was for the poor and for itinerant merchants; the wealthy ate at home, waited upon by servants. Eating out at venues such as The Ritz allowed the aspiring middle classes to emulate the gentry, with waiters dressed as servants, but in a thoroughly modernized setting, including the novelty of electric lighting. The Savoy, opened in 1889, was London's first hotel to boast electric lighting and electric lifts. At The Savoy, French chef Georges-Auguste Escoffier organized the kitchen on military lines. Courses were presented in a set order, unlike medieval banquets where all the dishes were put out at once. He invented Peach Melba ice cream and Melba toast, named after the operatic singer Dame Nellie Melba (1861–1931), not as dessert but as a palate cleanser between courses. The Lyons Corner House chain took the café habit further into middle-class territory; the first opened in 1909 and the chain remained until 1977. The Lyons Corner House chain closed as customers shifted towards modern, standardized chains with up-to-date entertainment, milk bars with juke boxes, burger bars, Wimpy and McDonald's outlets, pizza restaurants, and later to family gastro-pubs and wine bars. Since 2000, however, the idea of the coffee shop and snack restaurant has come full circle; a certain discontent with modernity has forced a refit of McDonald's back to a more muted subtle brown, beige and green colour scheme away from its brash modern red and yellow hues. The menu has changed to include healthier, more natural items such as salads. Family pubs are designed with mock-rural features like beams and gables, a faux-retro decor. The 2008 recession increased the demand for small 'village' coffee shops, as financially pressed consumers sought what economists call 'lipstick treats', little affordable luxuries. Lyons itself may not return but we have a new 'golden age' of the coffee shop, as customers seek a more authentic experience, both in what they eat and where they eat; a rejection of global standardization in favour of a genuinely local experience.

Food as geography. *Eating the land*

The French concept of *terroir* (Feagan, 2007) closely links food and soil. 'Terroir' may be defined as a small region of distinctive soil type and micro-climate, whose characteristics impart a unique flavour to a food product such as wine. 'Terroir' is connected to another French word, 'patrimonialisation', a sense of place where traditional production methods, a rich food heritage, is preserved. The French word *pays*, related to 'peasant', signifies the idea of localness in food, as does the Italian *nostrato*, but such concepts have no direct translation into Northern European languages. The closest word the English language has to *terroir* is the term foodshed, derived from watershed, although a watershed can be rather large, not local, and carries the idea of transportation, of food chains, not locality. The modern formal legalized version of *terroir* is found in the European Union's AOC, or *Appellation d'Origine Contrôlée*. AOC essentially states that a certain type of food can only originate from a certain geographical area. The idea of AOC pre-dates the EU; the earliest known example, from France, is a fifteenth-century law requiring that any cheese called Roquefort must come from the caves of the Roquefort area. Before World War Two a number of French wines were geographically protected, starting with the Bordeaux wines from 1855 (Trubek, 2008). Today a wide range of products come under AOC, including butter, cheeses, fruit, honey, lavender, lentils, olive oil and various meats and nuts. Even some types of potatoes are AOC-regulated, perhaps ironic for a food that did not originate within Europe. On the positive side AOC can imbue a food product with a halo of desirable attributes including environmental sustainability, low food miles, tradition, maintenance of rural society, organic, additive-free and cruelty-free. However, AOC may contribute towards a commoditization of place, towards 'ownership' of an entire landscape and way of life by corporate food producers. Sometimes the place name does not correspond with the place of origin of the product. Under the 1996 EU PDO (Product Designation of Origin) law, Stilton cheese cannot be made in the village of Stilton in Cambridgeshire, England. Stilton cheese is actually made further west in Leicestershire, according to a recipe developed by Frances Pawlett. The cheese was transported to the village of Stilton which before the railways came in the 1800s was on a major trading route and an important stop for stage coaches between London and the North of England. Cooper Thornhill, landlord of the Bell Inn in Stilton in the 1730s, sold the cheese, hence its association with the village of Stilton. There are suggestions that a version of Stilton cheese was indeed made in Stilton village, but adapted from and different to Mr Pawlett's recipe; Stilton village is attempting to amend the PDO but this process can take years.

Sometimes the nominative relationship is reversed; the food product names the region. Perrier Water comes from a spring called Les Bouillens in the South of France. The spring was bought by Dr Louis Perrier in 1898; he later sold it to Sir St John Harmsworth, who put the water in green bottles shaped like the Indian clubs he used for exercise and marketed the water as 'Source Perrier' to the middle classes of the UK and USA. In 1990 the Perrier brand suffered serious damage when minute traces of benzene were detected in the water, forcing a recall from supermarket shelves. In 1992 Nestlé bought the brand, planning to revive it. In 1996 Nestlé began producing a version of Perrier Water sourced from Egypt. The French village of Vergeze, where the Les Bouillens spring is located, were concerned about possible job losses, so they applied to change the name of the spring to Perrier les Bouillens. The French courts deemed the move legal, meaning Nestlé cannot market spring water from anywhere else as 'Perrier'. Meanwhile the Birmingham suburb of Bourneville has also been given its name by the chocolate manufactured there. The model village of Bourneville was created by the Cadbury family in the late nineteenth century. They wanted a greenfield site out of Birmingham, where the original chocolate factory was located, but with good access to canal and rail. The factory and village they built was named after the Bourn Brook; no settlement existed here previously. The 'ville' suffix may have been inspired by the Cadbury family's desire for a Parisian aspect to their business.

Regions have made food, and food has made regions; food can also regenerate regions. Food has an enormous range of attributes – colour, texture, shape, taste, history, tradition, name – that along with the attributes of its packaging and presentation can be linked in numerous ways to a particular locale. Wine labels include maps, pictures can be printed on food mats, leaflets can be given with free samples at tourist offices, recipe cards containers strategically positioned, environmental links forged in the minds of customers, or unusual restaurant venues may be built. In Rennes, France, the old slate industry is commemorated in the form of pieces of hard nougat, shaped like slabs of slate, dyed bluish-grey. In northern England the Ribble Valley Food Trail opened in 2008, promoting local food shops and restaurants; tourists are attracted away from more popular honeypot locations to Clitheroe's castle and river walks. Totnes in Devon has from 2007 promoted itself as the 'Nut Capital of Britain', with nut-bearing trees planted in public areas. The town advertises the environmental benefits, as CO_2 is sequestered and the trees provide timber (Steel, 2008: 232). Todmorden in Lancashire has adopted the slogan 'Incredible Edible Todmorden', with schemes to grow food in public areas, free for anyone to gather; visitors boost the town's retailing. The nearby town of Ramsbottom promotes the local speciality of Lancashire Hotpot, and has a Black Pudding throwing championship; using food as sport has, of course, a long history with events such as the annual cheese rolling competition at Cooper's Hill, Gloucestershire, celebrating the local Double Gloucester cheese industry, dating back to pre-Christian times.

Food can help in the regeneration of an entire city. Bell (2007) describes the policy of 'boosterism' adopted by many de-industrialized cities in the global North. These policies include 'spaces of hospitality' for the corporate sector, hotels, bars, gastro-pubs, restaurants with unusual and memorable features, such as revolving viewing platforms, the merger of food and entertainment in 'foodatainment', and the promotion of ethnically food-themed quarters such as Chinatown or Little Italy. Manchester has gentrified its former 'gay village' district, formerly an area of cheap bars and lap dancing, but now reinvented with a new metrosexual image more amenable to the business lunch or dinner. The annual Manchester Food and Drink Festival was inaugurated in 1998 to show the rest of the world that Manchester was no longer a grimy 'northern' decayed industrial city but a contemporary media-focused metropolis with everything for the modern business executive. Eating can even save an imperilled city. In 1977 the Pizza Express chain launched the Pizza Veneziana; for every Veneziana sold, Pizza Express donated 5 pence to the Venice in Peril Find, a sum raised over the years to 25 pence in 2008, the value today (2013) (Pringle and Thompson, 2001: 99). As with food and regional promotion, there is always some aspect of food that can link to a charity; in the 1970s Birds Eye printed tokens on its packets of fish fingers for which, when returned, Birds Eye donated 5 pence to the Royal National Lifeboat Institution. Food even promotes the tyre industry; the famous French Michelin Guides were a marketing initiative by the eponymous tyre company, to get motorists driving into the French countryside to sample its rustic culinary delights. And, of course, to wear out their car tyres. Entire diets can be regional; Scotland promotes its 'Natural Larder', covering its wide range of food products, from wheat and whisky to beef and strawberries. Fusion cuisines often focus on seas, not land masses; we have the Mediterranean Diet, Caribbean Cuisine and Pacific Rim Cuisine. The Nordic Diet encompasses a region from Iceland to Finland and therefore has a strong element of seafood from the Atlantic and Baltic. We perceive seafood as healthy, we like the mystery of produce emerging from the depths, of ships coming over the horizon laden with exciting new goods; the sea is fresh, clean, exciting. As with Stilton cheese, the nomenclature of origin of seafoods can be misleading; British tourists sampling the classic French dish *fruits de mer* are probably eating British food, as the UK exports 65 per cent of the shellfish caught in its waters, mainly to France, Italy and Spain. The favourite British shellfish, prawns, originates mostly from Far Eastern prawn farms. If these tourists order another French classic, *grenouilles* (frogs' legs), these too will be imports, from Eastern Europe and Asia, because the intensification of French agriculture has caused the draining of many French marshlands where the *grenouilles* once lived.

Food as symbolizing a region may become food as stereotyping a region, often unfavourably. Food can be used as synecdoche or metonymy. Synecdoche is the nominating of an entire object as a part of that object; referring to a vehicle as 'wheels' for example. So the British call the French 'frogs' while the French call the British 'les rosbifs', labelling each other by one of their symbolic national foods. In sophisticated tenth-century Persia, the neighbouring nomadic Arabs were denigrated for their alleged 'unculturedness' in food terms, as scavenging for whatever unpalatable food they could find; 'The Arabs of the desert eat locusts while the dogs of Isfahan drink ice-cold water' was a Persian proverb of the time. The name of the US biscuit Oreo, which consists of white cream sandwiched between black biscuits, has been appropriated by some African-Americans to label 'pretend-liberals' who are 'Black on the outside but White on the inside' (Belasco, 2008: 24) in the UK; the term 'coconut' is used similarly. Metonymy is a concept related to synecdoche; it means the act of referring to something by another concept closely related to it; for example calling the film industry 'Hollywood' or referring to the US financial sector as 'Wall Street'. Italy may be refereed to as 'spaghetti', perhaps with pejorative hints at the often-tangled nature of Italian governance. The German magazine *Der Spiegel* featured, on its 25 July 1972 cover, a plate of spaghetti with a pistol in it; the cover text translated as 'Kidnapping, Extortion, Mugging – Holidayland Italy' and featured a restaurant window with three bullet holes. Italians protested that their country also has a rich heritage of saints, navigators, intellectuals and poets, and anyway pasta did not originate in Italy but was brought to Sicily by the Arabs. Food stereotypes can become mocking to the point of racism; in one convoluted example, an episode of the British TV series *Goodness Gracious Me* featured a group of drunk Indians going for an 'English' and choosing the blandest dish on the menu; a satire of the relationship between Britons and Indian food. In an example of reverse-mocking of foreign ignorance of Indian cultural and economic achievements, of the sophisticated levels reached by Indian culture before the British colonial occupation, India's Finance Minister was reported as saying 'Before British investors came to India, we did not eat lizards' (*The Economist*, 2012a). When food interacts with geography, the relationship can easily turn from descriptive and promotional to mocking and false. However, food can be deceitful in many other ways, some of which damage not only national pride but individual health.

Food as deceit. *Lying through your teeth*

Urbanites have long been vulnerable to fraud through being sold food that is not of the expected standard. Four thousand years ago Babylonian King Hammurabi set out regulations concerning food standards; three millennia later King John of England addressed the same problems in the thirteenth century, as did his successor, King Henry III. Food fraud takes three basic forms: food that is underweight, food that has been treated to enhance or prolong its appearance of freshness, and food that contains inferior (and sometimes harmful) adulterants or has had some key ingredient removed (e.g. cream from milk). At least underweight food will not kill you. Food is very heterogeneous; a loaf of bread comes in a huge variety of shapes, colours and sizes, for example. With no 'standard loaf', consumers may be sold underweight loaves, and in 1327 a London baker, John Bird, developed an ingenious fraud. When customers brought dough for baking in his oven, Mr Bird placed it on a table with a hidden trapdoor; while he chatted to customers, an accomplice below surreptitiously removed part of the dough. A thousand years earlier, Roman wine merchants diluted wine with water. Long food chains between farmer and consumer raised the threat of food decay reducing the profits of food traders, so artificial methods of improving the appearance of food became common. Oranges would be immersed in boiling water, meat polished with fat, to enhance their appearance. The French langueyeur used to inspect meat at markets for ulcers and other imperfections; the Italians employed inspectors to check for stale fish. We still need the langueyeur; instances of farmed salmon being passed off as the more flavoursome wild variety, or sunflower oil being sold as extra virgin olive oil or non-organic food being marketed as organic, are regular news items today. In 2007 the Hungry Horse restaurant chain was caught selling Brazilian zebu as British beef; zebu is still 'beef' but is cheaper, and tougher, than British cows.

The issue of food adulteration raised most concern. Roman and medieval bread was bulked out, and its whiteness enhanced, with alum. King John addressed the issue of bread with ground peas added. As the range of foods, many unfamiliar, increased during the eighteenth and nineteenth centuries, the opportunities for adulteration also multiplied. Tea and coffee were adulterated with chicory, dried and ground up leaves, and mustard husks, bread with chalk and bone ash; these substances were also useful for filling out condiments like pepper. Chocolate and cocoa might include brick dust or iron oxide (rust). Brewers added salt to the beer, increasing demand by unsuspecting drinkers. These adulterants did little permanent damage to health, but other substances were more dangerous. Black lead was used to enhance the appearance of tea leaves, strychnine made beer taste more bitter, gin was diluted with sulphuric acid or turpentine, vinegar was acidified, also with sulphuric acid, salts of copper made pickles greener, and red lead made red food items such as meat and cheese rinds more attractive (Tansey and Worsley, 1997: 33). The Industrial Revolution further divorced consumers from the land, and people increasingly no longer knew what their food ought to taste like. As more artificial foods came onto the market in the nineteenth century, the fraudulent food chemists got busier; the colours of boiled sweets were brightened by salts of copper and mercury. Food adulteration and dishonest grocers were still a problem in early twentieth-century Britain, as this verse about food retailers by G. K. Chesterton suggests:

> *He sells us sands of Araby, as sugar for cash down*
> *He sweeps the shop and sells the dust, the purest salt in town*
> *He crams with cans of poisoned meat, poor subjects of the King*
> *And when they die by thousands, Why he laughs like anything*
> *The Grocer trembles: for his time, just like his weight, is short*
> from 'The Song Against Grocers', published in
> *The Flying Inn*, 1914, by G. K. Chesterton

Food adulteration and misrepresentation were rife in other countries too, as this verse, published in the *New York Times* in 1900, illustrates:

> *Mary had a little lamb*
> *And when she saw it sicken*
> *She shipped it off to Packingtown*
> *And now it's labelled chicken*

The sentiments here are echoed in the 2013 Europe-wide debacle about foods labelled as minced beef that contained horsemeat, or possibly donkey. In the 1820s a German chemist, Frederick Accum (1769–1838), highlighted the issue of harmful substances in food with his book *A Treatise on Adulteration of Food and Culinary Poisons*; for this Accum had to flee Britain. Food adulteration continued, and as often happens, one particularly notorious incident, what sociologists call a 'signal crime', forced the issue to a head. In Bradford, Yorkshire, in 1858 some 200 people were made ill and 20 died, as a result of consuming lozenges containing arsenic. In fact the manufacturer had meant to adulterate with Plaster of Paris, but bought the arsenic in error. Arsenic trioxide, a white powder not unlike Plaster of Paris in appearance, was then commonly used as an insecticide and pesticide, before the invention of organic pesticides like DDT. The UK government passed the Food Adulteration Act in 1860 (amended in 1875 by the Sale of Food and Drugs Act and in 1899 by the Food Adulteration Act). This made food quality the responsibility of the seller; it was no longer 'caveat emptor' or 'buyer beware', because in the industrialized age of food, the buyer *could not* beware. It became an offence to sell food 'not of the nature, substance, or quality of the article demanded'. Canada legislated against food adulteration with the Inland Revenue Act in 1875. The USA followed with legislation such as the Federal Food and Drug Act of 1906, superseded by the Food Drug and Cosmetic Act 1938. India followed with the Prevention of Food Adulteration Act 1954. However, food is chemically complex, so food adulterers can stay one step ahead of the scientists. Market pressure, the need to preserve a good brand image, often ensures that large food manufacturers maintain high food standards, but this works less well with smaller players; events such as the 2007 melamine in milk scandal in China illustrate this all too well. Food chains have never been longer than today's, and we have sophisticated laws and checks to eliminate as much food fraud as possible. Or we legalize it. All the three forms of 'food fraud' described above live on today, although they are perfectly legal. Oversized packaging conceals undersized portions, so long as the weight is correctly marked in small print, although as food marketers know we judge items by apparent size, not weight. Marketers have come up with numerous devices to enhance the appearance of the food we buy, or at least the appearance of the packaging it comes in; an ingenious example is lasagne packets that purport to show a perfect lasagne; in fact if one photographed this food item it would sag and look messy. So what appears on the outside of a packet of lasagne is meat layered between sheets of Styrofoam, carefully edged with cheese, the perfect (looking) dinner dish.

Food adulteration has not gone away either; it has just adapted to modern socio-legal norms. Or perhaps the food industry has succeeded in adapting modern socio-legal norms to accommodate food adulteration. In the 1930s the famous suffragette Sylvia Pankhurst described how women were employed to rub tiny pieces of wood into seed shapes, to insert in raspberry jam made without the use of real fruit, using artificial flavours. Food adulteration has become far more sophisticated since then. Germany was the centre of the chemical industry in the nineteenth and early twentieth century; in Chapter 1 we saw how German chemists in 1910 developed the Haber-Bosch method of fixing atmospheric nitrogen to produce fertilizer. Food flavours are intimately bound up with food scents, and twentieth-century Germany took the lead in food flavouring, using expertise from the great perfume houses of Britain, France and the Netherlands. The first artificial food flavour was discovered (like the first artificial dye, mauve) by accident when a German chemist synthesized methyl anthranilate and suddenly his lab was filled with the scent of grapes. Methyl anthranilate is in fact the natural chemical within grapes that gives them their flavour, but now grape-flavour drinks could be mass produced without grapes, which is how Kool-Aid is manufactured. Ethyl-2-methyl butrate smells just like apple. Ethyl-3-hydroxybutonoate gives a marshmallow taste. Natural flavours are chemicals; amyl acetate is the natural substance giving bananas their flavour; today the chemical is synthesized in a laboratory, by mixing vinegar and amyl alcohol, with sulphuric acid as a catalyst. The processed food industry increasingly positioned itself, economically and physically, near the heart of the chemicals and scents industries. After World War Two the perfume and fashion industries moved to New York, and the food flavour industry moved there too, opening large-scale manufacturing plants across the Hudson river in New Jersey. Food taste and smell are intimately linked, hence the affinity with the perfume industry; cosmetics and food also both need colourants. The same pigments do several jobs; titanium dioxide, the whitest chemical known, is used for white paint and for cake icing. Intricate flavours/scents such as coffee are made of thousands of different chemicals, but only in tiny amounts, so they are very cheap per unit of food despite being complex to synthesize. The flavour in a can of Coke costs less than one penny. The other physical components, the water and the can itself, are also cheap, as is the transport; what the consumer pays is mostly marketing costs and profit.

Food additives, some to modify flavour, some to enhance colour or some other attribute such as mouthfeel, raise many ethical issues. Carmine, which gives a red-pink or purple colour to foods, is derived from the dried carcasses of beetles from Peru and the Canary Islands; the beetles eat red berries and the red pigment accumulates in their bodies. It takes 80,000 insects to produce 0.5 kg of carmine. Consuming these beetles violates Halal, Kosher and Sikh dietary laws, but carmine is frequently used to colour red fruit drinks of strawberry yoghurt. Food additives blur the concepts of 'natural' and 'artificial'. We add corn syrup or sugar to 'natural orange juice'; the additives are natural but their presence in the orange juice is not, so is the juice still 'natural'? In Accum's day, making lemonade with citric acid would have been counted as fraudulent; in 2013, it is normal. If 'strawberry yoghurt' had been sold then, with no content of strawberry, Accum would have seen that as food fraud; we accept this. Where a 'real' or 'natural' version of a food exists, the legislators at least have some standard to judge food fraud by, but how can we decide what is fake when, as in the case of foods like cheese strings or squirty desserts, no natural version ever existed? Food has become a Baudrillardian simulacrum where the copy has become more real than the reality it seeks to copy; desserts are sweeter than nature, colours are brighter than nature, food textures are softer than nature. Food processors manipulate food in ways that are quasi-deceitful. Carrots are polished so they look fresh and have a deep orange glow after weeks in the food chain, and potatoes are similarly polished to remove the blemishes and fungi they acquire in the weeks between harvesting and reaching the consumer. Glacé cherries, which began life as red, would be beige after processing, but are dyed back red again, and farmed salmon are fed pink dye to regain that appetizing pink colour that wild salmon have, not the duller grey-pink of farmed fish. Margarine is not naturally yellow but grey-white; its name is derived from the Greek *margarites*, meaning pearl, because of its original pearly hue. In the 1930s margarine manufacturers successfully lobbied to be legally allowed to add yellow dye (some margarine manufacturers had been illicitly adding yellow colour since the 1880s). Now margarine, which had been developed as a cheap substitute for real butter, made from beef fat, cow's stomach and bicarbonate of soda and developed by Napoleon III as a spread that would not go rancid on long ship voyages, could compete as being more healthy than real butter.

Britain's modern equivalent to Accum was supposed to be the Food Standards Agency (FSA), set up in 2001 in response to the BSE crisis, because the Ministry of Agriculture, Food and Fisheries was unable to police food safety as well as monitor agricultural practices. The FSA has handled recent food crises such as the 2005 Sudan 1 incident, when a carcinogenic red food dye (also used in red shoe polish) was found in sauces and curries, and the 2006 occurrence of salmonella in chocolate products. The FSA also issues guidelines on diet, some more culturally and socially acceptable than others; one suggestion less likely to be taken up was for World Cup fans watching football in the pub to abstain from beer and drink fizzy water with a slice of lemon instead. The Conservatives, in the UK election campaign of 2010, promised to abolish quangos such as the FSA, but once elected they were unable to pass the legislation required regarding the FSA. Instead, the FSA was effectively broken up, with its health policy responsibilities taken over by the Ministry of Health, and its food labelling remit moved to the Department for Environment, Food and Rural Affairs (DEFRA). The FSA was left with responsibility for abattoirs, but not for the food processing plants further down the food chain. It was this fragmentation of governance over the British food chain that was blamed for the horsemeat scandal of 2013, with products supposedly made of minced beef, such as lasagne and burgers, being found to contain up to 100 per cent horsemeat. And some horsemeat may contain 'bute', or phenylbutazone, a horse medicine that in humans is a potential carcinogen. The reasons why horsemeat is generally unacceptable to the British consumer, while the French and Italians happily eat it, are discussed below, but, some 200 years after Accum, the consumer still faces the issue of adulterated food, cut with cheaper ingredients or, worse, with harmful chemicals. Expensive fish such as monkfish or sea bass may be mixed with cheaper hake or coley; Basmati rice is diluted with ordinary rice. The issue is largely economic; with such a huge range of processed foods, their original ingredients far from obvious, a huge range of potential contaminants and adulterants, and most tests designed to find just one illicit additive, the consumer can never be sure all food is what is supposed to be, and only what it is supposed to be.

When food is merely being described, pictorially in advertisements or verbally in food myths of origin, false representations abound even more. TV shots of breakfast cereals may have the cornflakes soaking in wood glue, not milk, so the cereal does not look soggy, aspirin powder is put into champagne to make it fizz more, while methylated spirits gives that Christmas cake just a bit more jolly glow (*The Observer*, 2004). We have become used to this hyper-reality, where celebrity photos are airbrushed to a perfection that nature, even when 'enhanced' with cosmetics, could never emulate. We expect the estate agent's shot of the house to be taken at an odd angle, with a slight fish-eye effect on the lens. 'Advertising puff' is even legally sanctioned, as to be anticipated and filtered out by consumers. We adapt to living in a Baudrillardian world where nothing is expected to be quite as it seems. However, when it comes to food our digestive system deals with what it gets, not what it ought to get or expects to get, and our health is affected accordingly. Food myths spread like viral advertisements altering concepts of food. Sometimes the disinformation is deliberate, to serve an ulterior purpose. During World War Two the British government spread the idea that carrots will help you see in the dark. Like all good myths, this one is partly true; carrots contain vitamin A, which converts to retinol, essential for night vision. But most of us have enough retinol for good night vision without extra carrots. The British government had to explain why RAF pilots were good at shooting Luftwaffe planes, without giving away the secret of radar. So effective was this food myth that the Germans fed their soldiers more carrots. Then we have food origins myths. Balti sounds, and tastes, like an Indian dish; it originated in Birmingham, England, in the 1970s, albeit cooked by migrants from India. The word 'Balti' means 'bucket' or flat-bottomed wok in Urdu, referring to the means of cooking this dish. The dish Teppanyaki is a food-related example of Baudrillardian reversibility; it originated in Japan in late 1945 when that country was under US occupation. American soldiers wanted fried beef. Fried (yaki) on iron plates (teppan), the dish was christened *teppanyaki*. When Teppanyaki restaurants opened in the USA, this 'Japanese' food was already somewhat familiar to American tastes, as it had been created by American soldiers (Cook, 2008). In similar manner the American food Spam entered Okinawa during World War Two, and is now a popular Okinawan dish, only stir-fried, Chinese style.

Food and the law. *Stealing the common from the goose*

Wright Mills (1956) argued that the law, far from being a set of rules to ensure fair play in a democratic society, was used by the political and industrial elite to maintain their position of power and keep the working class in their place. Food, or the restriction of its supply, is a powerful weapon used by such elites, past and present, to repress the working class. Often the political elite have connived in this by passing the required laws to enforce this oppression. A popular English folk-rhyme of the eighteenth century went:

> *The law locks up the man or woman*
> *Who steals the goose from off the common*
> *But leaves the greater villain loose*
> *Who steals the common from the goose*

This referred to the enclosure of common land, depriving the poor of the means to grow their own food, forcing them to work for the very landowners doing the enclosing. Thomas Rudge in his *General View of the County of Gloucester*, published in 1813, stated that medlars and other edible fruit-bearing plants should not be permitted in hedgerows for 'It is bad policy to increase temptations to theft: the idle among the poor are already too prone to depredation, and would be still less inclined to work if every hedgerow furnished the means of support.' Medlars are, unusually for fruit, available all through the year, including winter, and can be eaten even when blighted by rot. The nineteenth-century mine owners at Stiperstones, Shropshire, would have agreed with Mr Rudge. They resented the fact that mine workers also had smallholdings for growing vegetables because the miners were then not entirely dependent upon their mine earnings; miners then were paid on piece rates, by how much ore they could dig out. (Francis et al., 2000: 59). The same attitude prevails today in countries such as Guatemala, where the landowning elite feel threatened by any imitative helping peasant farmers improve yields, making them less dependent on low-paid plantation work (Lappe et al., 1999: 6). On a national scale the UK's Corn Laws represented a mercantilist effort to protect the interests of wealthy landowners. The Corn Laws, first passed in 1804, kept the price of food high by banning wheat imports unless the price was over 80 shillings a quarter. After the end of the Napoleonic Wars in 1815, landowners feared falling grain prices as imports flowed once more. In fact a poor harvest in 1816 caused the grain price to soar. The Corn Laws precipitated riots at St Peter's Field, Manchester, in August 1819 (dubbed Peterloo, after the Battle of Waterloo), where 15 protesters were killed and several hundred injured when the army opened fire. Economic depression and further poor grain harvests in the 1840s heightened opposition to the Corn Laws. The eventual motivation for repealing the Corn Laws was not concern for the poor, forced to buy expensive bread, but worries by the non-agricultural factory owners that hungry workers were less productive; high grain prices effectively raised the wages factories had to pay. As Britain industrialized, the influence of the industrialists eclipsed that of the landowners. The Corn Laws were gradually repealed in 1848 as the trigger price for import bans was lowered towards zero. Food initiatives by government have seldom been purely in favour of the poor. However, individual initiatives are another matter, as the next section explores.

Food as conscience. *They look in the dustbin for something to eat*

What you eat can make a powerful statement about your conscience and ethics, as can the manner by which you obtain that food. Freeganism was popularized by Adam Weissman as a protest, not just against food waste but also against sweatshops, rainforest destruction and unsustainable destructive production methods. 'The only point of freeganism is making the point that it shouldn't be happening in the first place' (quote from Stuart, a freegan, in *The*

Times II, 2011: 4). Freegans do not just recover food wasted by supermarkets, but also clothes and electronic goods, in perfect working order, discarded because superseded by more recent models. Supermarkets will dump a box of five perfectly good eggs because one is missing, or throw out jars of jam just because they are sticky when an adjacent jam jar broke (Earthwire, 2013). The issue of food waste, which if eliminated would mean the world already produces enough food for the expected peak population of 10 billion in 2050, is discussed further in Chapter 8. However, we can 'make a statement' about the food system without breaking into supermarket bins. Because food chains are now so long, food is the UK household's single biggest contributor to climate change (Jones et al., 2008). Concepts such as food miles, local food, locavorism and food patriotism are a powerful force in food politics. The Slow Food Movement and its wider effects upon society (the English town of Ludlow is virtually built upon Slow Food) are discussed in the next section of this chapter. Local food carries with it a bundle of ideas, each one appealing to a different sort of consumer. Older consumers may like the idea of food patriotism, of supporting 'Olde Englande' and its farmers, while younger radical consumers may like 'buying green'. Each group may be misled. Carrots grown for a major UK supermarket chain in Gloucestershire are transported to a distribution centre in Peterborough, 140 miles (225 kilometres) away, to be returned to Gloucestershire supermarkets and sold as 'local'. It is also possible that crops requiring hot-housing in the UK, such as tomatoes, are less energy-intensive if grown in Spain, without heating then transported to the UK, even by plane. The true environmental benefits, and disbenefits, of local food need careful unpacking. Overall the demand for 'ethical food' has grown strongly, even in the face of the global recession since 2007. Total global ethical sales in the UK have risen from £13.5 billion in 1999 to £35.5 billion in 2007 and £47.2 billion in 2012. Ethical food sales have risen from £1.0 billion in 2000 to £4.1 billion in 2006 and £7.5 billion in 2012; although this is still a small fraction of the total UK grocery market of £163.2 billion in 2012. Ethical food sales have risen faster than other ethical goods such as low energy appliances, cruelty-free cosmetics or ethical clothing. Sustainable fish sales have grown particularly well, suggesting consumers are attracted by a combination of environmental and health benefits. Fairtrade has experienced rapid growth. The Fairtrade label arrived in the UK in 1991, when the Cafédirect brand was launched, although Fairtrade Mexican coffee was on sale in the Netherlands from 1988. In 2000 Fairtrade sales in the UK amounted to £33 million. By 2006 annual Fairtrade UK sales were £273 million, reaching £1,530 million in 2012.

Organic food sales, having risen rapidly in the 1990s and 2000s, have fallen recently because consumers are unsure of the benefits in times of recession, as Table 4.1 shows. A small hard core, 8 per cent of UK households, buys organic food products more than once a fortnight, accounting for 54 per cent of all UK organic sales (Gerrard et al., 2013: 729), dairy products and vegetables being the most popular categories of organic food. There are signs of a rebound in 2013 due to the horsemeat scandal.

Table 4.1 Organic food sales in the UK, 1991–2012, selected years

Year	*UK organic food sales £ millions*
1991	60
1993	105
1997	445
2000	605
2003	1,100
2006	1,937
2008	2,100 peak annual sales
2009	1,850
2010	1,731
2011	1,670
2012	1,640

Source: Soil Association (2013).

Free range eggs have gained market share even during the recession, exceeding half of all UK egg sales in 2012; in 1995 four-fifths of eggs sold in the UK were from battery hens. Since the EU banned battery hen rearing in 2012 only 5 per cent of egg sales are now from these types of hens; 44 per cent of UK egg sales are from an intermediate rearing system known as barn hens. The popularity of free range eggs is despite a 10 pence differential per egg as against barn eggs. However, consumers may unknowingly buy battery eggs in sandwiches, cakes and ice cream, where the type of eggs used is not labelled.

Vegetarianism as food conscience is a blend of religious, ethical, health, environmental and socio-political concerns (Fox, 1999). Kalof et al. (1999) found that concern about the environment was the main reason for vegetarianism, but more recently Spencer et al. (2007) found health aspects have grown; this shift towards personal well-being concerns mirrors trends regarding ethical food generally. Vegetarians may object to terminating the life of an animal, regardless of any suffering pre-death. Vegetarianism may also be rejected for socio-political reasons, by non-white consumers as the diet of the privileged (Carolan, 2012: 149), although it is also the diet of (non-wealthy) Indian Jains, and Hindus who adhere to *ahimsa* (non-violence to animals). Similar class and ethnicity divides occur regarding soul food. The term 'soul' in black American parlance has connotations of black pride and culture. Soul food born from the exigencies of slave existence in America from the 1600s became in the 1960s a symbol of resurgent black culture. However, soul food was rejected by black Muslims in the 1970s as 'the diet of slavery' (Carolan, 2012: 147). Ethical concerns, moderated by class, are also affecting traditional Chinese foods. Shark fin soup is becoming less popular as Chinese consumers become aware of the endangered nature of sharks. Bear's paw has been largely substituted by beef moulded into a paw shape. A 600-year-old dog-eating festival in eastern China was cancelled in 2011 due to popular protest (*The Economist*, 2011a). Dog was stewed, known as 'fragrant meat', but

Chinese pet owners protested over the maltreatment of farmed dogs. Eating dog meat is a class issue because wealthy Chinese have pets and can afford to feed them, whereas the poorer Chinese might eat dog meat. Inevitably, when individuals choose food on the basis of conscience as well as taste, food becomes politicized.

Food as politics. *No land to eat*

The Bob Marley song 'No Woman No Cry' dates from the 1970s. One interpretation of the lyrics is 'woman' as 'motherland' and 'cry' as national anthem; a people without a homeland cannot form a nation, cannot have a national anthem. Without (mother) land, no food can be grown; 'without women we would not eat' is a common saying in Africa and Asia. Women are crucial to small-scale agriculture, feeding the family when the menfolk are employed away from home. As with religion and food, there is a close connection between woman, earth, food and love. For the oppressor, food represents control, tyranny. White settlers colonizing the American Plains forced the Indians off their buffalo lands onto reservations, guaranteeing their subjugation. White Americans themselves secured independence from Britain in a rebellion over another foodstuff, tea, at the Boston Tea Party. Meanwhile the history of the 'other India' of the East can almost be defined by rebellions over food. The Indian Mutiny of 1857 began when British colonials introduced ammunition where the tips of the rifle cartridges were bitten off before firing. The grease was rumoured amongst the sepoys (Indian soldiers) to derive from the fat of either pigs (unclean to Muslims) or cows (sacred to Hindus). The outcome of the Indian Mutiny was abolition of the East India Company and direct British colonial control. In 1930 Mohandas (Mahatma) Gandhi led a symbolic march to the Indian coast to make salt in defiance of the British salt tax. The British seemed to have learnt little from the Boston Tea Party of 1773; the Salt March led to independence for India in 1947. Eighteenth-century tea was not just a luxury but was necessary to make hot (sterilized) water palatable; salt was essential as a preservative in the hot Indian climate. Taxes on necessities have never been popular, and food is a basic necessity. Food in all its attributes – colour, name, origins, mode of manufacture and trading, to mention a few – has a long history as a political instrument. Food is complex, and so is nationalism; both frequently intertwine through a complex entanglement of attributes, as the following examples illustrate.

Orange carrots and Dutch nationalism

Carrots come in a variety of colours, white, purple, red, orange, yellow; yet today almost all are orange. The reason for this is the town from which William of Orange (1650–1702), champion of Dutch nationalism, originated.

Orange, in France, derives its name from a Celtic water god, Arausio. The English word for the colour 'orange' comes from the Arabic *naranj* or Tamil *narangh*, referring to the fruit we call an orange. This etymological dissonance, however, did not stop William from adopting orange as the national colour of the Netherlands, and encouraging the cultivation and export of orange carrots from there as a sort of national branding exercise. It is probably best not to mention this during an Orange Day Parade in Northern Ireland.

Margherita pizza, an American food

The Margherita pizza was developed by a Neapolitan chef, who, similarly to William of Orange, used the flag colours of the newly created State of Italy; red tomatoes, white mozzarella cheese, and green basil, and named it after Queen Margherita, wife of King Umberto I of Italy. Pizza itself is an ancient and geographically widespread dish, essentially flat bread with salt, oil and whatever else is available. The Margherita pizza became popular among Italian migrants to the USA from the early 1900s, but was largely confined to the US Italian community until the dish was reinvented for the American palate in the 1940s, given a wider variety of toppings and a thicker bread base.

Lithuanian Zeppelins, class, technology, geography and politics all in one dish

The food known as 'Cepelinai' or 'Zeppelin' has come to symbolize Lithuanian nationalism in a complex way. Its name derives from Count Zeppelin, a German who invented the airship, and its main ingredient, potato, is scarcely Lithuanian either. The Zeppelin consists of potato dumplings filled with mince or cheese, and is a popular family dish in Lithuania; it also symbolizes Lithuanian national pride (Mincyte, 2008). Lithuania, which once stretched from the Baltic to the Black Sea, has struggled to maintain a national identity in the face of greater regional powers, including Germany, Poland, Russia and Sweden. Lithuania gained independence from Russia in 1918. The Lithuanian peasantry began eating potatoes in the nineteenth century, but potato dumplings were the preserve of the middle classes because they were time-consuming to prepare. The 1920s Zeppelins captured the popular imagination, with many dishes in Germany and beyond being named after the machines. Lithuanian agriculture was extensively reformed under the Agricultural and Land Reforms of 1922, old manorial estates were reorganized, and the Cepelinai came to represent the new, independent, modernized, socially equalized Lithuania. Today, in the twenty-first century, the Cepelinai symbolizes the farming tradition of Lithuania within the greater European Union.

Soviet ice cream, command, eat and control

Ice cream was recruited by the Soviet Politburo in the 1930s as an unlikely instrument of social control. In the early formative years of the Soviet Union, soon after the 1917 Revolution, collectivism was supposed to triumph over individualism, and this ideology extended to the dining room. Eating privately as a family was discouraged in favour of communal dining in work cafeterias and school canteens (Smith 2009: 143). Lenin promised Soviet women that the drudgery of the kitchen would be banished as communal kitchens would feed all. To promote this change in dining habits, ice cream in 1930s Russia was produced in large catering-size tubs rather than individual cones. Ice cream was one of the few luxuries widely available at that time, and the Soviet state controlled food production as well as consumption; the first Soviet tractors, in use from the 1930s, were kept at 'district stations' and could only be used with Party permission. Only after the exigencies of World War Two did the Soviet political machine make privately consumable, individual-sized ice cream portions available as part of a promise that socialism could provide 'joy' for its citizens. The manufacture and distribution of Soviet ice cream had political overtones too. Ice cream, being a frozen product, was better able than most foods to withstand the creaky distribution channels across the vast Soviet Union. The raw materials of ice cream, sugar and milk were not easy to obtain at all times in 1950s Russia, a country that never possessed tropical colonies and sugar plantations. Milk was gathered from Russian farms in the summer, and freezing it as ice cream again eased distribution and storage problems. Sugar for the ice cream was sourced from Russia's tropical allies, Cuba and the countries of Indo-China, making these countries essential for Soviet food security.

Abstaining from foods, they eat horses, don't they?

Not eating certain foods, abstaining from them, may also be a symbol of national pride. There may be a pragmatic reason, linked to economics or resource availability, behind such customs. In Britain, Irish whiskey once enjoyed higher status than Scotch, but after Irish agitation for independence led to the creation of an independent Irish state in 1922, Irish whiskey found it hard to penetrate the British market. The ancient Egyptians despised the shepherds of the Palestinian grasslands because, as now, fertile land in Egypt was a scarce resource, a narrow strip along the Nile flanked by desert, and sheep require large swathes of land for grazing. Today, many consumers in the Anglophone countries, the UK, North America and Australia, would express disgust at the idea of eating horse. Yet consumers across much of the world, from Japan and China across Central Asia and Russia to Mexico and Argentina, and in European countries such as the Netherlands, Belgium, France and Switzerland, are happy to consume horse. Burger *au cheval* can be ordered in many provincial French towns. European prejudice against hippophagy can be traced back to Pope Gregory III, who in 732 pronounced that only pagan barbarians from the plains of Germany or further east would eat such food. Not just Christians but the other two great Abrahamic religions, Islam and Judaism, also despise horsemeat as *haram* or *treif* respectively. As with the pasture requirements of sheep, the grasslands necessary to sustain horses were abundant in Central Asia but scarce in the Arabian desert and on medieval European strip farms. Where horses are abundant you can eat some, ride some, fight with others; where they are scarce, you do not eat your military transport. Move forward a thousand years and we find Napoleon's army surgeon, in 1807, noting how wounded soldiers who scavenged horsemeat recovered sooner and did not suffer scurvy. As Europe industrialized, the demand for workhorses grew; the railways alone employed tens of thousands of them. Britain, with its large colonial empire, enjoyed abundant food imports; France was somewhat less privileged in this respect; Germany and Italy even less so. Hence the British horse became destined at death for pet food only; the cheval, the cavallo and the pferd became acceptable human fare.

Food as protest against Communism, a kiwi by any other name would not taste as sweet

It is unlikely that the leaders of the Cold War battalions facing each other across Europe's Iron Curtain ever considered Ronald McDonald as a combatant in that war. However, an alien visitor to the former Warsaw Pact countries after the fall of Communism in 1989 could have been forgiven for thinking that the red and yellow clown-like figure was chief in command of NATO forces, judging from the speed at which statues of Ronald went up as those of Lenin came down. McDonald's became the symbol of America, freedom and modernity for East Germans, and Romanians saw a visit to McDonald's as symbolizing their independence from the USSR (Schlosser, 2002: 230, 250). Ronald's conquests were repeated further east when China opened up to Western companies. In 1992 in Beijing McDonald's opened what was then its largest restaurant, with 700 seats and nearly 1,000 employees; this establishment set a McWorld record for the number of people served in one day, 40,000 (Ritzer, 1996: 5). The Moscow McDonald's, opened on 31 January 1990, also proved hugely popular and when the restaurant chain opened a branch in Kuwait in 1994 a seven-mile queue of cars formed at the drive-in window. Kiwis, the fruit not the flightless bird, also featured in the fight against Communism; once known as Chinese gooseberries, they were rebranded by New Zealand growers due to Cold War prejudices (Patel, 2008: 5). The USA also enlisted food nomenclature as a political weapon when, in 2003, some American restaurants rebranded French fries (potato chips) as 'Freedom Fries', following France's refusal to support the 2003 US-led invasion of Iraq, while the French themselves were castigated by some Americans as 'cheese-eating surrender monkeys' for their lack of military support in the 2003 campaign.

Coca Cola, another quintessentially American 'food' corporation, has been a target in the Middle East wars. In 2003 Dr Tawfik Mathlouthi, French-born entrepreneur, launched the Mecca Cola brand to cash in on anti-American sentiment and make a stand on the Israeli issue. 'It is all about combating America's Zionism and imperialism by providing a substitute for American goods and increasing the blockade of countries boycotting American goods,' said Mr Mathlouthi, in an interview on BBC News Online, 8 January 2003, 'Mecca Cola challenges US rival'. The slogan on the Mecca Cola bottles reads 'No more drinking stupid, drink with commitment'. Twenty per cent of the profits from Mecca Cola goes to charities promoting peace or development projects in the Palestinian Territories. In 2009 the UK government 'advised' UK supermarkets (not a legal requirement) to distinguish between foods imported from Israeli West Bank settlements and from Palestinian West Bank producers; previously food was just labelled 'Produce of the West Bank'. EU law already requires these two different food sources to be differentiated; food from pre-1967 Israel, also Palestinian-produced food, but not food from Israeli West Bank farms, gets a preferential import duty rate into the EU. From 2003 the USA has been pressuring Israel to freeze West Bank settlement construction under the peace 'road map'; however, Israel has not halted construction of these settlements.

The humble banana caused a trade dispute between the USA and the EU in the 1990s; the EU used the banana trade to support smaller economies in the Caribbean. Banana growers in the Caribbean, in former colonies of European countries, were at a price disadvantage against large US-owned plantations in mainland South America. The EU supported Caribbean economies via trade, to reduce the need for aid, giving them preferential access to the European market. In fact Caribbean bananas only accounted for 7 per cent of EU consumption; South America supplied three-quarters, and the USA did not directly export any bananas to the EU. Despite this, the USA took the so-called 'banana wars' dispute to the WTO and won in 1997. The USA was concerned about the size of its trade deficit (mainly with China) and wanted to eliminate trade restrictions faced by US-owned companies.

The big food corporations find themselves in the firing line of anti-capitalist protesters in a way that even the major banks seldom do; the big banks may symbolize the cold pounds and numbers side of global capitalism, but the big food corporations symbolize control over our very bodies. A new Tesco store will arouse far more opposition than a new bank branch because food retailing, like food itself, has a warm personal side, when that food is sold by a local, independent family-owned grocer with strong neighbourhood links, the Mon and Pop stores of the USA, the corner stores of Britain. Little local family banks do not work. Anti-corporate protests erupted in 2011 against a Tesco Express in a deprived part of Bristol in south-west England. Stokes Croft, where Tesco wanted their new local store, has a strong Bohemian hippy artistic culture and an annual street festival, while lurid psychedelic murals adorn many buildings, one called 'Telepathic Heights' by its occupants. Protests against Tesco began in 2010 after it applied for planning permission under a different name, Jesters Comedy Club, for six smaller retail units on nearby Cheltenham Road. A broad umbrella of concerns included the threat to local retailers and the six daily deliveries by large lorries that would not happen with smaller, non-food retailing. The local Green Party councillor, Gus Hoyt, told *The Guardian* newspaper that opening a Tesco in Stokes Croft was like 'putting a Whisky World in the middle of a Muslim area' (*The Guardian* II, 2011: 12). *The Guardian* reporter wrote, 'if Tesco is a Whisky World, then the local mosque can be found at the headquarters of the People's Republic of Stokes Croft'. Note the escalation in simile from a local retail dispute to a global ideological clash. Matters came to a head in April 2011 when police raided a squat opposite the new Tesco, with the raid attracting hundreds of onlookers, mostly not on the police's side. The Tesco was graffitied with poems such as

> *The silver swan in living had no note,*
> *when death approached, unlocked her silent throat,*
> *leaving her breast against the reedy shore,*
> *thus sang her first and last and sang no more*

The Tesco Express reopened after suffering considerable damage in May 2011; it had to, otherwise 'the mob' would have triumphed over a global corporation. The area still features a mural just up the road from the Tesco saying 'Think Local, Boycott Tesco', and advertising the website www.boycotttesco.org.uk, which features one product Tesco are unlikely to stock; a 'Tesco Value petrol bomb'. Even anarchists have adopted modern information and communications technology.

The opening of the first McDonald's in Rome in 1986, in the historic Piazza di Spagna, sparked similar sentiments to the Stokes Croft Tesco Express. An alliance of left-wing intelligentsia and chefs started the Citta Lente movement, which has grown to 100,000 members in 130 countries (Sassatelli and Davolio, 2010). Like the Stokes Croft protesters and other food activists, Citta Lente espouses a variety of concerns, from biodiversity to local food, rural vitality and sustainability; Citta Lente gave rise to the first Terra Madre (Mother Earth) event in 2004, held annually since then. The Italians have a term that, like *terroir*, has no direct equivalent in English: *la cucina povera*, literally 'food of the poor'. Whereas 'food of the poor' in England might mean burgers and Value ready meals, in Italy it signifies 'peasant food', local, home-cooked, delicious, uncomplicated, unprocessed (Steel, 2008: 320). Since 2000 the Slow Food movement has also 'defended foods at risk of disappearance' as part of its 'battle against homogenization of taste' (West and Domingos, 2012: 121); both rare food species and cooking processes are preserved. However, this has drawn criticism for 'romanticizing' peasant foods and customs, facilitating a sort of gentrification; it both glorifies the past and consumerizes it. Thirteen years after McDonald's entered Rome, its Millau branch in southern France was destroyed (or 'dismantled', depending on your ideological viewpoint) while under construction in August 1999, by a certain Monsieur Jose Bové, local farmer. At Mr Bové's trial in Millau in 2000, some 30,000 supporters turned out with signs reading 'Non à McMerde'. Mr Bové claimed he was not anti-American but anti-*malbouffe*; another word which has no direct translation into English, but which loosely means bad food or junk food. However, the anti-corporate dimension of his crusade inextricably linked class, politics and food.

Food as class conflict. *Posh nosh and grubby grub*

Although the dustman and the duke have the same biology, food is a highly class-ridden good; compare a Waitrose to an Aldi store, or visit a Tesco and contrast the 'Value' to the 'Finest' range, in price, packaging or ingredients. Contrast the subtle silver and black Finest livery with the stark blue and white Value branding; a branding that had to be redesigned in 2012 to a (still rather stark) orange and brown 'Everyday Value' colour scheme, because customers were eschewing the previous Value livery. Food as a signifier of wealth dates back at least to when Christopher Columbus brought the pineapple from the Caribbean. This fruit was impossible to grow in Europe unless you were could afford a heated greenhouse; the fruit is brightly coloured and looks unusual on a dining table. Hence the custom of carving pineapples on gateways and bedposts as symbols of prosperity. The television became in the 1950s what the pineapple was in the 1550s, when the Swanson Corporation launched 'TV dinners' in the USA. At this time only 9 per cent of US households possessed a TV; the meal was packaged to resemble a TV, and symbolized the aspiration of most households to own a television. When, in 1963, saturation point was reached with 100 per cent of US households owning a set, the Swanson Corporation stopped calling its meals 'TV dinners' (Patel, 2008: 263). Most societies have adopted distinguishing marks to divide off the elite from the hoi polloi, some signifier the plebeians cannot attain. As soon as this distinguishing characteristic becomes accessible to the poor, the wealthy find something else still unreachable to them; we could call this 'ascending aspirationalism'. Alternatively the wealthy may abandon a distinguishing characteristic, not because it has become attainable to the poor, but because it has become cumbersome, unsuited to newer social norms. The peacock's tail, so to speak, has grown too big. We could call this 'lateral aspirationalism'. British norms regarding skin colour are an example of 'ascending aspirationalism'. Once most peasants worked in the fields and acquired a tan through both sun and wind, pale skin was the mark of aristocracy. When the Industrial Revolution moved the poor into indoor factory work, giving them pale skins, it became harder to acquire a tan in dull wet smoky Britain; a tan meant you could travel to sunnier climes. In the days before mass air travel, that meant taking weeks away from home and expensive journeying by ship. Nowadays with cheap cosmetics, air travel and migration, skin colour has lost virtually all class significance. Cosmetics, in its widest sense, as the changing of the appearance or order of the human body (from *kosmos*, meaning 'the order of the universe'), provides examples of 'lateral aspirationalism'. The aristocratic Chinese used to bind their women's feet, as this would be a sign that such a woman did not, indeed could not, undertake manual labour. Western aristocracy would adopt extremely fancy clothes that were impractical for manual work, and expensive to maintain. To an extent we have moved laterally away from these peacock marks – although Louboutin high-heeled shoes are not easy to walk in, they force a very 'feminine' gait (Ekinsmyth, 2002: 57) – and the wealthy still drive ultra-expensive classic cars that require a chauffeur for safe parking. Women with the time and money can mark themselves out with extensive beautification regimes, the Baudrillardian 'rituals of insects' (Shaw, 2010), although cheaper beauty regimes are facilitating a fast catch-up by the less affluent.

Food features prominently in both 'ascending' and 'lateral' aspirationalism. The Health Select Committee Report (2004: 104) stated, 'We have observed an odd tension in society. The world of popular culture ... is usually dominated by fit and slim people ... Yet the average person is remorselessly moving away from the ideal.' Obesity, or rather its absence, may be poised to become the next distinguishing mark of the wealthy, particularly in an appearance- and celebrity-obsessed society. Obesity is strongly associated with poverty, because cheap food is high-calorie and low-calorie but nutritious foods are expensive. Bell and Valentine (1997: 26) observe that the gap between attainable reality and unattainable aspiration is growing; as obesity rates have climbed over the past few decades, the average weights of national and international beauty contest winners and fashion models have declined. In earlier times, when Calories were neither cheap nor plentiful, it was excess weight that marked out the rich and powerful. Nowadays we see the fat and obese as decadent, selfish, lacking in self-control; a slim body symbolizes discipline as fasting did in more religious times. Where people will not control themselves, society can step in to do the controlling; the tension between what society says it wants (slimness) and what it engenders (overweight) leads to eating disorders such as bulimia and anorexia, and then to medical intervention to fix within the body the damage that originates from outside it.

Bourdieu singles out certain foods, and the rituals that have been built around these foods by the wealthy elite, as acting as 'gatekeeper foods'; these foods with their unfamiliar tastes would not even be welcomed on the plates of the lower classes – foods such as caviar or dry red wine, that would seem perversely salty or sour in comparison with the compensating sweetness of sugar or fat that accompanies salty snacks for the poorer consumers. Tastes for such posh foods take time to acquire (Carolan, 2012: 131), as does learning the rituals and language of their consumption. Wine, for example, has an entire argot of taste descriptors like floral, spicy, woody, earthy; it should be physically handled in a certain way, swirled around the glass to test its bouquet before being spat out. The upper echelons of society have a panoply of annual dinners at revered and ancient institutions such as the Domus Dinner at Gray's Inn, the Law Tutors Forum at Lincoln's Inn, and the Formal Meals and High Tables of Oxford and Cambridge Universities, where those who have learned the requisite rituals of food can mingle easily; those who have not can be readily excluded. The ties of establishment, royalty and the church are reinforced at such events through a customary prayer and a toast to the monarch. Shark fin soup is an example of a food undergoing removal from the set of distinguishing marks of the wealthy. In China it was prized for centuries simply because it was rare and therefore expensive. In fact shark fin soup is stringy, gelatinous and without elaborate preparation including other ingredients it is rather tasteless. This soup is, or rather was, a Veblen Good, a commodity prized simply because it is expensive; rather like an exclusive restaurant that everyone want to dine at, simply because it is expensive. Such restaurants enjoy an upward-sloping demand curve; such prestige is fragile, however, and a slight change in fashion and demand brings it crashing back to earth. Shark fin soup has met such a change in fashion, as environmental concerns have taken hold in South-East Asian countries and the dish has been delisted by governmental agencies in China and Malaysia.

People buying hollowed-out pumpkins at Halloween are in fact celebrating lower-class or peasant food. The original character in this story was 'Stingy Jack', a resourceful, crafty, mean, drink-loving, hedonistic peasant who would do anything, even steal, to get what he wanted. Stingy Jack traps the Devil, only releasing him on promise that he will not claim Jack's soul for Hell when he dies; when sinful Jack does die he cannot go to Heaven either, so he is trapped in limbo, and the Devil gives him an inextinguishable ember from Hell to light his way, in a hollowed-out turnip or swede to serve as a lampholder. This tradition became incorporated into the Christian calendar on All Saints' Day, or All Hallows, when the souls of the dead were believed to be close to those living on Earth. The notion of leaving food for the souls of the dead at the end of October is common to many religions; in Mexico the *Dia de los Muertos*, a fusion of Roman Catholicism and pre-Columbian Zapatec Indian tradition, is held on 31 October, with *Pan de los Muertos*, bread adorned with sugar-coated faces, left out that night. In Europe the turnip represented the staple food, the life or body of the peasants, and the light within was the trapped soul; in America a pumpkin was substituted as it is easier to carve. Now the American tradition has come back to Britain and the original meaning of this ritual obscured.

Where we purchase our food is also class-burdened. Skeggs (1997: 3, 4) described the 'burden of class' as the efforts made by those of lower socio-economic status (SES) to be perceived as belonging to a higher social class, while those of higher class are more relaxed about such social signifiers and may adopt habits redolent of the lower social orders. Less-affluent shoppers may be reluctant to be associated with 'deep-discount' stores such as Netto, a Danish chain which formerly operated very cheap stores in the UK (the UK stores were sold to Asda in 2010). 'I'm not taking that [Netto] bag to school, they'll think you're shopping at second hand food stores' (a quote from a Leeds mother in Wrigley et al., 2004: 131). Generally, however, supermarkets provided a safely class-anonymous environment within which the working classes could shop with no obvious class signifiers, in contrast to shopping in smaller personal-service grocers where the paucity of their purchases would give away their lack of cash. However, the wealthy avoided the early supermarkets of America because the extravagance of their shopping baskets might attract gossip from low-paid shop assistants. What time you ate your food at and what you called your meals also signified your class. In the UK all classes called their first meal 'breakfast', but the midday meal was termed 'dinner' by the lower paid manual classes and 'lunch' by the upper classes (Teed, 1963). Class divisions in meals deepened as the day progressed. The working classes had their 'tea' at around 6 p.m.; this was a smaller meal than the midday 'dinner' and typically consisted of bread, fish or meat paste, a cup of tea and jam. Before bedtime a smaller 'tea' of a biscuit and a cup of tea might also be consumed. Middle-class suburbanites had 'tea' at 4 p.m., while the gentry had 'tea' at 5 p.m., both meals consisting of tea and biscuits. The upper-middle class suburbanites then had 'dinner', their largest meal of the day, at around 7.30 or 8 p.m., a two- or three-course affair, while the leisured upper classes might not partake of dinner until as late as 10 p.m.; their breakfast would be as late as 9 a.m. or 10 a.m. The higher your social class, the later your main meal and the later your daily schedule of going to bed and rising. The same pattern held for the Romans, with the wealthier citizens of the Empire eating smaller midday meals and a large formal meal in the evening. Medieval British peasants ate on an earlier schedule, with breakfast at 6 a.m., dinner at 10 a.m. and supper at 4 p.m. (Ferguson, 1971: 9, 12). When you are labouring in the fields you must rise with the sun, or even before it, to maximize your productivity. However, experiments suggest that our diurnal clock runs at nearer 25 than 24 hours, so lying in bed after dawn, and eating late, with romantic dim artificial lighting, is a pleasurable exercise, if you can afford it. Hence, the imposition of earlier mealtimes can signify subordination. The lowest 'caste' members of Western societies, prisoners, are fed much earlier than they would prefer or are used to at home, especially with their evening meal. A prison schedule might have breakfast at 6.30 a.m., lunch at 11.30 a.m. and dinner as early as 5 p.m. In part, these times are driven by staff considerations; they want to be off home for their dinner, so lockdown after the last meal of the day comes early, but this schedule also reinforces discipline and subordination. An extreme form of food discrimination manifested itself in South African prisons during the Apartheid era, when black prisoners were denied bread or jam as these were 'civilized' processed foods for whites, and also given to coloured/Asian prisoners as 'more civilized' than blacks (Patel, 2008: 267). Returning to modern Britain, we may have achieved the 'classless society' promised by John Major in the 1990s, at least in mealtimes; the popularity of quick, fast, convenient food now means that Britain now has no fixed mealtimes. At no time of the day in the UK are more than a fifth of people eating, in contrast to Spain where two-fifths are eating at 2.50 p.m. and a third at 9.30 p.m. (*The Economist*, 2013a: 25). Cookery methods are also class-based; upper classes grill or bake their food, whereas lower classes fry, boil or stew it (Bell and Valentine, 1997: 43). Frying causes odours that may spoil expensive clothes or home furnishings; frying can mask the taste of poor quality food or food past its best, as with fish and chips, discussed below. Boiling makes tough cheap meat edible, whereas grilling works better with more expensive foods. Also relevant is that grilling or baking demand more time and care, whereas frying is quick, and foods stewing or boiling can be left a long time without attention. So the poor, with little spare time, cannot afford the time-consuming cooking methods utilized by households wealthy enough to support at least one non-working member.

What we call our food also reflects class association. The 1066 Norman invasion of England subjugating the Saxons, and the subsequent ascension of French culture to hegemonic position in Europe, produced a division within the English language between upper-class words, derived from French-Latin and lower class words derived from Saxon-German. Meat consumption is associated with wealth but the poor eat more bread and vegetables, so Saxon animal-processing words like shambles, slaughterers or knackers have given way to 'butcher', from the French 'boucherie'. However, we have the Saxon words 'greengrocer' and 'baker' which do not derive from the corresponding French 'épicerie' and 'boulangerie'. The poor would have had access to meats from the pig, the chicken and perhaps the lamb, as these animals needed little land to rear; as in China today, pigs and chickens could be kept in backyards as handy recycling mechanisms, turning household rubbish into food. So English has words like 'swine' (German 'schweine'), pig (German 'bigge', a big animal), bacon (German 'bakke', meaning 'back'), lamb (Saxon 'lamm') and chicken (German 'kuken', meaning 'to cook'). However, consumption of cows, game birds and deer was associated with the upper classes, so in English we have beef (French 'boeuf'), pheasant (French 'faisan') and venison (French 'veneur', meaning 'hunter'; from which we also derive 'Grosveneur' or 'great hunter'). The English words 'mutton' and pork' are also derived from the French 'mouton' (sheep) and 'porc'; sheep require more land to graze than do lambs, and the wealthy would eat pork too. Likewise 'wine', an upper-class beverage, comes from the French 'vin' whereas 'beer' derives from the German 'bier'. We also use food names to distance ourselves from the soft, furry, warm cuddly animal that produced them; we eat beef not cow, pork not pig. But we only do this for soft furry mammals; we have no separate food word for chicken, turkey, cod or salmon.

Foods may be class-labelled but their class status is not fixed. Offal, cockles and whelks are all former working-class foods that have moved upmarket. Fish and chips has also moved up-class. Fish was once far more abundant than now, and its price was concomitantly lower. When nineteenth-century British trawlers began fishing as far afield as Iceland, the problem was that fish kept on ice darkens and acquires an unpleasant smell after 17 days, and the trawlers took 14 days to return to the UK. The resultant shop shelf-life of under three days was lengthened by covering the dark colour with batter, and removing the smell by frying. Battered fish and potato chips constituted an energy-dense midday meal for manual labourers. The first recorded British fish and chip shop opened in the 1860s, although Charles Dickens wrote of fried fish in the 1830s. Harry Ramsden took fish and chips upmarket with his first restaurant in Guiseley, Yorkshire, opened in 1928. Even the poor relative of fish and chips, 'scraps', has gentrified; these leftover fragments of batter were once given free to the poor, but may now be served with lemon juice, chilli or nutmeg as a posh starter. Foods may also de-gentrify. White bread in Roman times was a rich person's food, because it took more labour to sieve the stone-milled flour, to produce a more attractive loaf than the coarse brown bread the poor ate. The Industrial Revolution meant that white flour could be produced more easily, and the by-product now had an economic value as animal fodder. Then people recognized that brown bread was nutritionally superior in terms of fibre and vitamin content, and now white bread is the poor man's food. Changing technology, changing cultures and shifting geographies can take foods either up- or downmarket.

Food and gender. *Macho meat and girly grapefruit*

Food is heavily gendered at all household stages, from sourcing (shopping) through processing (cooking) to consumption (what is eaten). Shopping itself is often seen as feminine, frivolous, the flippant dispersal of household wealth; the opposite of the 'real, masculine' business of generating such wealth, an attitude often seen in the 1950s factories of a macho grimy industrial town. In Western society, this gender bias has intensified since the Industrial Revolution; women have retreated from the role of household production they occupied in pre-industrial times, when they produced textiles and grew food. In Proverbs 31:10 it asks 'a capable wife who can find?', followed by a list of roles such a 'capable wife' might undertake. These include procuring wool and dyes, producing garments for sale, trading in real estate, as well as obtaining food from remote sources. However, as the exploitation of child labour became unfashionable with the progress of industrialization, so there was also pressure to remove women from the factories, reassigning them to a household role of childcare and beauty maintenance; a role incompatible with gritty factory work. The British educational system of the late 1900s reinforced this division with the inclusion of 'domestic science' in the girls' curriculum; entrenching a firm separation from 'science' (the smelly, messy, dangerous, adventurous stuff), which was for boys only. This gendered outlook towards household provisioning persists today; most marketers agree that male shopping methodology differs considerably from female. Males minimize shopping time, doing 'commando shopping', in and out of the store in as short a time as possible, just picking up the essentials such as beer and barbeque requirements. When asked to obtain domestic goods by their partners, men may re-gender the shopping task; some stores report a peak sales time for both nappies and beer of late Friday afternoon. This is attributed to mothers asking their partner to pick up a weekend's supply of nappies on the way back from work, the alcohol purchase being a mitigating masculinization of this task. A 2006 advert for a Hummer 4x4 vehicle (YouTube, 2012) shows two men at a supermarket checkout; the green T-shirted guy being served has on the checkout conveyor belt some salad items and a large box of tofu, while the bloke behind (in a wasp-coloured, white, black and yellow T-shirt) is buying large outsized packs of meat, large ribs, obviously 'bits of animal', barbeque food. The first guy glances nervously and enviously at the 'real food' advancing to his rear. Then, the first guy sees a leaflet advertising Hummers. In a rather resolute, belligerent manner, the first guy rams his trolley into the trolley park, turns the key in his rather nondescript vehicle, drives to the Hummer showroom and promptly buys his large new 4x4. Tagline: 'Restore the Balance'. The message is that 'real masculine guys' not only drive 4x4s but also buy 'real' food, meat not salad and tofu. The only food sourcing procedure that is still male is going out for a takeaway, an echo of man as hunter-gatherer (Bell and Valentine, 1997: 73).

Once we enter the arena of food processing, gender divisions sharpen markedly, and these divisions are heavily reinforced by the media. In the unsung private home arena, cooking is low status and women predominate. An extreme version of this found in Atkins and Bowler (2001: 311), who report on a tribe in Chad where cooking pots are exclusively female property to the extent that any man using one is branded a transvestite. In contrast, high-status celebrity TV chefs are overwhelmingly male, despite the fact that the food they produce is all about presentation, visual decoration and fripperies, traditionally more feminine concerns. *Come Dine With Me*, a TV reality programme where four domestic 'food processors' compete to win the highest score for their cooking and hosting, occupies an intermediate level in status terms and the contestants are more balanced between males and females. TV shows regularly reinforce the idea that gardening, DIY and high status cooking are a male domain, but that cleaning and other repetitive domestic tasks are female. The two stars of the TV reality show *How Clean is Your House?*, which ran between 2003 and 2009 on Channel Four in the UK, were both female. The gardening (male) versus cleaning (female) split illustrates the artificiality of many gender divides; is mowing the lawn and clearing dead leaves so different from hoovering the carpet and removing dust? The former task, however, is external and therefore quasi-public, whereas the latter is private, behind brick walls. The word 'chef' (seldom applied to domestic food processing) itself derives from 'chief', a very masculine word. The job itself derives from the King's Cup Bearer, which became 'butler' (seldom if ever a 'butless'), and this Cup Bearer had to be, in pre-forensic days when poisoning was undetectable, a very trusted person. Women, from the days of Eve as temptress, were far too sneaky and unreliable to hold this post. Men are strong, fight openly as swordsmen, chivalrous knights on horseback, but women gossip snidely behind your back, are too weak with childbirth and the monthly cycle to fight openly, so must use underhand methods like poison. Despite the noble ideals of Proverbs 31, the distrust and subordination of women and hence female-oriented tasks have deep roots in the human psyche.

Food consumption is also gender-divided. Red meat, barbeque food, is firmly in the male domain; again a relic of man as hunter-gatherer. Barbequing is one of the few cookery processes seen as male whereas boiling or straining food through muslin is female. Modern man may hunt only as far as the nearest supermarket or takeaway, but taming fire, eating large, burnt roast portions, with excess alcohol (never a foetus to harm) and abjuring vegetables is a macho way of eating, signifying physical strength and control over wild nature. Macho foods should have a strong odour; real men may burp and fart; ladies never. In contrast, foods like fruit and salad are feminine; eating these signals 'I care about my attractiveness, complexion, weight, figure'; women may, indeed must, go to the length of denying themselves food while feeding the man and the children, when there is insufficient food for all in the cupboard. This serves the dual purpose of self-sacrifice (women's needs as subordinate) and figure maintenance (women must be slim). These considerations do not apply to the same extent to men who are supposed to be strong, hulky, tanned and muscular. Fish, soft and healthy, is feminine; so are sour dairy products (no odour), whereas smelly cheese is masculine. However, healthier foods can become less feminine, more androgynous, once men begin to worry about health and obesity too. Fish and 'lite' beer are becoming more acceptable for men to consume (Anderson, 2009: 41). Texture, colour and shape of food are also gender signifiers. Tough, chewy foods are male; soft runny ones are female. Red-brown-black (burnt) meaty foods are male; white-yellow foods are female. Red signifies danger, blood, adventure, whereas green-yellow-white signifies calm, purity, eggs, reproduction. Chocolate is gender-divided; dairy milk chocolate is feminine (milk, mothering), whereas dark, chunky, bricky chocolate is masculine. The wrapper on a bar of the hunky Yorkie Bar says it all – 'Not For Girls' – reinforced with a traffic-sign symbol of a girl in a red circle with a 'forbidden' diagonal line across. Yorkie Bar may be oriented to macho big-rig lorry drivers, but Flake, soft and crumbly and with a phallic shape, is female-oriented. It is advertised as being eaten by a woman in a long silky nightdress lounging on a soft sofa, or running with abandon (not purposefully chasing wild meat, rather without responsibility) in a field. What sort of man would put such a phallic-shaped confection in his mouth? *Real Men Don't Eat Quiche*, the title of a 1982 book by Bruce Feirstein, satirized the genderization of both food processing and food consumption; the message was that 'real men' would eat eggs and bacon pie (the eggs 'redeemed' by the meaty bacon) but would not cook eggy quiche for themselves (Goffman, 1979; Stein and Nemeroff, 1995; Sellaeg and Chapman, 2008).

Food as depravity. *Phwoar, tasty!!*

The mouth is, as noted earlier, an erotic area, both sensual and sexual; biting, sucking, kissing, licking, these are all sexual activities as well as food-related. The activity of licking a food such as chocolate off a partner's body bridges sex and food, and soft sweet lickable foods such as ice cream are frequently advertised in a romantic-erotic boyfriend–girlfriend context. If food is sexual then programmes like *Masterchef* are 'food pornography'. The root of *porne*, the Greek word for 'prostitute', means 'something bought and sold', such as a (sex) slave. The other half of 'pornography', 'graphein', means 'to write about'. So 'pornography' ultimately carries the idea of images that are unreal, unobtainable, images of something commercialized but seductive, erotic. Like the fruit in the Garden of Eden, it is tempting but forbidden. Cookery TV programmes like *Masterchef*, replete with arcane food jargon like joue, ragout, ham foam, en papillote, cerviche, julienne, dishes calling for ingredients such as lavender honey or gold leaf, unobtainable even at Waitrose, dangle dishes that can never be understood, let alone prepared, by 99 per cent of the population. Seductive but unobtainable, just as a naked model on a calendar (Bell and Valentine, 1997: 6) they make cooking inaccessible to the unskilled and so constitute 'food pornography'. TV cookery shows were originally more practical; in 1946 TV chef Philip Harben demonstrated to British housewives how to cook tasty meals within the constraints of rationing, which persisted until 1954. Fanny Cradock and others continued to teach Britons simple and practical cookery skills through the 1960s. Convenience foods, tinned and frozen, needing little culinary skill to prepare, were then available in the UK but of poor quality, 'TV dinner slop' in the words of Clinton Silver, leader of Marks & Spencer's food division 1975–87 (Seth and Randall, 1999: 125–6). Today's sophisticated range of cook-chilled ready meals, with exotic international cuisine, barely existed even in the mid-1990s in many wealthy countries (Wrigley and Lowe, 2002: 32). As cooking deskilled, TV cookery shows became more elaborate, sponsored by celebrity chefs like Heston Blumenthal or Jamie Oliver. These shows fitted the reality TV format; in 2002 British TV showed 4,000 hours of food programmes, and 900 cookery books and 25 million words about food and cooking were published (London Development Agency, 2005: 36). People bought these books but few could use them; they comprise a sort of food pornography, to peek into and leer at but not to produce real food, just as pornographic material is to leer at but does not constitute real love.

It is a short step from pornography to perversion, sadism or masochism, and food pornography occupies these areas too. Eating competitions have proliferated on reality TV, with shows like *Man Versus Food*, where contestants attempt to eat a huge amount of food in a limited time and then keep it down. The food is always calorific, fatty, filling (that's the whole point) and lesser mortals can practise with such delicacies as the 1,000 Calorie Stacker Quad burger or the even larger Dagwood. On the TV show *I'm A Celebrity,*

Get Me Out Of Here contestants attempt to eat so-called 'bush tucker', insects or animal parts such as the anus, eyes or testicles of kangaroos, while the viewers take sadistic pleasure in seeing if the contestants can stomach this. Meanwhile food masochists can visit Marks & Spencer's supermarket to buy a chilli sauce named 'Pain 100%'. Made from habanero peppers, 'Pain 100%', stocked by Marks and Spencer since 2012, scores 1 million on the Scoville Scale, a measure of the heat of foods based on their Capsaicin content. Capsaicin, a substance found in chillies and peppers, causes nerve endings in the mouth to release Substance P, which the brain perceives as burning, causing endorphin releases, a natural opiate, so excessive capsaicin consumption can give a 'high' and even become addictive. Capsaicin also excites the trigeminal nerve and enhances the taste sensation of other foods. Those dissatisfied with 'Pain 100%' can visit Tesco and purchase Dorset Naga; with a Scoville score close to the 2 million of police pepper sprays, it is the only foodstuff Tesco will not sell to children. Dorset Naga is painful even to touch and chefs using it must wear gloves. Drug users exploit the 'pink fix', snorting a mixture of cocaine and chilli, to stimulate the brain's release of endorphins, while more legal highs can be had at US hot food festivals such as the Fiery Foods and Barbeque Show in Albuquerque. For the ultimate capsaicin sensation one must visit the UK's Bindi Restaurant in Grantham, Lincolnshire, where a dish called The Widower is served; containing Naga Infinity chillies, this food scores an astonishing 6 million on the Scoville Scale. Three times stronger than a pepper spray, it can induce hallucinations from the massive endorphin release, and the chef requires gloves and goggles to make it.

Chapters 3 and 4 have shown how food is not just a nutritious substance but has deep psychological and cultural meanings as to how and why we buy and consume certain foods and not others. Chapter 5 looks at the changing way we buy our food, how these changes have affected access to healthy food, and the socio-cultural reasons for this change in the way we buy our food.

5 Grosser grocers, consumed consumers

From corner shops to supermarkets. *A nation of shopkeepers*

The word 'shop' is linked to the German word for shed, 'schuppe', where goods were manufactured for sale at the weekly market. The original meaning of 'schuppe' or 'shop' persists in terms like 'workshop'. The word 'schuppe' is related to the Saxon term 'chepe', meaning 'marketplace'; a meaning preserved today in English place names like Chipping Norton in Oxfordshire and Eastcheap in London. By the eighteenth century goods were being sold directly from these 'schuppes' (Pain, 1967: 6) rather than at market. The position of the small independent shop was strengthened by the Industrial Revolution. The urban working class, living in cramped terraced housing, had little storage space for food and no land to grow it themselves; they had to use their factory wages to buy food from shops. The development of the nineteenth-century industrial towns owed little to town planning; there was a laissez-faire attitude where anyone could do what they liked with their property (Davis, 1966: 300). In Britain, almost every street corner presented a good location to set up a shop, giving the UK the sobriquet 'nation of shopkeepers'. By 1900 European retailing consisted essentially of small independent stores serving the city suburbs, rural towns and villages and the urban centres hosting the innovative form of retailing called the department store, whose development was facilitated by a range of inventions from plate glass and lifts to electric lighting. In America a new form of retail was appearing, the out-of-town supermarket. Self-service was crucial for supermarkets, because the customer did most of the shopkeeper's work, selecting the goods themselves; a larger store became viable without high staffing costs and diseconomies of scale. The customers liked self-service, giving them more control over the shopping experience, as well as time savings. The Piggly Wiggly store, opened in Memphis, Tennessee on 16 September 1916, was the world's first self-service store; it was swiftly followed by out-of-town malls, the Lake Forest Mall near Chicago (also opened in 1916) and the Country Club Plaza at Kansas City, opened in 1922 (Marshall, 1995: 65, 178). As with European department stores, technological innovations paved the way for these new retail venues. The US had a prosperous car-owning middle class whose female half disliked jostling with the hoi polloi in cramped city centre stores; these women ordered goods by phone to be delivered to their home. The spacious malls of 1920s America were attractive to such people, and accessible only to car owners. The stage was set, first in America and later in Europe, for a departure of high-class retailing from cramped, impractical, expensive, dangerous, inaccessible, inner city venues to spacious clean suburban sites well served by roads that efficiently brought both customers and timely bulk deliveries of goods. Innovations such as self-service supermarkets did not reach the UK until 1950, when this form of retailing was adopted by both Tesco in Croydon and Sainsbury in St Albans, both wealthy south-eastern locations. The last UK supermarket to offer counter service was Sainsbury in the less-affluent London suburb of Peckham, which closed in 1982. A key stage in the migration of British retailing from town centres to out-of-town retail parks came with the election of Margaret Thatcher as Conservative Prime Minister in 1979. Her party's victory was due in large measure to the recession of the late 1970s, as British heavy industry moved to newly industrializing countries like Taiwan and Japan. The result was the appearance of large vacant sites where once stood steelworks, chemical works and dockyards. An iconic image of the 1980s was Mrs Thatcher's 'walk in the wilderness' as she strolled in the weed-infested ruins of a former steelworks in Middlesbrough in the industrial north-east of England. Mrs Thatcher designated this derelict land as Enterprise Zones (EZs), areas where businesses could set up with minimal planning regulations and tax burdens, like the laissez-faire planning of Victorian cities. Much of the EZ land was taken by large retail users, including supermarkets and regional shopping malls, the latter often having a big supermarket as an anchor store. Just outside Sheffield a former steelworks became Meadowhall Shopping Centre; in the West Midlands, another former steelworks became Merry Hill Centre; and just south of Newcastle upon Tyne a third steelworks made way for the Gateshead Centre. By the early twenty-first century every British city had its off-centre regional shopping mall, and most towns hosted one or more off-centre supermarkets. The average size of UK supermarkets was also increasing, as Table 5.1 illustrates.

Table 5.1 shows that stores being closed in 1980, probably due to lack of economies of scale, were larger than the average store being operated in 1974. Supermarkets have expanded in time as well as space; extended opening hours have intensified competition with small independent shops that were 'open all hours'. In 1994 the UK repealed its 1950 Shops Act which had outlawed trading on Sunday or after 8 p.m. on other days, except to sell perishable goods such as fresh fruit, vegetables and periodicals or newspapers; this meant you could buy a pornographic magazine on a Sunday but not a Bible. In practice small independent stores stayed open to trade in non-perishable goods like cigarettes, a trade seldom restricted by the authorities. From 1995 Sunday opening was legal for large UK supermarkets for up to six hours, and from 2000 Tesco instituted 24-hour trading, Monday to Saturday, at its larger outlets. These stores would be staffed anyway at night, for shelf stocking and

Table 5.1 Average size of UK supermarkets (all figures in square metres)

Year	*1974*	*1980*	*1988*	*2005*
Average size UK supermarket	260	700	1,000	4,000
Average size of Tesco store	600	1,000	2,200	6,000
Average size of new store opening	1,100	1,200		
Average size of store being closed	100	400		

Sources: West (1988: 35, 39); Gardner (1989: 177); Low Income Project Team (1996: 6).

Internet orders, so the extra cost of opening was low. Other innovations favouring large supermarkets over small independents include Internet trading, loyalty cards and sophisticated IT-based stock control methods facilitating just-in-time delivery schedules. The supermarkets have squeezed more sales out of their (increased) space and staff. Tesco, between 1997 and 2001, increased its annual UK sales per employee from £146,300 to £161,600 and its annual sales per square metre from £211.20 to £235.50. There are a number of reasons why consumers have found the supermarket so appealing: wider choice, convenience, the ability to do all the household shopping, food and non-food, under one roof, easy free parking, a reliable brand sold in a well-lit clean shopping environment, to mention a few. The main attraction, however, has been and continues to be price; supermarkets, with their huge economies of scale, can afford to undercut smaller independent retailers on staple goods or KVIs. A KVI is a Known Value Item, a staple good such as a litre of milk where the customer knows what it 'ought to cost'. Supermarkets can price their KVIs extremely competitively, while making higher profit margins on the luxury items that shoppers are less price-familiar with. From the beginning price was key; Mr Clarence Saunders, the proprietor of the Piggly Wiggly stores, promised to 'slay the demon of high prices'. Jack Cohen, founder of Tesco, was happy to acquire the nickname 'Slasher Jack' from his ruthless price cutting (Seth and Randall, 1999: 12).

All this extra supermarket retail capacity was bound to cause the closure of some smaller independent stores. Unless stores could specialize in some expensive niche product and had an affluent clientele to sell to, or they served a poor area where access to private transport was limited and could exploit this monopoly of distance by charging higher prices, grocery stores faced a major challenge from the supermarkets. As with the rise of the department stores and the advance of the American supermarket, underlying socio-economic factors played a major role in this transformation of the grocery retailing sector. Under the Thatcher government UK taxation shifted from direct (income) taxes to indirect (purchase) taxes, with extra rises on alcohol and tobacco. This hurt smaller independent shops in less affluent areas in two ways. First, this tax shift was regressive, because the poor spend a larger proportion of their income than do the wealthy, therefore spending power was withdrawn from less affluent areas and the shops that served the poorer car-less consumers in these areas. Second, the extra taxes on tobacco and alcohol damaged the trade of local convenience stores for whom these items were a staple, enabling them to offer a range of general food goods. UK car usage continued to rise and the Thatcherite policy of 'Right to Buy' saw many former council houses sold into owner occupancy. Inevitably it was the nicer rural village council houses that were sold, houses once built for low-paid agricultural workers. Now they were owned by wealthier commuters using the village as a dormitory but working in a distant town, where they would also shop, so many village stores closed.

Pensions also changed under the Thatcher administration; those with private or employer pensions gained while those relying on the state pension fell behind. Poorer pensioners remained in lower SES areas after finishing work because they could not afford to move to nice coastal retirement areas, and this further reduced the trade of local stores. Higher alcohol taxes, along with drink-driving law enforcement and raised energy costs, closed down many village pubs, so the threads of the community web that bound many rural communities together – the shop, the pub, the school – all began to unravel as birth rates fell and small schools were rationalized into bigger hubs. Bus services were privatized, and many rural routes vanished. More recently many small neighbourhood Post Offices have closed, and another thread that kept retail spending power within the village frayed. Mrs Thatcher also curbed the autonomy of local councils, reducing their funding; so when a big supermarket mounted a legal challenge against a council that had withheld planning permission, perhaps to protect local retailers, the council could less afford to resist the supermarket's lawyers. Indeed, the council, far from being seen as a local-economy hero, could be cast as irresponsibly employing legal expertise to resist, Canute-like, the inevitable arrival of an entity that would bring cheaper food and more choice to consumers anyway (Thomas, 1989: 208). Rising car usage negatively impacted small independent stores in another way. Town centres became congested and by-passes were built, directing traffic towards the out-of-town supermarket. Councils, starved of central government cash, sought income wherever they could, including increasing parking charges and charging businesses more for permits required for changes like starting a hot food takeaway. The number of Post Offices in Britain declined from 22,000 in 1981 (there were 21,900 post offices in the UK in 1900, serving a population two-thirds of what it was in 1981) to 20,000 in 1996 and 18,400 in 2000. Thereafter there was a sharp fall to 14,600 in 2005 and 11,500 in 2011. This decline was driven mainly by technological and economic factors, which conspired to erode the range of services offered at local Post Offices. For example, government benefits such as Jobseekers Allowance and State Pensions cost 79p per payment to process through the Post Office but just 1p to process through the banking system, so long as the recipient had a bank account. The new technologies and services offered by the Internet took over many former Post Office services, for example passport renewal, and many customers found the online method far more convenient than travelling to a

Post Office and trying to park nearby; especially as the Post Office network grew sparser and travel distances rose. Online, the queue was also avoided. As postmasters grew older and retired, it became harder to recruit replacements for a long-hours, low-pay job. The closure of rural and suburban Post Offices reduced footfall to nearby grocery stores; traffic fell by 15 per cent if the grocery shop was separate from the former Post Office, and by as much as a quarter if the Post Office had been inside the store. Shoppers wanting to visit a Post Office now had to travel to larger retail centres, and would do their grocery shopping there too. Besides loss of custom, small shops deprived of a local Post Office lost money due to the proprietors themselves having to travel further to access services such as stamps and cash depositing, and extra time spent queuing at these larger Post Offices – an estimated £270,000 per year increase in costs to rural shops (*The Guardian*, 2006). Rural bank closures had similar effects.

The expansion of higher education in the UK has also caused a reduction in grocery retailing in some areas, through a process called studentification. In areas close to large universities such as Headingley in Leeds or Lenton in Nottingham, large numbers of family homes have been bought by landlords to let as bedsit rooms to students. This may have adverse neighbourhood effects: gardens become unkempt, noise from cars and students at night increases, and the sense of local community falls away as the population of the area becomes transient. The locality may become semi-depopulated during the 20 weeks of the year when students are off campus. Headingley went from 80 per cent family households and 20 per cent student housing to 90 per cent student accommodation between 1992 and 2002. Not only did overall UK student numbers grow, but studentification carries its own momentum because the more houses become student lets, the more that family-oriented facilities such as schools tend to close, incentivizing more families to sell to student landlords. This affects local retailing as students may choose to eat takeaways. Pubs, bars and cafés increase, as do charity shops and 'landlord supply shops' selling cheap furnishings. Local grocery shops close, and those that remain open are increasingly reluctant to stock fresh fruit and vegetables, particularly during the summer when custom is down and these items spoil quickly (Shaw, 2006).

The trend in British grocery store numbers has not been entirely downwards. New types of grocery retailers have opened and others have expanded. The discounters Aldi, Lidl and Netto arrived in Britain in 1990, 1994 and 1990 respectively; the first two store chains were from Germany, the last from Denmark. These three 'hard discounters' offered very cheap groceries in a basic 'no frills' environment. Essentially unbeatable on price, it was possible to do a full household grocery shop at these stores, although they offered a very limited choice within product categories. The Netto fascia vanished from Britain in 2011 after Asda bought their UK stores from the parent company, Maersk Group; Maersk Shipping was also part of this group, and the shipping arm meant that Netto had enjoyed lower transport costs to its stores. Asda's acquisition of Netto was part of a trend by all the major UK supermarkets to open local neighbourhood stores in suburban and rural, small town and village locations. Tesco opened its Express store on a garage forecourt in Barnes, west London, in 1994, and Sainsbury followed suit with the first Local store in 1998 in Hammersmith, also in west London. Morrisons and Waitrose are also building local store networks, and Asda is using the former Netto premises as neighbourhood supermarkets. Factors driving this move back into smaller local stores by the big chains include a lack of further large sites to develop and the saturation of the grocery market in the UK, meaning that any sales growth in Britain must come from the local top-up market. On the demand side, customers are becoming more time-pressed and want the reliability and price advantage of a supermarket without the inconvenience of having to visit a large store just to buy a loaf and some milk. There has also been an expansion of supermarket grocery outlets at garage forecourts, where they function as local stores for people nearby visiting on foot. The Co-op has a significant position in suburban and rural retailing, where it competes with independent grocery stores. Areas of the UK where the Co-operative supermarket has spatial near-monopolies include north Lincoln, north Somerset, Copthorne in Shrewsbury and east Leicester. The growth in ethnic diversity in Britain has increased both the number and quality of ethnic minority-oriented grocery shops. The 2004 expansion of the EU into former Warsaw Pact countries meant large numbers of East Europeans arrived in the UK, and Polish food shops became common. These shops increasingly stock fresh fruit and vegetables, which they did not in 2008. Asian-oriented grocery shops, often with a Halal butcher, have also expanded and Asian supermarket chains, for example Pak Foods, are appearing on UK high streets. Chinese supermarkets are also becoming more commonplace, frequently located just outside town centres. There has also been 'category-blurring', with shop chains moving into each other's product ranges. Just as major chains like Tesco have diversified into clothes, electrical goods and indeed almost about every product and service line conceivable, chains like the off licence Bargain Booze and the hardware store Wilkinson frequently sell some food, although seldom sell fresh produce, just tinned foods.

The positioning of a supermarket branch near existing shops can enhance as well as damage their trade; much depends on the exact spatial relationship between the supermarket, shops and pedestrian flows. The clawback of trade theory says that locating a supermarket in a smaller town will keep local shoppers from travelling to a larger town and its supermarket; a 2006 study of Tesco Express stores in rural Hampshire locations in the UK suggested that the upgrade of these stores from former One Stop outlets did indeed reduce outshopping from the smaller towns and villages to larger centres like Winchester and Basingstoke (Wrigley et al., 2007). More intangibly, a sense of civic pride can be induced in an area if its retail centre hosts a full-scale supermarket, symbolizing a commitment by a major company to investing in the neighbourhood (Wind-Cowie, 2010: 16). However, it is crucial that the supermarket is very close to the smaller shops; if it is a hundred metres away, people will not visit the independent retailers at the same time as the supermarket, and the small shops will lose trade. Barriers to pedestrian flow between the supermarket and the shops, such as a main road to be crossed, or an unattractive pedestrian route between the two, prevent small retailers benefiting. In the market town of Brigg, in Lincolnshire, a Tesco supermarket offered two hours' free parking on the edge of the town centre while the council car parks charged for parking. There was nothing to stop Tesco car park users also walking to the town centre shops less than 500 metres away. However, few shoppers did this; the pedestrian route from the Tesco store passed the unattractive backs of shops and was not signposted at either end. Other forms of grocery shopping have also expanded in the past two decades. Farmers' markets in the UK numbered less than ten in 1997 but by 2002 there were more than 200 and in 2012 the UK hosted around 750 such markets. However, they are oriented towards the more affluent shopper, with high-end luxury goods on sale such as farm-made jams and cakes, and may only be held once a month; they will do little to improve access to fresh fruit and vegetables for less wealthy consumers, without cars. Farm shops number some 4,000 in the UK; some are situated on the edge of villages and function as village grocer. Many are too remote to be accessed except by car. As with farmers' markets, their main focus often is on sustainable local food at a price premium aimed at the more affluent consumer; poorer rural areas have fewer farm shops. Rural areas of the UK with few shops include mid-Wales, parts of Lincolnshire and large tracts of Leicestershire. More information on the spatial distribution of shops, in the UK and areas of other European countries, is available at www.fooddeserts.org/images/kontentMaps.htm.

There are forms of grocery retailing that in theory are open to anyone, however immobile, because the retailer comes to the customer: mobile shops and Internet-based retail. However, 14 per cent of UK adults have never used the Internet by 2013, down from 18 per cent in 2010. Internet non-use is concentrated among the elderly with 30 per cent of those aged 65–74 and 70 per cent of the over-75s never having logged on; the disabled, the less-affluent, the disabled and women are more likely to be non-users, and these groups may also experience difficulties accessing physical shops. Whereas 80 per cent of the wealthiest decile of the UK population had access to the Internet in 2010, only 38 per cent of the poorest decile did. Regionally, there are only four counties in the UK where over half of pensioners have Internet access; Surrey was highest at 63 per cent, followed by Bedfordshire, Buckinghamshire and Suffolk. The lowest proportion of pensioners with Internet access is in Tyne and Wear, 28 per cent. Going online is not free, there may also be a delivery charge for the shopping, and access to the Internet at public centres such as libraries is becoming harder as opening hours are curtailed to save money. Ordering groceries on a public computer is an unattractive proposition and demands a credit or debit card, which not everyone has. Other issues faced by the poor, elderly and disabled when shopping on the Internet include a limited time to unload the goods from the delivery van, and missing out on the social side of shopping (Townsend, 2003: 56). On the positive side, Internet shopping saves elderly people from standing in long checkout queues and, unlike in supermarkets, computers can enlarge the print for those with poor eyesight (Hare, 2003). There are also mobile retailers such as Milk&More, who can be telephoned; however, they are expensive – between 20 per cent and 50 per cent more than Tesco Online – and intended more for emergency top-ups than regular shopping, and their range of vegetables is limited. Mobile shops can extend the reach of retailing to remote, sparsely populated areas without sufficient numbers of people to sustain fixed shops; mobile shops and Post Offices are widely used in the rural areas of mid-Wales. However, their product range is necessarily limited, and the high cost of fuel means they do not venture far off main roads. Since rural fixed shops also favour main road locations, where more customers pass and delivery costs are lower, it is a case as with the Internet of serving those who already have access rather than reaching unserved areas. We still face the problem of providing good access to grocery retailing, especially fruit and vegetable retailing, for the poorest, the most remote and the least mobile consumers.

Decline in rural and suburban grocery shops. *Ailing retailing*

An easily overlooked feature of the transformation of grocery retailing from small independent shops to supermarkets and their local neighbourhood branches is the increasing size of the catchment area required by the supermarkets. Corner shops or convenience stores need a catchment population of 2,500 to 5,000, and a local neighbourhood shopping centre (group of small shops) needs 5,000 to 10,000. However, a large supermarket requires 25,000 to 40,000 catchment population (Barton, 2000: 94). A smaller supermarket such as the Co-op or a Tesco Express requires a catchment area of 10,000, so these supermarkets could take the trade of several independent grocery stores. In rural areas one Co-op may mean several smaller neighbouring villages losing their shop. Tables 5.2 and 5.3 show the decline in numbers of all independent single-store businesses in Britain from 1945 to 2000. The decline was steepest in the 1970s as the supermarkets were expanding. Grocery stores were less likely to close if part of a symbol group or buying group such as Spar or Londis. Members of these groups purchased groceries from wholesalers together, increasing their buying power; however, some shopkeepers resented the loss of autonomy since buying groups imposed conditions on their members, relating to opening hours, shop decor or sales of alcohol.

Villages and suburban centres, with fewer shops to begin with, have seen greater percentage declines in their retail facilities than have larger centres; as shoppers seek convenience and a wide range of shops, so smaller parades tend to be abandoned, except for a residual convenience store function. Many shops cease trading and become neighbourhood advice centres or offices; some suburban parades have been converted to housing. A tale of shop

Table 5.2 Total number of independent shops in Britain (single-store businesses)

Year	*Number*
1945	500,000
1950	450,000
1960	356,000
1970	330,000
1980	225,000
1990	215,000
2000	200,000
2011	148,200

Source: www.fooddeserts.org (author's research).

Table 5.3 Total number of independent grocery convenience stores in Britain

Year	*Total (indep)**	*Mkt share (indeps)*	*Non-symbol indeps*	*Symbol** indeps*	*Total (all)****
1900		80%			
1950	265,000	54%			
1960	135,000	51%			
1970	90,000	43%			105,300
1980	55,000	32%			68,000
1990	45,000	25%			
2000	41,700	18%	34,500	7,200	55,800
2010	36,600		21,900	14,700	48,700

* Total number of independent grocers (those in chains with fewer than ten branches).
** Symbol group stores are those in e.g. Spar, Londis, Nisa Today buying groups.
*** Total of independent stores, local supermarket branches (e.g. Tesco Express) and garage forecourt stores.

Source: www.fooddeserts.org (author's research).

closures could probably be told for every village in Britain; three typical cases are presented here. The village of Cottingham in south Leicestershire, population 730, had in the 1960s 12 retail premises, two bakers, a haberdashery, a Co-operative store, another grocer's, a Post Office, a garage (which also sold coal), a confectioner's, two fish and chip shops, an undertaker and a taxi office. In 2005 the village's last store, a combined Post Office and grocery store, closed. South Leicestershire, 90 miles (145 kilometres) from London, had become a London commuter zone as people were forced to buy houses further out due to rising house prices. Commuters, who shopped at supermarkets on the way home, replaced the village's older inhabitants who patronized the village shops; declining custom even forced the local mobile grocery store to close. In 2011 the local community managed to reopen a community shop, the Village Store (www.thevillagestoreandcafe.co.uk). However, in other cases the last village store is only hanging on until the current proprietor retires; nobody wants to take on a shop requiring long hours and only offering a low

Table 5.4 Retail facilities in Denholme, Yorkshire, 1950–2013

1950 (45 shops)	*2000 (10 shops)*	*2013 (9 shops)*
1 baker	1 baker	1 baker
3 barbers	1 hairdresser	
6 butchers		
1 chemist (with dentist)	1 chemist	1 chemist
1 clock and watch shop		
4 confectioners		
3 sweetshops		
5 drapers		
3 greengrocers		1 general grocers
8 grocers	1 Co-op supermarket	1 Co-op supermarket
1 hardware store	1 hardware and models store	
	1 electrical goods store	1 electrical goods store
1 jeweller		
1 ladies wear shop, milliner	1 ladies wear shop	
1 men's wear shop		
1 newsagent	1 newsagent*	
1 pies and peas shop	1 fish and chips shop	1 fish and chips shop
1 piano shop		
1 Post Office	1 Post Office	1 Post Office
1 pots and pans shop		
1 shoe shop		
		1 charity shop
		1 computer shop

*The newsagent (2000) was subsequently replaced by a sandwich shop, which itself had closed by 2013.

Source: Author's research.

income, so the premises becomes residential. South Ferriby, a small village in north Lincolnshire, population 660, has suffered a similar decline in its retailing. In 1950 it had ten shops, comprising two general grocers (one of which also sold curtains), a fish and chip shop, a butcher's, a cobbler's, a newsagent, a sweetshop (which also sold tobacco), a hairdresser's, a Post Office and a blacksmith. In 2013 it has just one shop, a combined grocery store and Post Office. Denholme is a larger village, population 2,976, eight miles (13 kilometres) west of Bradford, West Yorkshire. In 1950 it had 45 shops, a total that shrank to ten in 2000 and nine in 2013. Table 5.4 lists the retailers present in Denholme in these three years.

Village schools were closing at their fastest rate in the 1970s, when an average 77 per year were being lost from English villages. The closure rate slowed to 30 a year between 1983 and 1997, and just two village schools closed in 1999. In 1997, 49 per cent of UK rural parishes had no school. In terms of other fixed non-retail facilities, half the rural population of England did not have a GP (doctor's) surgery in their parish; three-fifths of parishes with a population below 1,000 lacked this facility, against two-fifths of rural parishes with over 1,000 population. One facility, the village hall, became more common, with 46 per cent of rural parishes lacking one in 1950 but only 10 per cent without in 1990. However, the absence of a school or doctor is more likely to force people to exit their village during working hours than is the absence of a village hall, often used for evening events. In 1997, 71 per cent of UK villages had no pub, meaning one less reason to visit or stay in the village during the day. Ninety-three per cent of UK villages have no rail service; unsurprising given that not only have many rural branch lines closed but the intermediate stops on many main lines have also been shut, to speed up inter-city services. Most rural stations remaining in Britain are commuter stops, taking people out of the village in daytime rather than enabling people to access the settlement. Village bus services declined after bus deregulation in 1986, resulting in greater bus competition on busy routes but lower subsidies for buses on quiet, uneconomic but socially useful rural routes. Two-thirds of rural parishes in 1997 had no daily Monday to Saturday bus service. In 2003, 9 per cent of rural UK parishes had no bus service at all, rising to 13 per cent for parishes of population under 1,000. Access to a car may be limited, with 14 per cent of rural pensioner couples and over half of single pensioners, most likely a widowed woman who never learned to drive, lacking access to a private car in 2003. Since it is the smaller villages that are most likely to have no shop, anyone living in these villages who is elderly, infirm or poor and therefore faces difficulties maintaining access to private transport will also find it hard to access grocery retailing. In rural counties of England, between 1 and 2 per cent of small settlements a year lost their last shop over the period 1965–90. The rate of attrition slowed after 1991 but the number of rural UK parishes with no shops rose to 42 per cent by 1997. This figure was 49 per cent for parishes with population under 1,000 (Countryside Agency, 2003; DETR, 2000).

A brief comparison with France shows the same retail trends there. France, with a similar population to Britain, has (2011) around 80,000 independent grocery stores, about twice the number in the UK. However, France too has seen rapid recent expansion by the supermarkets since the 1980s and Carrefour now has a 25 per cent share of the £149.2 billion grocery market, compared to the 30 per cent share of the £157.2 billion (2011) UK grocery market held by Tesco. Like the UK, France has seen its fishmongers decline from 6,500 in 1987 to 3,350 in 2000; épiceries (greengrocers) have declined from 125,000 in 1970 to 28,500 in 2000. Unlike the UK, France has stricter limits on supermarket expansion; the Raffarin Law (1996) allowed local authorities to ban the construction of a new supermarket of 1,500 square metres or more, or over 1,000 square metres in communes of population 4,000 or less. French supermarkets must locate outside town centres, preserving the traditional town square with its weekly market along with the épicerie, boulangerie, charcuterie, boucherie, traiteur, patisserie and fromagerie. French small town centres also often have free parking. France has fewer generalist convenience stores than the UK, but these are growing as ethnic minorities, from North Africa, the Middle

East and Indo-China, set up these shops, catering either for everyone or for a specific cultural community. Perhaps most ominously for the independent specialist stores, the French are acquiring the British habit of shopping at local small superettes, whose convenience, like Tesco Express, outweighs the slightly higher prices charged there compared to the vast Carrefours, Auchans or Leclercs.

The socio-economic causes of supermarket growth. *Driving a hard bargain*

A number of demographic, social and technological factors have combined to push shoppers away from independent stores and into supermarkets. Birth rates have declined and life expectancy lengthened; a less religiously bound, more hedonistic society has seen increasing divorce rates, so more people live alone at all ages into widowhood. More materialism and higher house prices, soaring beyond the means of most single-income households, have raised the number of dual-career households; high house prices have, as noted earlier, lengthened commuting times for many. When people prioritize leisure, live alone, have little spare household time or energy for cooking after long work hours, they abandon cooking from scratch, eating microwave meals instead. If perhaps for health reasons they abjure ready meals, they will still seek to shorten cooking times, using semi-prepared lazy foods such as ready-chopped joints of meat, ready-sliced fruit, pre-grated cheese, sliced onions, chopped garlic, fish already packaged with butter and sauce. La Doria make indolence part of the brand with their 'Lazy Fried Onions', pre-chopped. Cake making was simplified with shop-bought cake mix; now we shorten the process even more with the whole cake purchased from a supermarket. In 2013 Waitrose began selling ready-hard-boiled eggs, for those too lazy or too unknowledgeable to boil their own; at 69p each they are two or three times as expensive as the conventional kind. What we perceive as processed, pre-prepared or 'lazy' foods shifts up the 'processed' scale over time; in 1900 sausages and custard powder were seen as ready-made foods, but not so in 2000 (Glucksmann and Nolan, 2007).

Traditional butchers or greengrocers might supply a full range of meats or vegetables; however, small convenience stores cannot compete with the range of ready meals or prepared foods in supermarkets. Increasing numbers of holidays abroad have also led to a demand for sanitized, ready-prepared versions of dishes such as paella and spaghetti bolognaise. In the UK and USA, the average time spent cooking per day per household has fallen dramatically (Table 5.5) (Cutler et al., 2003; Propper, 2005; *The Economist*, 2012b: 31).

In the UK, the average time spent cooking rose slightly in the past decade as some households took on concerns about healthier eating due to TV programmes featuring celebrity chefs like Jamie Oliver. However, in 2011 only one in four home meals was actually cooked at home from raw ingredients. Ready meals also save on washing-up time. Since the 1960s time-saving household

Table 5.5 Average time spent cooking the main household meal, UK and USA

Year	*UK (minutes)*	*USA (minutes)*
1940	120	
1960	100	120
1980	60	
2000	33	50
2010	38	35

Sources: Cutler et al. (2003); Propper (2005); *The Economist* (2012b: 31).

Table 5.6 Percentage of households possessing selected appliances, various years

Year	*Microwave (USA)*	*Microwave (UK)*	*Fridge (UK)*	*Freezer (UK)*	*TV (USA) (sets per h'hold)*	*TV (UK)*	*1+ Car (UK)*
1950			2%	0%	9%		13%
1956			8%	0%	72%		24%
1960			22%	0%	87%	75%	30%
1970			66%	3%	99%	91%	50%
1980		0%	93%	50%	99% (1.6)	96%	58%
1983	33%				99% (1.7)	96%	59%
1986	67%	25%		67%	99% (1.8)	96%	60%
1990		51%		82%	99% (2.0)	97%	67%
2000	88%	85%	99%	90%	99% (2.4)	97%	70%
2010	95%	93%	99%	96%	99% (2.9)	97%	70%

Sources: Clarke et al. (2006); French et al. (2001); author's research.

appliances have become more widespread; these appliances encourage consumption of pre-prepared food. The microwave has perhaps done the most to advance the consumption of ready meals. This appliance was invented by chance when a technician, Dr Percy LeBaron Spencer, at the Raytheon Corporation, was experimenting with microwaves for military radar and found that a chocolate bar in his pocket had melted. The first commercial microwave was produced in 1954; weighing 0.3 tonnes, at two metres high it was useful for ships' canteens, hotels and commercial restaurants but was a little too large for household kitchens. The first domestic microwave went on sale in 1967 and by the late 1970s they were cheap enough for mass ownership. In Australia in 1997 81 per cent of households possessed a microwave, rising to 91.6 per cent in households with children under five. Microwaves were popular in households with two people working and in those with children (Clarke et al., 2006; French et al., 2001). Table 5.6 shows the penetration rate for selected appliances in the USA and UK.

Fridges and freezers also encourage larger, less frequent, shopping trips, steering consumers towards larger stores. Because fresh produce often does not freeze well but ready meals do, this pushes diet towards more processed fare. Televisions also promote the consumption of ready meals because a traditional meal such as meat, gravy and two vegetables demands a stable surface such as a table and the use of a knife and fork, whereas a ready meal can be eaten with a fork on one's lap. Increasing car ownership has also tilted the balance towards supermarkets. Concomitantly the average distance walked per person per year in the UK fell from 255 miles (408 kilometres) in 1975 to 192 miles (307 kilometres) in 2003, and the average distance cycled per household fell from 51 miles (82 kilometres) to 34 miles (54 kilometres) (Butland et al., 2007). As car use rose, town centres became more congested and parking charges were increased by councils seeking to raise revenue. This enhanced the attraction of out-of-town supermarkets with free parking. By the end of the 1990s 77 per cent of UK shopping trips were made by car, 8 per cent by public transport and 13 per cent on foot (Whelan et al., 2002). The car has greatly improved access to retail facilities for the fortunate majority, both in terms of what retailers and supermarkets can be accessed and in terms of what amount of shopping can be carried home. However, for the less affluent, less physically able, older minority, retail access has worsened. They are often left with the smaller, more expensive, limited-range convenience stores that can be accessed on foot or by bus. The time and effort required to access even a limited-range discount supermarket is such that, especially for those with children or the elderly, the local takeaway or pub becomes a more attractive choice despite the food there being less healthy. There are options such as taxi-sharing that mitigate the cost of reaching a full-service supermarket; these are discussed further in Chapter 7, but these options demand a high level of social organization. The next chapter examines the issues surrounding access to food retail and healthy foods, and who is most likely to be affected by these issues.

6 Mapping food access and obesity

The phenomenon of food deserts. *Burgers burgers everywhere, and not a veg to eat*

Many of us have a mental image of a desert, probably a vast expanse of sand dunes, almost devoid of life, an occasional green oasis of a few palm trees by a pond. So a desert must be big; but how big? Ask people the minimum size of a 'desert' and they often link their answer to the capabilities of life, saying 'It's a desert if it can't be crossed in a day' or 'It's only a desert if it is big enough to have its own ecosystem.' The former answer varies considerably depending on whether one is travelling on foot or in a jeep with spare water and fuel. On foot, what can be crossed depends on your fitness, survivability skills, navigation abilities, tools, clothing, the ambient temperature and local terrain. These same personal capability and circumstance factors apply also to the concept of food deserts. The English word 'desert' derives from the Latin *de-serere*, meaning 'abandoned, not farmed, not served'. Deserts can be green or even brick-red as well as yellow. The English town of Leighton Buzzard derives its name from the Norman French *Beau-Desert*, a beautiful but uninhabited place, without what we might call 'facilities'. This was the sense of 'desert' used by Baines (1973: 3) when he wrote, concerning the large residential areas then recently built in England:

> The large suburban estates that are a recent feature of the townscape are epitomized by the regular rows of similarly styled houses that have earned for themselves the title of suburban deserts. They often lack the shops, churches, public houses and social centres that allow a community life to develop.

This sentiment was echoed by Duany et al. (2000: 60), stating, 'It is near-impossible to imagine community development independent of the town square or the local pub.' At the same time as Baines was writing about suburban deserts, the Women's Institute was becoming aware of problems faced by widows in British villages without access to the everyday shops they needed. The 1970s were a time of major transport change in the UK, with personal transport effectively being privatized. Britain's railways could not run economic branch line services in the face of increasing car ownership, and between 1900 and 1980 the route mileage of the system practically halved. The Beeching Report of 1963 was merely a chapter in an ongoing process of passenger service withdrawal, a process mirrored in many other European countries as new motorways and by-passes speeded up the growing volume of road traffic. These transport changes isolated women who had attained adulthood in the 1920s at a time when driving was an almost exclusively male preserve. Now as widows they had lost their personal transport, with no guarantee that the replacement bus service would continue to run as car ownership by younger villagers continued to rise.

The Conservative administration that governed the UK from 1979 to 1997 was ideologically in favour of the free market and reluctant to intervene in poverty issues. However, the election of New Labour in Britain in 1997 saw a renewed focus on urban deprivation. Another concern for the UK government was the rising obesity rate, up from 6 per cent of adults in 1980 to over a fifth by 2000. The term 'food desert' was born during a study of a socially deprived housing estate in west Glasgow by the Low Income Project Team (LIPT) in 1996; a local resident used the phrase to communicate their perception of the lack of good quality, reasonably priced food in the area (Cummins and Macintyre, 2002). The LIPT described food deserts as 'areas of relative exclusion where people experience physical and economic barriers to accessing healthy food' (Reisig and Hobbiss, 2000: 138). The term was taken up by both policy-makers and the media, despite the lack of any precise definition for food deserts at the time. *The Independent* (11 June 1997) described food deserts as 'Those areas of inner cities where cheap nutritious food is virtually unobtainable. Car-less residents, unable to reach out-of-town supermarkets, depend on the corner shop where prices are high, products are processed and fresh fruit and vegetables are poor or non-existent.' *The Observer* (13 September 1998) stated that 'Many poor housing estates were left as food deserts by the closure of local food shops and that in the few local food shops left, prices were up to 60 per cent more than in the supermarkets.' *The Guardian* (17 March 1999) said, 'On the poorer estates of Coventry, low cost, good quality, food is not available to the poorest. These people either have to shop at expensive local stores or pay for transport and lug small children for miles and back with shopping.' A UK Government report (Acheson, 1998: 65) described food deserts as 'Areas where cheap and varied food is only available to those who have private transport or are able to pay the costs of public transport if this is available.' Coventry today (2013) still has large areas without easy access to fresh fruit and vegetable retailing for those without cars.

Food deserts in 2000 had not been formally defined, and today there is still no generally accepted definition of them. However, by 2000 we knew the following about food deserts:

(i) There were few shops selling food that nutritionists would recommend as healthy; many shops that once sold this type of food in the area had closed.
(ii) The local shops that did still exist were small and therefore expensive; the food they sold was largely not fresh, and high in sugar, fat and salt.
(iii) Despite the costliness of the food in local shops, many local residents were in lower income brackets.
(iv) Furthermore, many of these residents, due to low income, lacked access to private motor transport.
(v) Additionally, other obstacles to travel, such as the presence of children, or ill-health, made travel to distant supermarkets where healthy food could be bought cheaper, physically difficult. The bus service was hard to use, perhaps due to infrequent service, the need to change buses, or it did not go near some residents' homes.
(vi) Travel to distant supermarkets was also financially difficult because travel costs took a relatively large fraction of disposable income.

There is a strong focus here on urban food deserts, although the access factors above could equally apply to rural food deserts. There was also little discussion as to whether, had cheap healthy food been available locally, all consumers would have chosen such food. Lack of culinary skills or personal preference for unhealthy foods can be just as strong a barrier to consuming fruit and vegetables as can physical or financial obstacles to accessing them. The existence of food deserts depends as much on the personal attributes of the resident as it does on the geography of the area. A household that can afford a car, and possesses cooking skills, will perceive a very different foodscape from a household next door that lacks these assets. Food deserts, like their physical counterparts, have fuzzy boundaries. However, just as no one denies the existence of the Sahara Desert, this fuzziness is no reason to doubt the existence of food deserts. Unequal food access also occurs within households. Historically, when households lack sufficient funds to feed all members, the wife has made do with the cheapest and least healthy foodstuffs while the husband and children consumed any more wholesome foods that can be afforded (Miller 1998: 37). In nineteenth-century Britain working-class men had first call on any meat available while their partners subsisted on Calories from bread, sugar and jam (Belasco, 2008: 51). In the 1930s Depression the British government was concerned about a rising maternal mortality rate of 4 per 1,000 births, attributed to poor maternal nutrition, particularly in the 'Special Areas of England and Wales'. In the poorest areas, such as the Rhondda Valley, a coal mining area of South Wales, hard hit by the 1926 General Strike, maternal mortality was as high as 11 per 1,000 births. The National Birthday Trust Fund (NBTF) delivered food supplements, mainly Marmite and dried milk products like Ovaltine to pregnant women in these areas from 1935 to 1939 (Williams, 1997: 99). A similar attitude to female nutrition was manifest in America during World

Table 6.1 Food insecurity in the USA (millions), 1999–2010

Year	*Individuals*	*H'holds*	*Per h'hold*
1999	31.0	10.5	2.95
2000	33.2	11.0 (10.5% all Hh)	3.02
2003	36.3	12.6 (11.2% all Hh)	2.88
2010	49.0	17.2 (14.5% all Hh)	2.85

Source: United States Department of Agriculture, various dates.

War Two, when US food policy assumed meat for fighting men but protein substitutes for women.

In the USA the idea of 'food deserts' has been extended to include 'food oases' where there is easy access to healthy food, and 'food swamps' where there are numerous takeaways selling obesogenic salty food, but few outlets selling healthy food. As in the UK, financially constrained households tend to be located in areas with poor physical access to healthy foodstuffs such as fresh fruit and vegetables. These 'food-insecure' households lack access to enough food to fully meet basic needs at all times due to lack of financial resources. Households that are black, Hispanic, or comprise disabled or elderly people living alone, in inner cities, are likely to be affected by food insecurity. In 2000, when 10.5 per cent of all US households suffered from food insecurity, 20.5 per cent of African-American households and 21.4 per cent of Hispanic households were food-insecure, as were 31 per cent of households headed by a single woman with children. By 2010 the proportion of food-insecure households in the USA had risen to 14.5 per cent, the highest ever recorded. The food insecure are more likely to have higher BMIs; 'Women in food insecure households, compared to those in food secure households, had a BMI of approximately two units greater, on average' (Olson and Holben, 2002: 1842). Also, the prevalence of overweight (BMI > 27.3) was 32 per cent for the food secure, but 41 per cent for the 'mildly food insecure' and 52 per cent for those 'moderately food insecure' (Olson and Holben, 2002: 1842). The severely food insecure, however, have lower BMIs. Table 6.1 shows how food insecurity has evolved in the USA, 1999–2010.

Measuring food access. *Cooking up the ingredients of a food desert*

We will never be able to draw a line in a city and say, 'This is where a food desert begins', any more than we can fix a point where the Sahara Desert starts. However, a common definition of a physical desert is a region that receives less than 25 cm (10 inches) of rainfall a year. There can still be some rainfall in a desert, as very few areas get no rain at all. Similarly most convenience stores sell some fruit and vegetables, but mostly in frozen or tinned form, because these have a much longer shelf-life than fresh produce. However, frozen vegetables can lose some micronutrients, and tinned fruit and vegetables are commonly high in sugar or salt. Fresh is better, if obtainable. Some fresh vegetables are sold by most convenience stores; the hard sorts – carrots, onions – that retain a saleable appearance for longer. Unfortunately carrots may look edible but their vitamin content declines with age; they are physically present but nutritionally absent. There may also be bananas and apples, items that also have a relatively longer shelf-life than softer fruits. Independent shopkeepers often sell fresh produce they can eat themselves if just past saleability; the shop's FFV offer is then linked to the ethnicity and dietary habits of the proprietor's family, which may be different from the majority of their customers'. However, in most convenience stores in deprived areas you will look in vain for blueberries, strawberries, courgettes or broccoli. One measure of whether a store sells a good range of fresh fruit and vegetables is, does it normally stock at least ten different kinds of these items? At a level of ten, there will almost always be some healthier green vegetables such as broccoli or cauliflower. This threshold of ten was used by *The Grocer* (2008) and is also used by www.fooddeserts.org to map the location of 'green' stores, and identify urban and rural areas where 'green' retailers are absent. In the USA, stores classified as 445110 under the North American Industry Classification System, supermarkets and other grocery stores but not convenience stores, count as 'green' or 'fresh produce' stores. A complicating factor is that many local independent shops will pass the 'ten' threshold when the weekly delivery has come in, but not on other days; local shoppers wanting fresh produce will know the delivery day, and adjust their shopping routine accordingly. These shops too should be counted as 'green'. In rural areas, villages may have no shops but there may be a farm shop half a mile (a kilometre) outside the village that sells fresh produce, so these shops too need to be counted, as do small informal roadside stalls if they are permanent features.

A food desert is 'two-sided' in that it must contain many households that eat unhealthily as well as have a shortage of green retailers. Otherwise affluent areas of British cities such as Four Oaks Park in the Sutton Coldfield area of Birmingham or the Bishops Avenue area of Hampstead Heath, London, would count as food deserts because there are no shops there. A metric of healthy eating is the Five-a-Day guidance adopted by the UK government; this advice originated from the World Health Organization (WHO) which in 1990 stated that adults should consume 400 g of fruit and vegetables (FV) daily. The WHO set a portion size of FV at 80 g, essentially about a handful, so five portions were needed to get to 400 g (NHS, 2012). Other national governments have adopted similar daily consumption guidelines, for example:

Australia: 2 serves fruit and 5 serves vegetables; 1 serve = 150 g fresh fruit or 75 g vegetables
Canada: 5 to 10 portions FV
Denmark: 6 portions FV

Germany: 5 portions FV
Hungary: 3 portions FV
Netherlands: 4 portions FV
Sweden: eat FV with every meal
USA: 2 portions fruit and 3 portions vegetables; 5 to 9 portions daily

Despite the simplicity of Five-a-Day there is some confusion among consumers as to what counts towards this target. Fruit and vegetable juices (portion = 150 ml or 175 g) should not contribute more than 1 portion a day; neither should beans or pulses because of their higher salt content (Nelson et al., 2007: 16). Frozen, canned, chilled or dried fruit and vegetables do count as well as fresh; however, some of these more processed forms may be higher in sugar or salt, or have lost some vitamin content, compared to fresh. Starchy vegetables such as potatoes, yams or cassava do not count. Jackson (2003) reported that in Dudley (Birmingham, UK) some consumers thought you had to eat five portions of fruit and five of vegetables a day, while others thought a whole large fruit such as melon was one portion. Such overestimates of the Five-a-Day requirement will deter people from following it. Others underestimated the amounts, thinking that chips or just a sprinkling of herbs counted as a portion. Even greater misconceptions about Five-a-Day were demonstrated by some residents of deprived areas of Birmingham in 2009, where some thought that jam, orange squash or even Jaffa Cakes (orange flavour centre) counted. A respondent in North Wales (2013) said 'eating green vegetables gives you gallstones'.

Although less precise, Five-Handfuls-a-Day might be a more comprehensible guideline. Five-a-Day needs adapting to local meal cultures; for example in Norway the meal culture is one large hot meal and two or three cold meals a day. Norwegians are more likely to eat fruit than vegetables with the cold meals, so their guidance is three portions of vegetables with the main meal (Vejrup et al., 2008). In the UK, the actual number of portions of FV consumed varies over time, and by class, age and sex. In 1976 the wealthiest in the UK consumed an average 2.5 portions a day, as against 2.0 for the least affluent; by 1984 the figures were 2.8 and 1.7 respectively (Joseph, 1991: 228). The average daily UK FV consumption was 3.0 in 1986, rising to 3.9 in 1999 (Wrigley et al., 2003); however this fell back slightly to 3.7 in 2003. For those on benefits, equivalent to the 'least affluent' of 1976 and 1984, daily consumption was 2.1 for men and 1.9 for women. *The Grocer* (2008) reported an average daily UK consumption of 2.4 in 2004 and 2.5 in 2005, with the least affluent 1.9 million consuming just under 1 portion daily. In 2009 the UK managed a daily average of 3.55 portions FV (3.7 for men and 3.4 for women). Only 8 per cent of men and 9 per cent of women attained the full Five-a-Day in 2005 (Nelson et al., 2007). *The Grocer* (2008) stated that these figures were based on consumption, not sales data; the latter would suggest a UK average of 3.5 a day, indicating that consumers discard an average of 1 portion of FV a day per person.

To summarize, we have a rise in average daily UK FV consumption through the 1980s and 1990s, but this rise has halted after 2000. We also have a gap between high levels of consumption for the wealthy and lower levels for the poor; a gap that has been widening since the 1980s. The wealthy–poor FV consumption gap persists whether one looks at poor classes, poor regions or poorer ethnic groups; for example the 2009 average daily figure for Scotland was just 2.4 in 2009. The gender gap trends in FV consumption are more ambiguous, but suggest a slight disadvantaging for women. *The Grocer* (2011: 6) reported that women's daily FV consumption fell from 2.83 in 2007 to 2.80 in 2009 and 2.78 in 2010, due to the recession, whereas men's daily consumption remained stable at 2.51 over this period. These figures are well below those given by Nelson (2007), perhaps because as noted earlier there is a difference between purchasing and consumption; Nelson also had men consuming more, whereas *The Grocer* puts women higher. Perhaps single men buy more FV but also discard more; Donkin et al. (1998) stated that in 1997 single men ate 2.66 portions of FV a day against an average for all UK men of 4.1. The decline in women's consumption is probably due to the typical pattern in food- or financially stressed households whereby the woman prioritizes the diet of the man and the children first, hers last.

Geography of food access. *How green is your high street?*

We can plot on a map the location of 'green' food retailers, but we also need a measure of what counts as 'distant' from such a retailer. There are several complications regarding the determination of what households are 'distant' from green retailers, as detailed below.

- Some households have access to private motor transport; others have no car but can use buses. Some households with no car also do not have good public transport connections and must walk, or employ other coping strategies such as arranging a lift from a neighbour, walking to the shops or hiring (or sharing) a taxi home. What is 'distant' for a 'walking' household may be close for a car-owning household.
- Poorer households are usually doubly disadvantaged because they often have no car and may live in an area where retailing is low-quality with few shops selling fresh produce. However, rural households, because public transport is poor, will make efforts to obtain a car even on low incomes. Then the issue becomes, with recent increases in fuel prices, can the household afford to run the car to distant supermarkets? Bus fares can also be expensive for less-affluent households (Hallett IV and McDermott, 2011).
- For car-less households, how far is 'too far' to walk, either to a shop or to the bus stop that gives access to shops? This distance is mediated by a wide range of factors, including geographical (steep hills, busy main roads hard to cross), personal (how able-bodied the shopper is to walk

and carry heavy shopping, whether they have children that retard mobility) and social (whether the local roads, or short cuts across parks, are safe to walk at all times). Rural households may have a longer acceptable walking distance than urban ones.

- How do we measure 'distance'? The simplest approach is a straight line between home and shop, but people do not travel in straight lines. Measuring along street lines is computationally intensive, and demands a level of IT expertise that not everyone possesses. Alternatively we can take statistical data areas or tracts and ascertain which of these blocks contains both a large proportion (what percentage?) of both less-affluent households and/or few green retailers. However, shoppers do not shop according to boundaries of statistical census areas, so food deserts can be misidentified where clusters of poor households live close to such a boundary, or major retailing centres are not located towards the centre of a census area.

There is no agreement even on the simplest metric of how far is 'too far' to walk to the shops. In the UK in 2000, Beverley Hughes, then Parliamentary Under-Secretary of State in the Department of the Environment, Transport and the Regions, at a speech to the Third Annual Local Food Retailing Conference, said an ideal maximum distance would be 5–7 minutes, or 500 metres (Wrigley, 2002: 2034). Other benchmark distances used by researchers have been ¼ mile (400 m), ½ mile (800 m) or 1,000 metres (Apparicio et al., 2007). 'Distance' may be to the centroid of the census area, or from shops to households. If we take actual shop-to-household distance, in older UK urban areas with a terraced street layout, or older areas of US cities with a grid block layout, the ratio of actual walking distance to straight-line distance will vary from 1:1 (direct walk) to a maximum of 1.4:1 (e.g. 400 metre walk east, then 400 metre walk south, 800 m walk vs. 566 m direct). A ratio of 1.2:1 is typical here. In more modern suburbs, with complex winding street layouts and many cul-de-sacs, 1.2 might be both too low and unreliable. However, even here shops tend to be located on main through-roads that give more direct access, excepting the last few tens of metres to cul-de-sac households, and in such suburbs, pedestrian-only walkways often provide a more direct route to retail centres than is available for cars. Shop access maps by White et al. (2004) and Donkin et al. (1999) consistently suggest a ratio of between 1.1:1 and 1.2:1 for ratio (actual walking distance):(straight-line distance), depending on the street layout and connectivity, which in turn is correlated to the age of the suburb. Overall then, without invoking complex computer procedures, we can generally assume a working ratio of 1.2:1 as a rule of thumb.

Alternatively we can use as a metric the numbers of green stores within a set distance of the census area centroid (Apparicio et al., 2007). This has the merit of making it possible to incorporate measures of deprivation. A census block centroid with many poorer households that is 1,000 metres from a supermarket is more 'food desertified' than an affluent block 2,000 metres from supermarkets; the latter is a frequent situation in low-density suburbs where houses are spaced apart with large gardens. However, the affluent area may contain people who are infirm and less mobile, people medically unfit to drive, people whose cars have been stolen or broken down, those disqualified from driving, and people who are asset-rich because of owning a large house but on a low income (pension). So even in better-off areas not everyone has adequate access to a healthy diet. We can also set multiple distances, as food desert thresholds, for shoppers travelling on foot, cycling or by car (Raja et al., 2008). Alternatively we can measure number of stores per 10,000 residents or number of stores per census area (Ball et al., 2009); in many national statistical datasets, census areas at a certain level will all have broadly similar numbers of households or residents. In this case the level of census area chosen needs to be small, or the boundary errors noted above mean misidentification of food deserts, but the smaller the census area level chosen the fewer data may be available on poverty, because at small-area level it may be possible to identify individual households with certain less-common characteristics, e.g. belonging to a small ethnic minority group. The census tract and distance approach may be combined by dividing up the study area into 250 metre squares, assessing which squares are residential and which contain green retailers (by straight line distance x 1.2) and then fitting census area boundaries to the 250 metre grid (H. Shaw, 2012); the principal source of error here is along the census area boundaries, where households may be misallocated from their actual census area. However, errors in the social ranking of households 'misallocated' to neighbouring census tracts this way will be small if, as likely, neighbouring tracts have similar socio-economic status. Nottinghamshire County Council (2007) used a graphic of bar charts, the height of each bar indicating a socio-economic factor, superimposed on a conventional map indicating both green shop locations and census area boundaries. This made the combination of shop distance and wealth information easy to read, but would only be suitable for relatively small study areas, with fewer census areas, or the information would be too small to read. Other innovative combinations of census data and shop distance are provided by Block and Kouba (2006) and Larsen and Gilliland (2008).

The United States Department of Agriculture has achieved the most spatially extensive mapping of food deserts on its website, www.ers.usda.gov/data/fooddesert, indicating across the entire USA which areas are food deserts. Combining socio-economic data with food access, USDA defines a food desert as 'A census tract with a substantial share of residents who live in low-income areas that have low levels of access to a grocery store or healthy, affordable food retail outlet'. Low income means 'a poverty rate of 20 percent or greater, or (b) a median family income at or below 80 percent of the area median family income' and low access means 'at least 500 persons and/or at least one third of the census tract's population live more than one mile (1.6 km) from a supermarket or large grocery store'. Identification of a tract as a food desert renders it eligible for funding and intervention projects to increase access to healthy food retailing. In 2009 that put 23.5 million people in food deserts. However, USDA, by extending the distance criterion to 10 miles (16 km), reduced the number of Americans in food deserts by 13.5 million; a tenth of the 65,000 US census tracts were now food deserts. But according to *The Economist* (2011b), only 15 per cent of US citizens shop for food within their own census area, and USDA concentrates on supermarkets, ignoring some other outlets such as roadside stalls and farmers' markets. Renton, for example, a low SES suburb of Seattle, is counted by USDA as a food desert but has a thriving roadside fruit and vegetable stall, patronized by shoppers from well outside the census tract. Conversely, the opening of a full-range supermarket in a poor area does not mean the less affluent or obese will start shopping healthily there. There are many other factors influencing the choice of food and supermarket that people make.

Physical access to healthy food. *Bringing home the bacon*

Physical access to food retailing is far more than simply distance to shops, or even distance to a bus stop. As noted earlier, physical geographical features, from steep hills to busy roads, can prove major barriers for some shoppers, the elderly and those with children, but not for others. Access, to shops and other facilities, may be improved by anti-crime initiatives such as better street lighting and policing, and even a more effective judicial and prison system. In Southampton, UK, pensioners in Swaythling were left vulnerable to crime when their local Post Office closed, forcing them to walk under a gloomy railway bridge to the nearest Post Office at Portswood; muggers knew Monday was a good time to rob people coming back with pension money. In turn the grocery shop in this part of Swaythling saw trade drop as these pensioners would rather spend their pension money near the Portswood Post Office than carry it home. A large rise in crime can deter walking as much as a 6°C drop in temperature (Janke et al., 2013); as noted below, climatic extremes may also create barriers to food access.

Barriers can arise even inside a grocery store. Many smaller urban independent convenience stores are very densely stocked, with aisles barely 18 inches (45 cm) wide, too narrow for someone using a walker frame or wheelchair. The disabled might not make it inside the shop, although the UK's Disability Discrimination Act (DDA) 2004 was supposed to ensure all public places were disabled-accessible. Shops in inner urban areas of the UK are often converted from houses, with steps into the door, and these were supposed to be replaced by ramps under the DDA. Grants were available, but in cramped and hilly inner city areas there is no room for a ramp, and in 2013 many such shops remain 'inaccessible'. Inside shops, shelves may be too high to reach for the elderly or disabled, especially those in scooters. Coveney and O'Dwyer (2009) details a similar situation in Adelaide, Australia, where busy roads with narrow uneven pavements debar access to the disabled and mothers with pushchairs. Such people may also find it hard to cope with bus transport to distant supermarkets where disabled facilities are better. Local shopping parades, often incorporating a takeaway, may become gathering places for youths who, even if not malevolent, scare elderly people; some pensioners have osteoporosis, meaning that a fall can result in bone fracture, necessitating a long stay in hospital at that age and even a move into sheltered accommodation. This reduces trade at independent stores as pensioners make efforts to reach supermarkets, and access to grocery retail for all is curtailed if these independent shops then close.

There is also a range of other less-obvious physical barriers to food purchasing and consumption. Food packaging such as security seals, tight jars and fiddly tabs may be difficult to open for those with arthritic hands. This may push some people into less-healthy eating, at takeaways, pubs or social service-provided meals for example. Aids for the disabled are available, such as special tin grips, but these tend to be expensive, perhaps because the size of the market is limited, and many disabled are not wealthy. Then there is a concept called 'disposable carrying capacity' (Shaw, 2006); akin to 'disposable income', a person on foot has a certain carrying capacity but certain essential items must be transported home: toilet rolls, pet food, washing-up liquid for example. Healthier foods tend to be lower both in Calories per kilogram and Calories per pound or dollar. An adult should consume 400 g of fruit and/or vegetables a day which, allowing for packaging, skin and peelings and wastage, equates to 2 kg a day for a family of four, or 14 kg a week. A disposable plastic supermarket bag will hold around 3 kg if it is to be lugged on and off buses or walked with, rather than simply loaded in a car. So to meet the 400 g a day target entails transport of five bags a week, before any other food or essential non-food items are bought. A fit person might manage five bags on a bus journey; less for a pensioner. So the 400 g a day rule will entail one extra shopping trip a week, against the alternative of more calorie-dense foods such as biscuits or microwaveable meals. Re-usable bags are an improvement as they do not rip, but the weight still has to be carried. The bus itself may be relatively expensive for those on fixed low incomes such as pensioners and unemployment benefits; a return bus journey in the UK will probably cost £3 even for a short distance, so two journeys a week is approaching a tenth of the income of a claimant on Jobseeker's Allowance. In the USA, Rose and Bodor (2009) reported how New Orleans consumers who had to travel over 2 km to a supermarket paid an average US$34 more in travel costs than those consumers living closer to the store. The bus may also be slow; an average speed of 8 mph (13 kph) in UK towns and 15 mph (25 kph) in the countryside because bus routes are often indirect, taking long detours around village housing estates. So the total time spent on the bus, including walking to the stop and waiting, may be an hour each way, resulting in a three-hour total shopping trip which would have taken an hour and a quarter by car. This is a problem for mothers with small children. Coveney and O'Dwyer (2009) also note other deficiencies in the bus service, such as having to wait in the cold and rain, which is not good for pensioners, and an absence of seats at many bus stops. The bus stop at many supermarkets is also often sited at the far end of the large car park from the supermarket doors, so large buses are not manoeuvring around cars and pedestrians. This means anyone with limited mobility, perhaps needing a scooter, will face difficulties as the scooter has to be left inside the supermarket. Even the climate can create barriers to shopping on foot; in Oklahoma, USA, cold winters make walking to the shops unpleasant and hot summers mean food can spoil on a long walk back home. This also pushes people into shopping at convenience stores close to home, selling few FFV. Local 7–11 stores sell bananas and apples for 50 cents each, no other fruit or vegetables, but also sell Pop Tarts for 50 cents each or eight for US$3. At a little over 100 Calories per banana or apple, against nearly 200 for a Pop Tart, the choice for the poor is obvious.

Many studies have found a correspondence between the dietary health of an area and the type of retail outlets selling food in that area. Where there is good access to supermarkets selling a wide range of fresh fruit and vegetables, people tend to eat healthily, and where there are fewer supermarkets but more convenience stores selling few fresh items, and many fast food outlets, diet tends to be worse and obesity higher. Nelson et al. (2007: 42) wrote that '[W]omen in [UK] households that shopped at a large supermarket consumed significantly higher amounts of fruit and vegetables compared with other women.' This correspondence between diet and type of local retailer is partly geographical, partly economic. As noted earlier, low income is strongly linked with poor diet and obesity. Supermarkets tend not to locate in less-affluent areas, for reasons discussed in Chapter 7. *The Economist* (2002) found that in Sandwell, one of the most deprived areas of Birmingham, UK, '90 per cent of the households were within 500 metres of a shop selling junk food and fizzy drinks. Less than 20 per cent of the houses were within 500 metres of a shop selling fresh fruit and vegetables.' In Newcastle upon Tyne, 'There were more multiple supermarkets in the more affluent parts of the city [however] there were more greengrocers in the more deprived parts of the city' (White et al., 2004: 215). This is likely because 'greengrocers' includes ethnic minority-oriented food stores. A major study of the effects of the insertion of a large supermarket (Tesco) in a deprived part of Leeds found that fresh fruit and vegetable consumption rose in areas with good access to this new store (Wrigley et al., 2004). Similarly O'Neill (2005: 1) found, for Stafford, that 'Local shops are over-priced and low on choice and quality. In high-risk areas, the lowest-priced items in local outlets are, on average, 37 per cent more expensive than the equivalent items in a town supermarket. A "healthy diet" could be up to 88 per cent more expensive.' The food retailing situation in Stafford was very regressive, with less-affluent consumers facing higher prices for healthy food options locally than the prices in shops serving the more affluent areas of the city. This regressive pricing of healthy food is replicated in many cities, in Britain and elsewhere. In Melbourne, Australia, Ball et al. (2009) found that the poorer the consumer, the further they had to travel to access fresh fruit and vegetables. Likewise in the Australian city of Adelaide where fresh produce could be accessed easily from lower SES areas, lack of knowledge on preparing it together with lack of money to buy it precluded its purchase. With some low-income households in Adelaide spending two-fifths of their income on rent, food was seen as an optional purchase, after fuel, transport and utility costs had been met. Other Anglophone countries have similar access/poverty barriers to a healthy diet. Larsen and Gilliland (2008) found worse access to supermarkets in less affluent areas of London, Ontario, and Pearce et al. (2007, 2009) discovered a similar situation in New Zealand cities. The poorer New Zealand districts did, however, have a greater density of fast food outlets. In the USA, Hendrickson et al. (2006) also noted that food costs were highest in the poorest areas, and the quality of this (expensive) food was lower, nutritionally. Powell et al. (2009) found that fast food restaurants were prevalent in less affluent areas and that each additional fast food restaurant per 10,000 people was associated with a 5 per cent drop in fruit and vegetable consumption. There is an international parallel with poorer countries consuming a worse diet; low-income Pacific Island nations like Papua New Guinea and Fiji import cheap 'flap meat', belly meat, from New Zealand, and this food has displaced traditional fish dishes. Wealthier nations will not import this meat (Lawrence, 2005: 287), but Ghana has successfully legislated to ban all meat imports containing over a quarter fat by weight. This hit imports of turkey meat from the USA. Ghana succeeded, whereas a similar ban in Fiji would contravene WTO rules, because the ban was against retail sales of fatty meat. Fiji has no domestic sources of this type of food, so the ban by Fiji, unlike Ghana's restriction, was deemed equivalent to an import ban. The outcome is that smaller nations will find it more difficult to restrain imports of poor-quality food without incurring the wrath of the WTO and the USA.

There is also a significant body of research denying a link between poor diet and absence of supermarkets, or presence of fast food retailers. Pearce et al. (2009) found no correlation between the density of fast food outlets and obesity in the USA, and Ronald Sturm at the Rand Corporation likewise found no relationship between what students ate, their weight and the type of food retailers present within a 1.5 mile (2.5 km) radius, using self-reported data from 13,000 Californian schoolchildren. Morland and Evenson (2009: 493) reported from a study of Forsyth County, North Carolina and Jackson City, Mississippi that 'Each mile [1.6 kilometre] closer to a supermarket was associated with a 6 per cent higher prevalence of obesity and each mile closer to a fast food restaurant was associated with a lower prevalence of obesity.' Meanwhile Helen Lee (Lee and Nieman, 2013), at the Public Policy Institute of California, found that low income neighbourhoods had three times as many corner stores per square mile (as better-off areas), and nearly twice as many supermarkets and large-scale grocers; again perhaps due to the presence of ethnic-minority food retailers. In Edmonton, Canada, Smoyer-Tomic et al. (2006) also found that low SES areas had possibly better access to supermarkets than better-off districts, as did Apparicio et al. (2007) for Montreal, and in Brisbane, Australia, Turrell et al. (2004) found similar degrees of access to supermarkets and other food retailers for rich and poor areas.

It is difficult to reconcile these two schools of research; there is no common factor between the venues in either camp that might explain the contradictory findings. It may be a matter of scale; at an individual level one can always find single households in poor areas who are food-insecure or face poor spatial food access; at a city level the findings may be affected by type and level of census area chosen, the degree of social mixing in that city, the precise location of food retailers, the selection of respondents, and the importance attached to exercise as a calorie-burner, although as we saw in Chapter 2, exercise alone may not prevent weight gain in the face of high energy intake. A nationwide study at a detailed statistical area level may shed further light on the issue, but this would be a large research commitment that has not as yet been undertaken or funded. What is more certain is that, for individual households, the cost of food can be a significant barrier to healthy eating, as can lack of knowledge about food preparation.

Economic access to healthy food. *Pinching the pennies, expanding the waist*

The trend towards increasing food affluence was sharply halted for many as the global economic crisis known as the Credit Crunch began in 2008. Other economic developments associated with the Credit Crunch include the rise in oil prices mentioned earlier, a shrinkage in world food surpluses caused by a range of factors including a shift of diets in developing countries towards higher meat consumption, loss of farmland to urbanization and biofuel production, loss of crops to extreme weather events that appear to be increasing in frequency and severity, and a general fall in purchasing power for many as the debt-fuelled consumer economy of the 1990s shows signs of unravelling. In the UK the price of an 800 g loaf of white bread, having been steady at 50–55p from 1993 to 2002, reached 90p in 2007 and in 2013 costs £1.25–£1.30. From 2007, food manufacturers have been imposing 'hidden' price rises on consumers by reducing the quantity or quality of their products while keeping the price the same, in contrast to the increase in portion sizes in the 1990s discussed in Chapter 3. In 2009 a pack of Maltesers shrank from 140 g to 120 g, and in 2011 the Dairy Milk bar suffered the same weight reduction. The Mars Bar shrank, but the package size remained the same, so the reduction was less obvious. Toblerone Bars lost a triangle in 2010, and boxes of Tetleys tea bags at Poundland went from 100 to 88 bags although the price stayed at £1. In 2012 tins of John West tuna shrank from 185 g (drained weight 130 g) to 160 g, –11.1 per cent (drained weight 112 g, –13.8 per cent) with no price reduction. Sometimes the size reduction was accompanied by a price rise. In 2011 Thorntons Mini Caramel Shortcakes were sold at 12 for £1.40, but changed to 10 at £1.50, a unit price rise of 28.6 per cent. Birds Eye Original Beef Burgers with Onion went from 16 per pack at £3.98 to 12 at £4.29, a unit price rise of 43.9 per cent. Prices rose in more clandestine ways, as Bourneville removed the more expensive chocolates from its packs of Heroes. Manufacturers of sugary obesogenic foods such as chocolates might claim they were helping to reduce obesity but the smaller pack sizes and higher prices overall represent a squeeze on household budgets that is likely to push more consumers onto cheaper, more fattening, diets; an alternative outcome of smaller pack sizes is unsatisfied consumers buying more packs of sweets. The factors behind the recent global rise in food prices are further explored below. Food surplus pushed us towards unhealthy and unsustainable food consumption habits; however, the current retreat in affluence is unlikely by itself to return us to more sustainable healthier dietary habits. On the contrary, it is still the less wealthy, the less educated, the less mobile in society who are the most prone to the new diseases of food consumption, much as in past eras they were most liable to the diseases of food production. Food-associated illnesses may have changed but the social anatomy of food and its diseases is more persistent. As personal budgets for many are squeezed, we still want convenient (fast), and we definitely want cheaper, so it is the good (healthy) aspect that is often sacrificed. Just as the wealthier elite were, despite their relative food security, at risk in past centuries if the masses were starving, so today the implications of increased food consumption illnesses threaten to bear down on all, especially the wealthy, if unhealthy food choices continue to produce rising obesity rates and hence rising healthcare costs in countries rich and poor.

Donkin et al. (1999) first suggested that economic access was a bigger barrier than physical access to fresh fruit and vegetables. Nelson et al. (2007: 10) note that 'Successive [UK] Government reports over the last 15 years have highlighted a persistent nutrition-related health disadvantage amongst the poor.' Back in 1936 Sir John Boyd Orr reported that in the UK the poorest had the worse diet, spending 2½d (1p) a week on fruits compared to 1s 8d (8p) per week on fruits by the wealthiest, a sum eight times greater. Overall the poor spent 4 shillings a week on food as against 14 shillings for the wealthiest, a sum just 3.5 times greater (Ferguson, 1971: 74). The UK's 'health premium', the difference between a healthy and an unhealthy basket of food, has widened since the 1980s (*Food Magazine*, 2008: 6). Furthermore this health premium is higher in low income areas, and the differential between high and low income areas has grown, as Table 6.2 shows.

The health premium has widened because in the UK the price of unhealthy foods rose by a third between 1989 and 2004, whereas the price of healthier foods rose by half; there is also a rural/urban gap, with healthy produce costing 34 per cent more in rural areas, where it is produced, than in cities (*Food Magazine*, 2004b: 11). Dawson et al. (2008) discovered similar differentials in Scotland; the price of a healthy basked of foods was £37.48 in larger retailers, £40.30 in medium-sized stores, and £47.83 in small retailers, the ones mostly used by poorer and rural consumers. In deprived rural areas of Scotland this food basket cost £52.75, in deprived small towns £47.25, and in the very

Table 6.2 The UK's health premium, 1988–2007

Health premium	*1988*	*1995*	*2007*
Affluent area	16%	31%	39%
UK average	18%	35%	48%
Less affluent area	20%	41%	58%

Source: Adapted from *Food Magazine* (2008).

remote rural islands the cost of this basket reached £49.18. Relative food price movements in the USA have also produced a widening health premium. Between 1985 and 2003 the real price of fresh fruit and vegetables rose 39 per cent; the price rise for all fruit and vegetables over this period was 20 per cent, implying a lower rise for frozen, canned or otherwise processed foods. Over the same period the real price of meat and poultry fell by 3 per cent, prices of sugars and sweets were down by 7 per cent, and the real price of soft drinks fell 22 per cent (Butland, 2007). One does not have to be an economist to see what foods the lowest-paid consumers are going to be shifting towards. In the UK, *Food Magazine* (2007: 19) calculated the cost of 100 Calories from a variety of foods on sale at a Lidl (discount) store in a low-income area of south-east London in 2007 (figures in Table 6.3, in price order).

As food prices have risen, consumers have indeed shifted to cheaper, less healthy foods. Comments from individual organizations included (author's research): 'People on very tight budgets, convenience food is cheap, they eat a lot of frozen food' (Christians Against Poverty, Birmingham, 2009); 'Chips are cheaper [than fresh fruit and vegetables]' (Community Centre, Birmingham, 2009). 'As grocery shops close here, a fast food outlet opens up. Fast food, pizzas, curries, are "ridiculously cheap", lack of parenting skills, life skills, young people don't know how to peel a potato, or that you can eat one with the skin on' (Youth and Community Centre, Birmingham, 2009). In Ireland, Friel et al. (2004: 23) calculated that 'Two adults with two children, a single mother with one child and an older person living alone, on social welfare benefits as their only source of income, would have to spend 69 per cent, 80 per cent and 38 per cent respectively of their social welfare entitlements to eat healthily.' Poverty factors tend to interlock and reinforce each other, and those relating to diet are no exception. Low-income households in the UK tend to be single person or single parent families, so less likely to eat healthily; in 2004, 12 per cent of households were single-person but nearly 30 per cent of low-income households were single-person (Donkin et al., 1999: 44, 50). A poorer diet predisposes to more illness, limiting income potential, and it is harder to concentrate and study when you are hungry. Poorer families cannot afford to waste food, so they only buy items they know the children will eat; children then get unhealthy sugary foods, and poverty persists down the generations. The poor live in smaller accommodation and that limits dietary options. They may have no room for a large fridge; that, along with lack of a

Table 6.3 Cost of 100 Calories (2007), healthy and unhealthy foods

Food item	*Cost of 100 Calories*
Digestive biscuits	1.3p
Frozen chips	2p
Vanilla ice cream	2.1p
Crisps	5.5p
Baked beans	5.9p
Potatoes	8.4p
Beef burgers	9.6p
Skimmed milk	16.1p
Battered haddock	16.5p
Carrots	17.3p
Fresh sausages	17.4p
Back bacon	18.2p
Fresh minced beef	21p
Tinned tomatoes	22.1p
Peas	29.8p
Grapes	*32.8p*
Green cabbage	*36p*
Iceberg lettuce	*45.7p*
Broccoli	*51p*
Fresh beef steak	*59.5p*
Fresh tomatoes	*63.7p*
Cucumber	*116.3p*

Note: The italicised terms represent those items beyond the budget of a single consumer on the minimum wage in 2007 (£5.35 an hour) who works 40 hours a week, consumes 2,000 Calories a day, and is spending no more than a fifth of their gross income on food.

Source: Adapted from *Food Magazine* (2007).

car, predisposes to eating from takeaways or purchasing groceries from local convenience stores that do not sell many fruit and vegetables. At the extremes of poverty, those in bedsits, bed and breakfast accommodation or hostels may have no access to their accommodation during the day, so have no choice but to eat from cheap takeaways. Smaller homes may also lack space for a dining table; when children eat as a family at a dinner table they are more likely to eat healthily. Without this furniture, they will likely eat ready meals on their lap while watching TV or on the computer, a sure route to obesity.

Food is an inelastic normal good; consumption rises as price falls, but the quantity change may be small. The price elasticity of fresh fruit and vegetables has been estimated, in the USA, at –0.32, meaning that a 1 per cent drop in price raises demand by 0.32 per cent. Elasticities for younger people are higher; the figure was –0.72 for young adults from middle-class families (a 1 per cent price drop raises demand by 0.72 per cent), for young adults of lower SES status the price elasticity was –0.66, and for lower educated mothers it was –0.41. In other words, for less affluent mothers a 1 per cent price drop would only raise demand by 0.41 per cent, probably because these mothers would still be unwilling to buy foodstuffs their children might reject (Powell et al., 2009). In 2012 the US state of Mississippi had the lowest average household income (US$37,790), the highest proportion of people living in poverty (20.8 per cent), and it also consistently scores highest on obesity rates. In Val de Marne, France, Darmon et al. (2004: 25) found that 'Energy-dense diets tend to be those with a high proportion of fats and sweets, whereas energy-dilute diets are those with a higher proportion of dairy products, vegetables and fruit.' For the poor 'higher dietary energy was associated with lower diet cost'. In all countries, the average proportion of income that is spent on food declines as average wealth rises. As we become richer, we spend our disposable income on other things. This relationship is known as Engel's Law, which states that the income elasticity of food is between 0.0 and 1.0, and that this elasticity falls towards zero as income rises. The income elasticity of food is defined as % increase in food spending / % increase in income. So in a poor country, a 10 per cent rise in income might result in a 7 per cent rise in food spending, giving an elasticity of 0.7. In a wealthier country, a 10 per cent rise in income might only result in a 3 per cent rise in food spending, giving an elasticity of 0.3.

Rises in food spending in wealthy countries may occur because we may trade up in food, buying more meat and fewer potatoes, or buying more microwave ready meals, paying a food company to do our cooking. But we can only eat so much food, as rising incomes enable us to spend more on luxuries such as cars and holidays. In real terms, consumer expenditure rose in Britain between 1963 and 1993 by 104 per cent. Over this period the proportion of consumer spending devoted to durable goods and to services rose from 6 per cent and 39 per cent respectively to 10 per cent and 45 per cent. Meanwhile the proportion taken by food fell from 20 per cent to 12 per cent (Ennew et al., 1995: 3). The overall trend for the UK is shown in Table 6.4.

However, what is good news for consumers overall can be bad for poorer households, when these households are faced by a sudden rise in food prices from a low base. The differentials over time between less-affluent consumers in earlier years spending more on food and more-affluent ones in later years being devoting more spending to non-food luxuries are replicated between less and more affluent consumers at any one time period. In Ireland the proportion of income spent on food fell from 38 per cent in 1951 to 20 per cent in 2000 (Friel et al., 2004). In the UK in 2006, the wealthiest quintile spent just 7.5 per cent income on food; the poorest quintile spent 16 per cent (Donnelley, 2009: 35). In Australia in 1989 the average household spend on food and beverages was 18 per cent of income; the poorest decile spent 56 per cent of their income on food and beverages, the wealthiest decile spent 12 per cent (Tansey and Worsley, 1997: 164). In South Africa the poorest consumers spend 53 per cent of their income on food, as against an average of 30 per cent for all consumers (Battersby, 2011). Similar trends are observable in the USA, where the proportion of income spent on food fell from 38 per cent in 1924 to 11 per cent in 1998 (French et al., 2001). In 1999 Americans on earnings of US$10–15,000 spent 14.8 per cent of income on food, whereas

Table 6.4 Percentage of income in UK spent on food (average, all consumers)

Medieval England	*80*
1800	67.7*
1910	57.7
1920	50.7
1939	46.6
1950	30.0
1960	28.0
1970	19.0
1980	15.0
1990	12.0
2007	10.5
2011	11.3

* In 1800, for a labourer in Kent. For every £100 income, cottage rent took a further £8.80, fuel £5.40, clothing £10.20, shoes £1.70, candles £1.50, soap £1.50, leaving £3.20 for other goods after food (Richardson, 1976: 105).

Sources: DEFRA (2012: Table 2.1); Pollard (1963: 178); Ferguson (1971: 80); HMSO (1990: 24); HMSO (1996: Table 6.1); HMSO (2003: Table 6.2); Butland et al. (2007: 55); Ponting (1991: 316).

those earning over US$70,000 spent just 11.4 per cent (Consumer Expenditure Survey 1999 by US Department of Labor, Bureau of Labor Statistics). Significantly, less-affluent consumers will likely derive a higher proportion of their income from state benefits than more-affluent ones, and state benefits are frequently raised in line with price inflation, not wage rises. The price indices upon which inflation rates are calculated are based upon all consumer spending. Therefore a significant price rise in foodstuffs, such as occurred worldwide from around 2008, will tend to have a lower impact on price inflation generally. A 5 per cent rise on food, in a society where food accounts for 10 per cent of consumer expenditure, will raise inflation by just 0.5 per cent, if non-food prices remain constant. Using Donnelly's figures quoted above, the wealthiest quintile would feel an inflation rate of just 0.375 per cent, but the poorest quintile will experience inflation of 0.8 per cent, from a food price rise of 5 per cent. Yet state benefits would rise by just 0.5 per cent. Over time this differential will amount to a significant squeeze on the poorest; not just those on benefits, but also the lower-paid, because pay rises too are linked to overall inflation, not the higher inflation experienced by the less well-off. Because food represents a considerable fraction of a poorer household's expenditure, they will respond to this squeeze by cutting back on food spending; they will buy calorie-rich but nutrient-poor foods, because these are cheaper. For those on lower incomes, outgoings such as rent and utility bills represent non-discretionary spending; they must pay these items, or be evicted or cut off by the energy company. Therefore food spending is frequently cut back by cash-strapped households. Later on, society pays the food bill when these households create public health demands. Governments, especially in wealthier countries, are frightened of hunger amidst their urban poor. There is a political aphorism that 'Every society is three meals away from a riot', meaning that if large numbers of people are deprived of three meals for whatever reason – transport breakdown, poverty or sharp food price rises – rioting will ensue. An old Hungarian proverb goes 'An empty stomach is the Devil's playground'. Lagi et al. (2012) noted that the global food price spikes of 2008 and 2012 closely correlated to peaks in global unrest, riots and revolutions. The echoes of the Arab Spring, sparked by poverty in Tunisia, continue to reverberate across the globe; a food shortage in Russia in 1917 sparked riots that led to the abdication of the Tsar and the Soviet Revolution. Dwellers in rural areas, especially farmers, where population density is too low to sustain a riot, are forced by government policies and by corporate buying power to subsidize the food bills of the less affluent in the cities. A sick and obese 'urban peasant' is less of a threat to the social order than a fit, lean and hungry one. However, cheap Calories are not a total social panacea; they simply shift the bill for maintaining social stability from the present police budget to the future health bill.

A range of factors have combined to produce the so-called 'perfect storm' of soaring food prices across the globe since 2007. In the long run, global population is still rising at around 75 million per year, although this is predicted to slow from now on. Not only does this mean more mouths to feed, but most of the growth is taking place in less-developed country urban areas, which often sprawl out over fertile farmland, because these cities were founded in the first place in fertile regions. Agriculture across the world was hit by unusual weather events from 2007 onwards, including severe floods in the UK and droughts in Russia's grain-producing regions. These events may be part of the global warming phenomenon, in which case they will become more severe and more frequent. Crops of the future may have to be engineered to withstand alternate periods of both drought and flood, of both unseasonal cold and frost and severe heat waves. These constrictions on supply caused the global wheat price to rise from its average of US$120 per tonne in 2000 to a spike of US$430 in 2008; a subsequent fall, back to US$160 in 2010, was not sustained and the price in 2013 now hovers around US$300 per tonne. The volatile wheat market attracted commodity speculators like moths to a flame, and their market activities drove the price still higher, much as the global house price spike of 2007 and subsequent collapse was in part caused by house buyers betting that prices would continue to rise and by their very frenzy to enter the market, driving prices yet higher, a classic bubble scenario. The 'just-in-time' nature of today's food distribution chain, with very little slack or spare capacity, also magnifies the price effects of any shortages.

The world oil price also soared in 2007. Static at around US$20 a barrel throughout most of the 1990s, crude oil prices began to rise from 2000, partly due to increasing unrest in the Middle East. In 2008 prices spiked at US$140 a barrel; as with the wheat price, a fall back to around US$40 in 2009 was not sustained and the 2013 price is around US$110 a barrel. Increased energy prices feed into almost every stage of the food chain, from fertilizer prices, farm energy costs, transport of food and packaging prices to supermarket distribution costs. Consumers must also pay more to reach the shops, if they travel by car or public transport. Part of the reason why food prices rose was the diversion of agricultural land to biofuel production, hailed as part of the environmental solution to global warming; from the point of view of food-insecure households struggling to meet the food bill, biofuels were exacerbating the very problem they were supposed to solve. In a sense, the biofuel events of the 2000s mirrored an earlier UK biofuel crisis of the 1890s and early 1900s, when horsepower was at its peak. Horses were used extensively in late Victorian Britain, not least by the railway companies to distribute goods from the railheads, as well as on farms to power machinery. The UK's horse population consumed 4 million tons of oats and hay a year, demanding some 15 million acres (6 million hectares) of land; similarly the USA in 1900 devoted 90 million acres (36 million hectares) of cropland to feeding its horses, a quarter of the US cropland area. Without cheap food imports from its Empire, Britain could never have fed both its human and horse populations (Ponting, 1991: 274). The adoption of the internal combustion engine to replace horses actually freed up much cropland, by changing the source of energy from East Anglia and the Midwest to the deserts of the Middle East. We now need another source of abundant cheap energy to replace oil, and the possibilities for this are discussed in Chapter 8.

In the long run, oil prices would have risen as demand began to outrun dwindling supplies, but a major short-run impetus for the commodity price spikes of 2008, including wheat and oil, was the economic growth of China (Shaw and Shaw, 2012). China provided the world with cheap goods and so acted as an engine of deflation until around 2005 when its spectacular annual GDP growth of around 12 per cent created a huge Chinese demand for oil, steel, copper and much else, forcing up global prices for these commodities. As China became wealthier, as its GDP per capita rose from around US$500 in the 1990s to around US$4,000 now, another factor kicked in that raised world food prices: the shift in Chinese diet from vegetables and rice to meat. Meat is an inherently inefficient way for humans to obtain Calories because most of the Calories consumed by the cow or pig never make it to us; they go to maintain the animal itself. To produce 1 kilogram of fish takes 1.5 kg of fish food, or 3 kg for a top-level carnivorous fish like salmon; 1 kg of poultry demands 2 kg of feed. Larger animals are less food-efficient; 1 kg of pork necessitates 3.5 kg of feed, and bovines are the least efficient source of food, with 1 kg of beef necessitating 8–10 kg of feed. This feed demands land, energy and water; to produce 1 kg of grain takes some 1,500 litres of water. One kilogram of pork demands 3,680 litres and 1 kg of beef demands 9,680 litres, compared to 1 kg of tomatoes or onions which require just 140 litres and 130 litres respectively. This presents countries where water is often scarce with a dilemma: should water be used for agriculture, industry, for domestic

Table 6.5 Kilograms of meat per year per capita consumed in China

Year	*Kg meat per capita per year*	*Population (millions)*	*Total meat tonnes*
1962	4	720	2,880,000
1980	14	1,000	14,000,000
1985	20	1,030	20,600,000
1989	22	1,090	23,980,000
1997	29.4	1,190	34,986,000
2003	46.2	1,290	59,600,000
2008	54	1,300	70,200,000
2012	60	1,340	80,400,000

Source: Collingham (2011: 5).

use, or should river levels be preserved for wildlife? In China the water used to produce US$200 worth of beef could produce US$1,400 of industrial output (Earth, 2002: 37), which implies a huge rise in food prices if the agricultural sector is to claim the resources it needs to boost production.

Meat demand in China has risen sharply because meat consumption per capita has risen and the total population is still growing, as Table 6.5 shows.

The global per capita demand for meat was 42.3 kg in 2011, down slightly from 42.5 kg the previous year. Two factors are causing this reduction: a growing vegetarian lifestyle in the wealthier countries, and economic recession hitting the purchasing power of the poor worldwide. Meat consumption rises with affluence (Lavik and Kjørstad, 2005), and the current Chinese figure of 60 kg/person/year is eclipsed by the UK consumption of 85 kg, 124 kg in the USA, and 146 kg in Denmark. The developed world consumed 78.9 kg meat per capita in 2011, compared to 32.3 kg in the less-developed world in 2011, up from 25.5 kg in 1999 and just 10.2 kg in 1964. Over time, meat consumption has risen in both the UK and USA, as Table 6.6 illustrates. The UK figures show the historical results of wartime supply restrictions and subsequent reductions caused by rationing and economic distress, and how meat consumption rebounds again when the economy improves.

From a perspective of maximizing global food availability, meat consumption is not all bad. Animals such as pigs and chicken can recycle household organic waste back into edible nutrients, and in arid areas goats can similarly produce food out of inedible grasses. We also get other goods from animals such as clothing and dairy products. More intangible benefits from farm animals include companionship and education for children. If we have to eat meat, grass-fed animals are better than grain-fed ones, if we are to maximize food availability and minimize price and resource consumption. However, some companion animals also create huge demands on the world food supply. The UK has (2009) 8 million dogs and 8 million cats; the USA hosts 113 million cats and dogs. A medium-sized dog can have the same ecological footprint as a Vietnamese person, because cat and dog owners like to

Table 6.6 Meat consumption per capita per year, UK and USA (kilograms)

Year	*UK*	*USA*
1800	16	
1880	40.5	
1910	58	45
1914	50	40
1925	57.3	
1935	57.3	
1941	44	
1947	42.7	
1960	60	95
1985	72	110
2012	85	124

Source: Author's research.

feed their pets a high-protein diet. Here also, China is adding to world food demand because by the late 1990s Chinese pet ownership was diversifying from the traditional caged birds and crickets into kittens and puppies (Avery, 1999: 6). The global–nutrition benefits of a falling birth rate may be cancelled by increasing pet ownership, as more single-person and childless households adopt a pet for companionship. For a sustainable future food system, we may need to change our attitudes in many ways, some of them not directly related to human food consumption.

Food ignorance. ***Because they spend so much time out of the house earning money, many young women in cities like Manchester have never learned to cook. Sometimes their households scratch along, ill-fed. (Frederick Engels, Communist and associate of Karl Marx, 1845)***

When people have good physical access to healthy food, and it is within their budget, there is still no guarantee they will actually eat healthily. The disengagement with, and sanitization of, our food discussed in Chapters 1 and 3 has now produced a degree of ignorance about what we are putting into ourselves that would have been astonishing to our ancestors a couple of centuries ago. In the 1970s butchers found it necessary to have pictures of cows, sheep and pigs on their walls with the various parts labelled, along with cooking instructions, because customers no longer possessed this knowledge (Scott, 1976: 17). By 2007 food ignorance in the UK, although by no means new as the 1845 quote above illustrates, had increased to the point where a TNS poll of 1,700 adults found that a fifth of respondents did not know that bacon came from pigs. In deprived parts of Birmingham, UK, some schoolchildren thought bacon came from sheep and cows laid eggs. A community centre worker in Birmingham commented, in 2009, 'The younger generation have grown up on burgers and chips, not been taught how to cook. The younger could learn (about healthy eating) from the elderly but don't come into contact with the older ones much. The older generation have a good idea of a well-balanced diet but the young don't. If the vegetables are badly cooked they lose the nutrients anyway.' A 2006 poll by the British Heart Foundation, surveying over 1,000 8- to 15-year-olds, discovered that whereas 99 per cent were confident with the DVD player, only 43 per cent knew how to boil an egg. The level of food knowledge among the young has scarcely improved since then. A 2013 survey of 27,500 schoolchildren by the British Nutrition Foundation found that

- One in ten secondary school children thought tomatoes grew underground.
- One in three 5- to 8-year-olds believed bread and pasta were made of meat.
- One in three primary school children thought cheese grew on plants.
- One in five children aged under 11 thought fish fingers were made of chicken.
- One in five children had never visited a farm.

On the positive side, 90 per cent of secondary school pupils were aware of the need to eat five portions of fruit or vegetables a day, although 67 per cent of primary school children and 81 per cent of adolescents admitted they actually consumed four portions or less daily. France, home of the World Heritage Dinner Table, hardly does better, with 87 per cent of French schoolchildren unfamiliar with a beetroot and a fifth unable to identify an apricot, according to a recent survey by ASEF, France's public health organization. Attitude and knowledge are crucial to the consumption of a healthy diet, evidenced by the fact that the strongest (inverse) predictor of the level of obesity in Britain is the proportion of the population with university degree level qualifications. Attitude towards fruit and vegetables may be 'negative but necessary'. In Dudley, UK, some respondents thought the only way to improve their diet was to consume more salad, even though this was not a preferred foodstuff; other people had come to see Calories as an economic bad, having negative value: 'I'd be thinner and healthier if I could afford to eat those low Calorie meals all the time. I have to make-do with meals that are higher in Calories so it's hard to lose weight' (Jackson, 2003).

In today's leisure-oriented society, eating healthily often takes second place to saving money, even for those who can afford a healthy diet; in turn saving money may take second place to saving time, this time being then available for leisure pursuits or relaxation. An extreme example of this was reported in *The Independent* (2010: 33) which reported a Californian stating that non-drive-through restaurants were a waste of time because you have to find a parking space, get out of your car and order your food. Another motorist complained that queues of cars at his local drive-through made it impossible for him to drive there – from his workplace just across the road from this restaurant – so he had to leave his metal cocoon behind and actually walk across the road to eat in the sit-down section. Food attitudes in Birmingham, UK, were not much better. 'It's easier to go to the chippy than cook' and 'There's a chip shop in the middle of this area, sells £1.25 specials so it negates the need to cook', were among comments made at a community centre in 2009. Smoking may be prioritized over food: 'Smoking causes poor diet, it suppresses the appetite, also money for food goes on cigarettes instead of food' (Age Concern, Birmingham 2009), and even convincing some that their diet needs improving may be difficult: 'People here prefer to spend their time at the pub, we have lifestyle sessions here, they are poorly attended as people don't consider themselves unfit, even if they are obese. Many people here on benefits, they prioritize the pub first, food second' (Community Centre, Birmingham, 2009). Time constraints appear to impact most heavily on the working poor, those on low wages. Some people may put in more overtime or take on more than one job simply to make ends meet or to satisfy a need to conform to consumer society-fuelled aspirations such as beautification rituals, relentlessly generated and advertised in the media. Although in most areas obesity was negatively correlated with employment, in less affluent areas more employment went with higher obesity rates (H. Shaw, 2012). The unemployed in these lower-SES areas had more time to visit markets at times when food bargains were to be had, typically at close of market around 3 p.m. when the employed were still at work, and had more time and energy to cook rather than resort to ready meals or takeaways when tired after work. The London Development Agency (2005: 33) reported that those in employment spend an average 40 per cent less time cooking than the unemployed. Meanwhile Butland et al. (2007: 58), in a study of 21 OECD countries, found that as annual work hours for men rose from 1,400 to 1,900, male obesity rates rose from 9 per cent to 21 per cent. Similarly Smith et al. (2008) found that in Salt Lake City, Utah, obesity was lower in older inner city areas because these neighbourhoods had shaded sidewalks and local shops close by, whereas in outer suburbs a drive to the supermarket was often the only option. Interestingly, factors that were positively associated with obesity in affluent areas such as being a full-time carer or being in poor health did not reverse to become negatively associated in poorer districts, because these factors limit time and mobility in any economic situation (H. Shaw, 2012).

By 1980 'the death knell was being sounded for the Fordist social wage where one income supported an entire household' (Herbst and Stanton, 2007: 649); rising real house prices and costly social aspirations, as well as changing societal expectations regarding women working and child-rearing, meant an increasing number of women were joining the workforce, and more of these women held full-time, not part-time, jobs. In the USA the proportion of adult women holding jobs has risen markedly (Table 6.7); simultaneously household work has declined. The inevitable result was a greater share of food being sourced from takeaways. In 1977, 18 per cent of total dietary energy originated from takeaway food in the USA; by 1995 this proportion had risen

Table 6.7 Percentage of adult US females with jobs

Year	*% women with jobs*	*Average weekly hours spent on cleaning, cooking (average all adults)*
1900	21	44
1950	31	20
1975	46	
2001	72	
2012	75	14

Sources: Jabs and Devine (2006); Forbes (2013); US Department of Labor (2013).

to 34 per cent. Takeaway food is more obesogenic than home-cooked food, French et al. (2001) estimated that if takeaway meals had the same energy content per kilogram as home-cooked food, Americans would be consuming an average 197 Calories fewer per day.

We have a dromology of food, with its own idioms: 'deskfasting' and eating 'al-desco' for example, signifying the practice of leaving home without breakfast but grabbing a quick snack on arrival at the office. At the other end of the day the average time taken to cook the main meal in Britain has fallen from 60 minutes in 1980 to 33 minutes in 1990 and 14 minutes in 2006. In 1996 the sound of Britain cooking was characterized as 'hum, ping, rip' (Moran, 1996); as our addiction to microwave TV dinners grew, Oxo, in 1999, dropped its image of a family eating a roast dinner together as too outdated (Blythman, 2006: 85). The proportion of people agreeing that 'it is difficult to find time to prepare meals' rose from 33 per cent in 1980 to 45 per cent in 1999. Adults with children are more prone to obesity than childless adults, as they eat more sugary foods and have less time for exercise; snacking while doing other things such as watching TV, working on the computer or chatting on the phone all promote obesity. Children are targeted by food manufacturers selling high fat, sugary and salty (HFSS) foods and the presence of these foods in the house encourages adults to eat less healthily too. Working mothers rushing to get the child off to school as well as get themselves to work often have no time for breakfast, and skipping breakfast increases the propensity to consume a sugary obesogenic snack later on. The concept of the 'family meal' was created by Queen Victoria; it was then an idealized myth, because the children of the Victorian aristocracy would in fact be fed in the nursery by the servants, while the children of the poor would be working long hours along with their parents to maximise family income. Mrs Beeton (1836–65) spread the 'family meal' idea to the emerging Victorian middle class, who were keen to differentiate themselves from the poor while being unable to afford a large body of servants. The concept of ready meals, pre-prepared food that simply needed reheating, did not reach Britain until 1962 when the Vesta Chicken Curry appeared. Spending on ready meals rose from £62 million in 1963 to £220 million in 1973, a rise after inflation of 105 per cent. Per capita consumption of frozen food in the UK rose from 3.7 kg to 8.3 kg, as frozen food chains like Farm Foods emerged. An interesting measure of the changing social attitude in Britain to convenience foods is provided by Scott (1976: 13), who describes two surveys done on people's attitude towards instant coffee. The first survey, done by Haire in 1950, involved showing respondents two shopping lists, identical except that one list had instant coffee, the other real coffee. In 1950 the instant coffee users were negatively labelled as lazy, bad mothers, slovenly housewives. In a repeat of the Haire study in 1968 by Webster and Pechmann, attitudes had reversed. The real coffee user was now perceived as dull, phlegmatic, lacking elegance and imagination, whereas the instant coffee user was seen more positively, as quick, energetic, outgoing, friendly, physically active and busy. The 1968 study was just before the big rise in obesity that began in many developed countries in the 1970s.

We also lack time for exercise. Gentle exercise walking is better for weight loss, as intensive bouts will not only increase appetite but put strain on the joints. However gym workouts can burn Calories more quickly. In two hours one might expend 400 to 500 Calories in a gym, depending on weight, but a kilogram of fat equates to 9,000 Calories so shedding one kilogram takes 20 hours of gym work. In fact the time taken to travel to the gym, change, shower and travel back afterwards, probably extends this time to 30 hours. Walking will burn off 130 Calories an hour over and above sitting down, and involves no showering or changing; a time cost per kilogram of fat of almost 70 hours. Shedding weight will extend life expectancy, and especially extend healthy life expectancy, but this benefit is uncertain in terms of amount and far in the future. Most people discount future rewards heavily so that when choosing between a gift of £100 now and £120 in a year's time, the majority take the £100 now, although they are spurning a 20 per cent interest rate. If your aim is to lose 5 kilograms and you can spare three hours a week for exercise, it will take you between 50 and 120 weeks to achieve this. Not everyone feels they can spare three hours a week, and not all of those that can are able to keep this schedule up for a year or more. There may be a way to incentivize people to eat more healthily, long term. Whitehead et al. (2011) found that for most skin types, attractiveness to the opposite sex was enhanced by the golden-yellow colour produced by carotenoids, antioxidants found in most vegetables. Moreover, the carotenoid glow was distinguishable from a (less-attractive) bronze hue produced by suntanning. The carotenoid tint disappeared within a few weeks if vegetable consumption ceased. So perhaps healthy eating, which will contribute to weight loss through replacing calorific foods (and being grossly overweight is not sexually attractive either) needs to be promoted with a more socio-sexual message rather than a health agenda.

The increase in ethnic diversity and rise in longevity seen in Britain and many other developed countries over the past two decades have created new issues of obesity. Muslim women tend to be less adventurous in their shopping than their non-Muslim counterparts, not travelling to distant supermarkets on their own but going in groups to local smaller Asian food stores. There may be language barriers in a diverse culture to understanding food labels, along with a psychological tendency to eat sugary food and high calorie Western-type snacks because these are perceived as higher status than the food consumed pre-migration (Winham, 2009). Without full understanding of the nutritional labelling, migrants may be exposed to high calorie diets unwittingly. Migrant men may be pushed into occupations such as taxi drivers or shop assistants, where they get little exercise, because these jobs use 'transferable skills', not requiring academic qualifications that may be unrecognized in the host country if acquired abroad. Men, of all races, are prone to resist both dietary advice and cooking lessons, some seeing cooking as 'women's work'. Some pensioners can afford healthy food but choose cheaper unhealthy fare so as to save money to leave to their children, or save for a rainy day not realizing that day has come (Age Concern, Birmingham, UK, 2009). The grandchildren may come 'like harbour sharks' to claim their inheritance (Elderly Centre for the Afro-Caribbean Community, Birmingham, UK, 2009). Older people may have cooking skills but be too frail to cook; if they rely on a carer, the carer will likely purchase a ready meal, and Meals on Wheels may be unpalatable to some (Elderly Daycare Centre, Birmingham, UK, 2009).

Food deserts have three layers of access. The first layer is physical access; there are some households, mainly in rural areas but in some urban areas too, that are distant from green retailers selling a range of fresh fruit and vegetables. These urban areas tend to be the less affluent housing estates on the periphery of towns, where supermarkets are scarce and independent retailers are reluctant to stock fresh produce because it goes bad before it is sold. However, the vast majority of urban British households are within 1,000 metres of a retailer selling fresh produce. The second layer of access is financial. Many households in less affluent areas can physically access healthy food but cannot afford it; and find that fast, takeaway, processed, sugary, fatty foods are cheaper. These households may be interspersed with higher-income families even in lower-SES neighbourhoods, constituting large but hidden food deserts. There may even be financial food deserts within households, if as often happens the adult female of a cash-strapped household prioritizes the husband and children's dietary needs while eating junk food herself. The third layer is even harder to see: those households who can access fresh produce, and can afford it, but do not want to eat it. George Orwell's comment in *The Road to Wigan Pier* is interesting: 'A millionaire may enjoy breakfasting off orange juice and Ryvita biscuits, an unemployed man doesn't.' The unemployed, the poor and those who are unhappy want indulgence foods as affordable treats while the millionaire has many other means of attaining satisfaction. Psychological attitudes are elusive, changeable and hidden, but can produce a poor diet along with all the associated health issues just the same as for a household that faces physical or financial barriers to the consumption of a healthy diet.

Figure 6.1 is a schematic representation of the locales in Britain where food deserts may occur. Twelve areas where food access may be problematical for

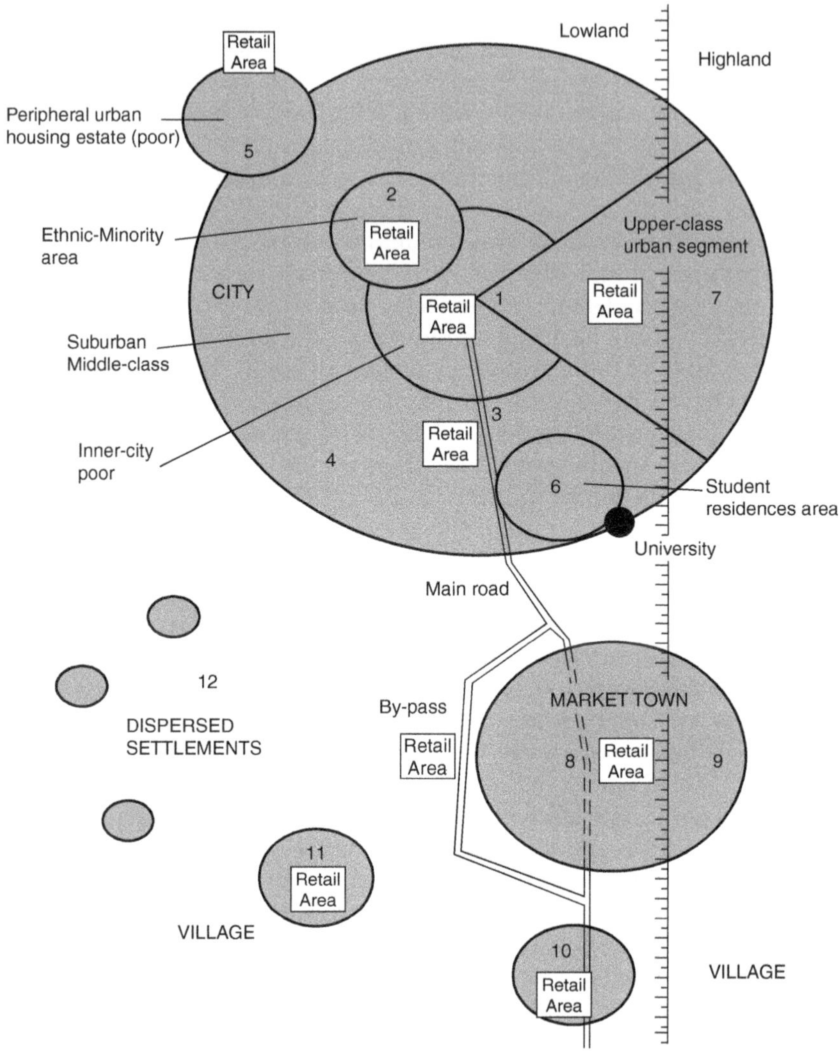

Figure 6.1 Schematic representation of food desert areas

some households are highlighted; food access is improving in some of these areas but worsening in others. Table 6.8 summarizes the attributes of these 12 areas.

There are other settings where eating a healthy diet may be difficult, settings that cannot easily be marked on a map. We have noted that institutionally provided food, in schools, hospitals and prisons, may be nutritionally poor. Individuals living in hostel-type accommodation may have no access to a kitchen, or indeed to the premises at all, during the day, forcing them to

Table 6.8 Food desert areas, as shown in Figure 6.1

Number, area type	*Food access issue*
1. Inner city executive flats	Prefer to save time, eat pre-prepared food.
2. Inner city ethnic minority areas	Cost of fresh food vs. wages. Availability of culturally acceptable vegetables (improving).
3. Inner city, access to shops severed by main roads	Crossing barriers (road, railway, park) difficult for vulnerable (mothers with pushchairs, disabled, elderly) due to fear of crime, physical barriers such as stairs. Local independent shops poor in fresh food.
4. Suburban small shopping parades	Declining use of smaller parades as footfall shifts to larger centres, to local supermarket branches. Shops in smaller parades cease selling fresh produce as it goes bad before sale.
5. Planned low SES status housing schemes on urban periphery	Often a centralized retail area, some homes distant, with poor bus service and low car ownership. Local stores do not sell fresh produce as it goes bad before sale.
6. Student residence areas	Students prefer takeaways, replace local residents so fresh produce shops decline; when students away from university, area semi-depopulates, shops lose trade.
7. High SES area, often at higher elevation than city centre	Many older people, may be asset-rich but low income, may be disabled, unable to drive car. Poor bus service. Getting shopping home on foot difficult if journey home is uphill.
8. Market town centre	Decline in retail facilities if passing trade lost to by-pass retail park. By-pass acts as barrier so shoppers do not use retail park and town centre together.
9. Market town suburbs	Suburbs extend 1–2 miles (1.5–3 km) from centre, too far to walk but not far enough for viable bus service. May be uphill back home.
10. Smaller rural centre	Lacks full range of shops so shoppers with cars travel to market town. Local shops at risk of closure; bus service may be poor.
11. Remote village	Off main road, so little passing trade and poorly served by mobile shops. Poor bus service.
12. Dispersed settlement	No village centre, so nowhere viable for shop to operate. Also poor bus service.

eat unhealthy cheap takeaway food. The homeless, single mothers, the repossessed, those just out of prison, recovering substance abusers, all those disadvantaged in other ways, are liable to suffer the disadvantages of poor diet too. Just as the causes of food deserts are multi-faceted, so are the solutions. Actors at all stages of the food chain from farm to fork, as well as gatekeeper and governmental agencies such as schools, local councils and dieticians all have a role to play in improving the quality of people's diet. The next chapter examines the various means by which diet might be improved and food deserts eliminated.

7 Getting back into shape

Introduction

In Chapter 1 we described four stages by which we have become divorced from the origins of our food: industrialization, globalization, supermarketization and dromology. We saw that the innovation of farming, replacing an earlier and simpler hunter-gatherer mode of life, set in train a complexification of society that led to specialist trades, government, army, a hierarchy of classes and much else. A key issue with food and obesity is that, as in Accum's day, those who produce, process and sell us our food have little interest in making it more healthy; in fact the greater commercial rewards often lie in manufacturing, advertising and selling less healthy, more processed, foods. Those who bear the financial costs of unhealthy food lie outside the food chain, because the costs of obesity described in Chapter 2 fall mainly on government and the healthcare providers. Therefore Chapter 7 starts with central government as the agent with the most potential to curb obesity and promote healthy eating, and then examines the possible contributions from other organizations lower down the power chain, including local government, health providers, schools, the private sector, parents and how we ourselves can take greater responsibility for our diet and health.

Governmental initiatives. *An army marches on its stomach*

Governments have long seen the need to intervene in the food chain; in Chapter 4 we saw how the Babylonian King Hammurabi saw a need to legislate on food standards, as did King John of England in the thirteenth century. These rulers were not especially altruistic; they had an interest in a reasonably healthy workforce and especially in having a recruiting base for their armies that was fit to fight. From the early Middle Ages through to the nineteenth century soup kitchens were provided by a combination of government agencies, altruistic nobility and religious charities. Besides a moral obligation to feed the starving poor there was a fear that these hungry citizens would riot, turn to crime, or simply be unfit for work. However, there were counterbalancing concerns that free food would demotivate the unemployed from seeking work, and the soup kitchens were periodically closed down to redirect the indigent into workhouses. In 1753 Dr James Lind demonstrated that scurvy in sailors could be prevented by including citrus fruit in their meals, hence the nickname 'limeys' for the British. As emerging chief sea power of the world, Britain could not afford to have its traders and naval might compromised by a malaise whose symptoms are lethargy, jaundice and oedema. A few decades later Napoleon, realizing that a well-equipped army is nothing without food, offered a prize of 12,000 francs to whoever could preserve food in a portable form. The Frenchman Nicholas Appert initially solved the problem by sealing heated food in bottles; this led the Englishman Brian Donkin to use metal cans to preserve food, in 1812. However, the food still rotted as some bacteria were left alive; it was only after Louis Pasteur's work in the 1870s that canning food became a practical means of preservation.

With increasing urbanization and continued rampant food adulteration the problem of unfit army recruits only intensified, so that when the Boer War (1899–1902) broke out, the British Army discovered that half those volunteering to fight were medically unfit. In Manchester in 1899 only 1,000 out of 11,000 turning up to enlist were fit enough to be accepted (Ponting, 1991: 320). Overall, 34.5 per cent of all volunteers for the British Army who turned up between 1893 and 1902 had to be rejected on medical grounds (Teed, 1963: 35). While middle-class ladies from the more affluent parts of West London ventured into the impoverished East End to teach cooking skills, the army health recruiting crisis was a major stimulus to the British government setting up a State Health Insurance scheme in 1911. However, the unfit recruit problem persisted, so that in 1935 some 62 per cent of volunteers to the British Army were rejected on medical grounds. These volunteers came overwhelmingly from the poorer classes (Buchanan, 1982: 110), signalling a large underlying dietary problem among the poor. Even in 2012 the Pentagon complained that rising obesity was shrinking the pool of potential US Army recruits. In 1937 the Political and Economic Planning Committee advised the UK government that the health of the nation should not be left solely to the medical profession, but that lifestyles, the built environment, transport, work practices and the food industry must also be involved (Fraser, 1980: 187). Free market-oriented governments may be reluctant to force changes on industry but many have, perhaps belatedly, implemented dietary improvement schemes and seen the improvements. Schemes such as the EPODE programme (*Ensemble, Prévenons l'Obésité des Enfants*), operating across nine European countries as well as in North and South America, Australia and New Zealand, the UK's 'Change 4 Life' and 'Healthy Towns' initiatives, Australia's National Child Nutrition Programme improving access to healthy food in rural and impoverished north-western communities, and Canada's Action Plan on Food Security have all played a role in improving diet and promoting exercise as a means to reduce obesity-driven illnesses.

In the USA First Lady Michelle Obama has started an initiative to combat food deserts and reduce obesity called 'Let's Move'; this has a goal of

Table 7.1 Food Stamp / SNAP recipients USA (millions)

1996	25.5
1999	18.2
2000	17.2 (lowest since 1979)
2003	22.0
2005	25.0
2007	37.0
2011	45.0 (1 in 7 Americans)

Sources: Olson and Holben (2002); United States Department of Agriculture (various dates).

Table 7.2 US ethnic breakdown; general population and SNAP recipients, 2005

Ethnic group	*% Overall US population*	*% of SNAP recipients*
Afro-American	12.3	31.3
Hispanic	12.5	13.0
White	75.1	45.4

Source: Adapted from Alston et al. (2009).

eradicating food deserts by 2017 with a US$400 million input from the federal government focused on providing tax breaks to supermarkets that open in areas designated as food deserts by USDA; as noted earlier in Chapter 6 this may not be the entire solution to improving diet among the disadvantaged. The world's biggest food assistance programme today is the SNAP (Supplemental Nutrition Assistance Program), known as the Federal Food Stamp Program until October 2008. In the 1990s over 25 million Americans were in receipt of Food Stamps, a number the federal government sought to reduce under the welfare reform law known as PRWORA, or Personal Responsibility and Work Opportunity Reconciliation Act. Passed at a time of strong economic growth (Olson and Holben, 2002), the aftermath of PRWORA was a reduction in Food Stamp recipients to a low of 17.2 million in 2000 (Table 7.1). Economic growth was credited with two-fifths of this fall, and welfare reform the other three-fifths. A major aim of PRWORA was to get single mothers off benefits and into employment.

However, from 2000 the number of Food Stamp recipients began to rise; the economic boom continued until 2007, but rising housing costs outpacing wages began to push many lower paid into poverty. Unsurprisingly, ethnic minorities were over-represented in the 25 million SNAP recipients, as Table 7.2 illustrates.

This uneven breakdown is mirrored in the distribution of diabetes, diagnosed and undiagnosed, within the USA (Lee and Nieman, 2013: 13); the Hispanic population being slightly worse off than whites, and Afro-Americans considerably worse off than the Hispanics. Worryingly, the ethnic-based health gap appears to be growing for the Afro-Caribbean community (Table 7.3).

Table 7.3 Adult diabetes rates, USA, 1988–2008

	1988–94	*1999–2002*	*2005–2008*	*Increase*
Male	9.6%	10.8%	11.7%	21.8%
Female	8.7%	8.8%	9.2%	17.2%
White	8.0%	8.3%	9.2%	15.0%
Hispanic	14.9%	13.2%	16.9%	13.4%
Afro-American	16.0%	16.3%	19.9%	24.4%

Source: Adapted from Lee and Nieman (2013).

By 2011 the number of SNAP recipients had soared to 45 million, one in seven Americans, and the cost to the government had risen from US$35 billion in 2008 to US$65 billion in 2010 and US$86.6 billion in 2013. The United States Department of Agriculture estimated that only two-thirds of those eligible, those with incomes below 130 per cent of poverty level, have signed up for SNAP. Many US benefits are time-limited; Unemployment Benefit can be received for a maximum of 26 weeks, a period cut from 99 weeks in 2012. However, SNAP is not time-limited, but has a ceiling value of US$200 for the poorest recipients, and tails off with any income so the average SNAP recipient gets US$133 from the scheme. Able-bodied and childless people can get SNAP for a maximum of three months a year, but this restriction is lifted in times of high unemployment; then, only recent immigrants and drug offence convicts are ineligible (*The Economist*, 2011c: 45). A nutritional flaw with SNAP is that in low-SES areas the recipients can, and likely will, use them to buy unhealthy sugary food and carbonated drinks from non-green retailers. As in the UK, poorer areas of US cities have fewer full-range supermarkets. A non-profit organization called Wholesome Wave is attempting to steer SNAP recipients back to healthy food by arranging for their food assistance vouchers to have double value when redeemed at green retail outlets such as farmers' markets, because fresh produce is more expensive than unhealthy food. More coercively the US government has proposed making SNAP benefits eligible for healthy food only. However, this might raise the price of healthy foods where they are scarce anyway due to monopolies of distance and lack of consumer transport options (Alston et al., 2009); this might worsen the diet of non-SNAP recipients. It might also make unhealthy food seem more attractive by making it more unattainable; as discussed below, people often exhibit perverse responses to financial bribery and coercion. Other food banks exist to serve specific communities with unique dietary requirements and financial circumstances. The Yad Ezra food bank (http://www.yadezra.org/) served 250 families a month when founded in 1990, but in January 2013 was feeding 1,400 families in the Detroit, USA, area. Deeply Kosher families may be more prone to poverty as they bear the expense of running Jewish schools, rather than using state-provided education, and have more children than average. Meanwhile Halal food banks have been set up in Australia and Canada.

Food banks and food pantries have also appeared in the UK and Europe since the 2008 Credit Crunch began, a development sparked by the same factors as in the USA: rising housing costs, stagnant wages, job losses and stubbornly high housing costs, and these factors combine with political pressure to reduce social welfare costs in European countries as in the USA. European governments, however, give joblessness benefits as cash, not Food Stamps or SNAP entitlements as in America (US churches also operate food banks). Some food banks have gardens for producing food, as well as taking donations of tinned food. UK food banks have appeared in formerly thriving industrial towns like Swindon, and even prosperous Tunbridge Wells has one; by 2012 Britain had 190 food banks, of which 88 opened in 2011 alone. They serve those on benefits and low-income working families hit by some crisis such as a boiler malfunction or car breakdown, they help widows facing funeral costs and households facing sudden demands for small weekly benefit overpayments that may have built up for months, or self-employed people facing illness. Some UK supermarkets allow food bank collectors to canvass donations in their foyer, giving out leaflets asking shoppers to buy a bit extra for donations, listing both food items (cereals, tinned food, rice, etc.) and non-food items (toiletries, nappies) that can be given to the poor. The UK and many other developed countries have a large number of households whose income only just meets outgoings, who cannot afford to save, and for whom any sudden crisis will tip them deeply into debt. By 2013 the Trussell Trust alone operated over 300 UK food banks, and weekly food recipients had risen from 29,000 in 2009/10 to nearly 300,000 in 2012/13. UK benefits policy looks set to boost these numbers still further, as the so-called Bedroom Tax started in April 2013. Under this 'tax', social housing tenants face a housing benefit cut if they occupy premises with too many bedrooms, and fail to move to smaller accommodation, but smaller accommodation is not always available, in the right area, and some disabled benefits claimants need regular visits from distant relatives. Overall benefits rises are capped at one 1 per cent per annum, when UK inflation is 2–3 per cent; as we saw earlier, poorer people experience higher than average inflation.

Community centres that provide a range of benefits for attendees, as well as improving their diet, work well in the UK. In King's Lynn the St Augustine's Healthy Living Centre combined cookery lessons and gardening classes with a crèche, café and benefits advice centre, and speakers may be invited to give talks on cooking and nutrition. Similarly to St Augustine's, the South Side initiative in Syracuse, USA, hosts a grocery store selling locally grown produce, a café, computer and Internet facilities and runs a community newspaper; the City of Refuge in Atlanta, Georgia, provides raised planters for growing fruit and vegetables as well as a kitchen where the poor can receive free meals. Overall a holistic entire-lifestyle approach is often needed, focusing on wider issues than diet alone.

Fiscal

In free market economies prices are set by supply and demand, but the free market price of a good only reflects the private costs of its consumption, not any externalities. Externalities are the costs paid by third parties outside the transaction. For example, a motorist buys petrol based on their need to travel, a cigarette smoker buys cigarettes based on their need for pleasure; the driver and the smoker do not consider the costs of pollution to third parties, the costs of traffic noise or second-hand cigarette smoke. Because of this failure of the market to charge the buyer for all the costs of their driving or smoking, more driving is done and more cigarettes are smoked, than is optimal for society. Governments can rectify this failure by taxing petrol or cigarettes, to the point where smokers pay not only for their pleasure now but for their future medical treatment, and for the inconvenience imposed on others by their smoke. If smokers continue consuming cigarettes, they pay tax contributing to health costs; if they cut back, national healthcare costs fall. Taxing unhealthy food seems as logical as taxing cigarettes. Like smoking, people who eat unhealthily are opting for present gratification but seldom take into account future healthcare costs. A number of countries have introduced such taxes. Finland taxes sweets, and Norway and Sweden are considering this move. In 2011 Denmark also introduced this so-called 'fat tax', imposing a 16 Kroner (£1.85, or US$3.00) per kilogram tax on foods containing more than 2.5 per cent saturated fats, but abandoned the tax in 2012 as too complex, requiring an assessment of the fat content of all foods. France announced plans, in 2008, for higher VAT on foods rich in sugar, fat and salt, but abandoned these plans; Hungary went ahead with such a tax in 2011 as did Romania. In the UK Professor Jebb advised the government, in 2012, to tax sugary drinks, and Sustain and the Royal Society for Public Health have urged the UK Chancellor, in 2013, to impose a 20p tax on cans of sugary drinks. In the USA a report entitled *Local Government Actions to Prevent Childhood Obesity* similarly demanded taxes on junk food and sugary soft drinks. Some US states do tax sugary drinks. Arkansas levies 2 cents (1.3p) on a 12 oz can of cola, and California imposes a 7.25 per cent sales tax on soft drinks.

As often happens when economic theory meets real society, the result is considerable controversy. Economists themselves worked out that if the UK imposed a 10 per cent tax on sugary drinks then demand for them would fall by just 7.5 millilitres per capita per day, about 3 Calories' worth, scarcely denting the UK obesity figures. The Danish fat tax appeared to reduce demand for fatty foods, but economists suggested demand for these foods was down simply due to pre-tax hoarding. Nutritionally, the taxes in Arkansas and California were ineffective; from Chapter 2 we saw that each person who becomes obese may cost their national government some £500 (US$800) in extra healthcare costs per annum. To raise a person of average height from BMI 25 to 30, the threshold for obesity, would entail a weight gain of 15 kg, from 72 to 87 kg.

That 15 kg of fat equates to 135,000 Calories, or the Calories in 950 12 oz Coke cans (142 Calories each), which would bring in a total of US$19 or £12 in tax. Even the proposed UK's 20p per can tax would only raise £200 for that weight gain. The food and drink industry would aggressively oppose such a tax, and even the Scottish Whisky Association has fought against such taxes, because it fears the principle of a health tax on less-healthy drinks. In 2012 the US beverage lobby spent over US$2.8 million to oppose a soda tax in the city of Richmond, California, population 105,400 (*The Economist*, 2013b: 53). The soda sellers wanted to avoid the establishment of any kind of precedent for this tax. A fat tax would be inflationary, and drive shoppers abroad; one reason Denmark cancelled its fat tax in 2012 was that consumers could avoid the tax by shopping in Germany or Sweden. Danish consumer choice was reduced; one blue-cheese manufacturer in Denmark, faced with a 25 per cent rise in the price of their product, cut their range. The Danish tax seemed to favour larger supermarkets against small shops, because the former could spread the tax price rises more thinly across a range of products (*The Economist*, 2012c: 42). Fat taxes are regressive; because the poor eat less healthily than the wealthy, the tax impacts them more. The World Health Organization has warned Romania of the impact on the poor of a food tax where the average income is 350 euros per month and the average household spends half its income on food. Fat taxes may damage the local economy in less affluent areas, the food deserts where there is little local food sold that is not unhealthy. If the poor are deprived of spending power, they may economize on food even more and eat even less healthy foods. The poor without cars, who cannot readily access distant supermarkets, are especially penalized. This raises the question of what exactly we should be taxing to combat obesity: lack of exercise, too much car usage, long work hours preventing healthy cooking? Do we tax overtime, or car manufacturers, or TV and computer sales?

There are also sociological arguments against a fat tax, or its equivalent, a reverse fiscal measure whereby healthy foods are subsidized. Too much meddling in the market system and there will be accusations of the 'nanny state'. What else might the state get involved in: taxes on pet ownership, because they consume resources and may spread disease? Should the state effectively 'pay us to eat well'? If so, any fiscal incentives, subsidies for healthy food or taxes on healthy food, will impact more on the poor than the wealthy, so we are condoning state discrimination between rich and poor, leaving the latter with autonomy but regulating, coercing, the former. Once we start rewarding 'good' behaviour (which is equivalent to penalizing bad), we may be committed to this course of action forever, because once the incentives are removed then good behaviour could easily revert. Moreover, rewarding a shift from bad to good behaviour may be unfair on those who were good to begin with, and could be seen as a reward for previous bad behaviour; so state or health service rewards for losing weight, for example, may be morally wrong. If such 'rewards' for good are wrong, then perhaps so are 'penalties' for bad, such as refusing some health therapies for the overweight; is the role of the health service simply to cure disease, or to change lifestyles too? Instituting a financial reward for 'doing good' may crowd out moral considerations, even to the point where immoral, or unhealthy, choices simply become simply a financial transaction; one buys 'good' as one might purchase a coat, or not. In *Freakonomics* (Levitt and Dubner, 2005: 15–19), an Israeli crèche was regularly inconvenienced by the late arrival of parents picking up their offspring at the end of the day; at least one carer had to stay late, looking after anxious children, so a US$3 fine per late arrival was added to the US$380 monthly care fees. Within a few weeks, the number of late pick-ups had doubled. The fine had replaced moral guilt with an affordable economic penalty. When the lateness fine was revoked, the high number of late pick-ups stayed high. Guilt had been eliminated and there was now no financial penalty. Similarly, paying for donating blood reduces the number of donors, because a good deed is converted into a painful way of earning a few dollars, and the pain and inconvenience are not worth it (Levitt and Dubner, 2005: 20). If the payment was large, the dark side of incentivization would emerge; people would steal blood, pass off pig blood as their own, damage their health by over-donating, creating societal costs in the form of medical bills.

As noted in Chapter 6, demand choices are often heavily influenced by short-term factors. People greatly prefer the benefits of food now, taste, sweetness, pleasure, against some uncertain extra life expectancy, and young people expect to live for many more years anyway. The 'nudges' of good looks derived from a carotene-rich diet may have more impact on diet; other emotional nudges might include a longer life with your children; smokers have been incentivized to give up, not through benefits to their own health but through lessening the risk to their partner's or children's health, or even their pet's well-being. Interestingly, non-financial or indirectly financial incentives seem to work better. These incentives range from discounts on health insurance for the non-obese, cheaper holidays if you regularly visit the gym or lose weight, or distributing vouchers that give discounts on fresh fruit and vegetables. From a fiscal viewpoint, these incentives are often less costly to the government. In the UK, the Low Income Project Team proposed (1996) giving tax exemptions on profits made from home sales of fresh produce, and more significantly, allowing benefits recipients to keep any gains from such sales without loss of benefit. The UK benefits system has been criticized for stifling entrepreneurism among claimants, which might have led to more permanent employment, by deducting almost pound for pound any income the claimant receives from other sources. Allowing claimants to boost their income by sales of produce from their gardens would probably not cost the UK government a huge amount, but there would be worries that this could open up a sort of 'money laundering' where other undeclared income could be hidden this way.

Restricting advertising

If advertising did not have a powerful influence on consumption choices, developed countries would not be spending over 2 per cent of their GDP on this industry. Unfortunately, because the greatest profits in the food industry lie in less-healthy processed foods, that is where the majority of advertising is directed. In 2007 the UK's Food Standards Agency criticized the use of cartoon characters such as Bratz dolls, the Simpsons, Spiderman and characters from the film *Flushed Away* to promote the consumption of HFSS foods by children. Because advertising is so successful at altering consumer psychology it can have undesirable social side-effects; Bratz dolls are highly sexualized, with pouting lipsticked mouths, blonde bouffant hair, large eyelashes, long legs and prominent breasts. These dolls have contributed to the 'adultizing' of children and reducing parental influence, including parental influence on children's diet. Consumer behaviour is far from simple, and regulating advertising can have unintended side-effects. One example of this is the heavy regulation of alcohol advertising, which forced the alcohol advertising industry to become far more sophisticated in its tactics, to the point where some adverts have become iconic much-watched pieces in their own right. For example, the Guinness 2013 'Clock' advert with its hauntingly classical music, black and white imagery and nostalgia appeal, by June 2013 had been watched over 1.1 million times on YouTube. In 2006 the UK's TV watchdog Ofcom banned junk food advertisements from programmes broadcast before the 9 p.m. watershed if over 23 per cent of the programme's audience was aged under 16. This ban caught *The Simpsons* because 27 per cent of its 2.1 million viewers, total 567,000, were aged under 16. However, junk food ads could still be shown during *Coronation Street* because just 9 per cent of its 10 million viewers, total 900,000, were aged under 16. It is not hard to guess which programme a junk food manufacturer aiming at young children would choose to advertise on. Other programmes, such as *I'm a Celebrity Get Me Out Of Here*, *The Bill* and *Emmerdale*, also escaped the ban, despite having many younger viewers. Children's toys are often a major marketing feature of fast food restaurants; generally a series is produced, creating a 'swap-market' within schools and encouraging children to demand further visits to the restaurant to acquire the full set. The swap market effectively gets children doing (unpaid) advertising work. In 1999 McDonald's produced no fewer than 80 different types of 'Furby', a cute looking speaking robot resembling a cross between an owl and a hamster, with multiple variations in fur colour, beak, eyes, tummy, paws and ears. Fast food restaurants frequently link with the children's film industry and the computer games industry as well as amusement parks like Disney; games, toys or sets of swap cards are given away at these venues. Pokemon Cards, Tamagotchis, Teenie Beanie Babies and Cabbage Patch Kids all induce children into free marketing initiatives for the film, toy, gaming and fast food industries together (Schlosser, 2002: 47).

The supreme cartoon fast food character is of course that happy avuncular clown Ronald McDonald. In Beijing, schoolchildren told researchers that they liked 'Uncle McDonald' because he was 'funny, gentle, kind, he understood children's hearts'. Quite an achievement for a fictional character, though he did conquer the former USSR.

Advertising can also be used to steer consumers towards more healthy food choices, although a frequent complaint by health-conscious parents is that the bulk of TV adverts, especially those aimed at children, are for unhealthy foods. The cartoon character Popeye was used in the 1920s in the USA to make children want to eat spinach. In 2003 the Food Dudes quartet of kids, fighting a galactic war against General Junk, promoted fresh produce consumption in British schools. Children in schools in northern England were greeted by a giant vegetable called Chris P. Carrott, an initiative designed by People for the Ethical Treatment of Animals in an imitative to combat obesity and promote vegetarianism. However, most food adverts promote less healthy items. In 2000 28 per cent of the UK food advertising budget was spent on promoting HFSS foods such as cereal bars, biscuits, crisps and other snacks, while less than 1 per cent went on promoting fresh fruit and vegetables; 99 per cent of adverts during UK children's programmes were for HFSS foods (Food, 2003: 30). In 2003 £2.8 million was spent on advertising fresh fruit and £1.2 million on advertising fresh vegetables, against £15.2 million on confectionery adverts. In the USA in 1997, food manufacturers spent US$7 billion on advertising and food retailers and restaurants spent a further US$4 billion. The total, US$11 billion, was second only to the total ad-spend by the automotive industry (French et al., 2001). Of this US$11 billion, US$227 million was spent by Coca Cola, US$572 million by McDonald's and US$408 million by Burger King. This compares with US$30 million spent on the 'milk mustache' and 'get milk' campaigns, or the US$1 million spent by the National Institute of Health and the National Cancer Institute to promote Five-a-Day. In 1997 USDA spent a total of US$333 million on nutrition education. Ireland and France are considering banning HFSS food adverts aimed at children unless accompanied by a health warning, but there are doubts about the efficacy of these warnings.

Planning laws and retailing

Preserving physical access to local green retailing has been the aim of a number of legal planning initiatives. In the UK, there are five grades of usage for retail premises, which are quite widely drafted, namely:

A1 = shops: includes all shops; e.g. undertakers, hairdressers, greengrocers, sandwich bars, dry cleaners, Internet cafés.

A2 = Financial and professional services: includes banks, estate agents and betting shops.

A3 = Restaurants and cafés.
A4 = Drinking establishments.
A5 = Hot food takeaways.

An A1 shop can change without planning permission from a greengrocer or butcher to a coffee shop, hairdressing salon, sandwich shop or Internet café, something the Greater London Authority (2010) would like to prevent. Under the present system, banks can change to betting shops because both are 'financial services', and banks have closed as customers migrate to Internet banking. However, the substitution of a betting shop for a bank can erode the character of an area, remove access to cash for some shoppers, and generally accelerate the closure of everyday food stores. Changing shop sizes can affect retail choice; some planners have suggested banning the amalgamation of units into one large shop, when the rent may become unaffordable to an independent grocer; however, many independent general grocers have only survived by gaining the economies of scale that come with a larger premises. If planners intervene to 'freeze' retail units in one usage, the shop may become a charity shop or just lie empty. The UK has also promoted FFV sales by independent retailers through the Change 4 Life initiative; from 2009 shops could apply for grants to install shelves and chiller cabinets to stock fresh produce. The scheme also funded advertising, and participating shops saw profits rise by up to a fifth; however, by July 2009 88 shops had joined, as against target of 120 by May 2009. Furthermore, by 2013 many retailers had ceased holding fresh vegetables because sales were low, and the chiller cabinets now house sandwiches, pre-packed meats and alcoholic drinks. Meanwhile the Countryside Agency and the Vital Villages organization will help communities set up local grocery shops, selling locally produced foods and boosting local employment; again the issue is how to make sales of such foods profitable and self-sustaining in the long run. The demand side, consumer choices and lifestyles, needs to be tackled as well as the supply side.

More localized schemes include Chicago's plan (2012) to require any retailer with multiple mobile vegetable stalls to operate at least half of them in areas designated as food deserts, so everyone in Chicago is within 1 mile (1.6 km) of an FFV retailer; stallholders have expressed concerns that this would put some of them at risk of street robbery and assault. In the UK, Leicestershire Council runs (2013) classes teaching residents the benefits of home cooking and how to make best use of leftover food. There are a huge number of disparate schemes, operating for a while then lapsing, with varied aims, and a key issue must be how to coordinate these nationally and monitor the results in a standardized way to identify best practice and maintain funding for the successful initiatives. However, in some areas, existing laws actually militate against FFV provision. In Cape Town, South Africa, by-laws require food retailers to obtain a permit only if they sell perishable food, so many avoid this by not selling such foods: the so-called 'tuck shops'. Healthier FFV is sold by mobile traders, using small trucks (bakkies), but these are less accessible and offer a smaller product range than fixed shops could.

Regulating sugar as we do harmful drugs

Robert Lustig, professor of paediatrics at the University of California, has noted (*New Scientist*, 2011c) that we do not generally regulate substances that are harmful but not (often) abused, like bleach or glue. We do not regulate substances that are abused but not harmful, like coffee. We only regulate if the substance is both harmful *and* abused, like alcohol, drugs or cigarettes. Lustig proposes that sugar should be in this last category. Sugar alters brain chemistry in similar ways to addictive drugs (*New Scientist*, 2010: 38–41). The hallmark of addiction is when a new substance causes dopamine release in the brain, the dopamine creates a sense of pleasure, and subsequent consumption of that substance causes further dopamine surges. In non-addictive situations, substances like food do not stimulate excess dopamine production. Cocaine addicts shown a bag of white powder, even after months without cocaine usage, still get a dopamine release and desire the powder they have just seen. Some obese people exhibit dopamine surges when they see food, and sugar can have the same effect on the brain. An alternative addiction pathway is when habituation occurs and subsequent substance intake fails to produce the same dopamine release (pleasure sensation) as earlier, or dopamine receptors have become desensitized, so more must be consumed to achieve the pleasure as before. HFSS food can produce an addiction effect via either of these pathways.

Dietary advice

Rather than imposing regulations, on advertising, on property usage, or on what substances people may consume, a free market-oriented government may prefer advice schemes that leave it to individual, hopefully informed, choice, as to what to eat. Dietary advice schemes are usually communicated to the public via food labelling, as that is where a consumption decision is made, although further material can be made available at healthcare points such as doctors' surgeries. Like regulatory schemes, dietary advice schemes are open to misuse and misinterpretation. Traffic Lights are the simplest system, using a universal code of red = bad, green = good, and amber = intermediate. Traffic Lights are supported by a range of retailers, including Sainsbury, Marks & Spencer, Waitrose, Asda and the Co-op. Using a standard 100 gram portion of food, Traffic Lights give a unidimensional rating to the foodstuff. This 100 g standard is the major flaw with Traffic Lights because it demonizes foods that are usually eaten in smaller amounts; cheese is typically consumed in 30 g pieces, but 100 g of cheese is high in fat and salt. Marmite, if consumed 100 g at once, would deliver 9.8 g of salt, compared to the recommended daily amount of 6 g, but a typical serving contains just 0.4 g of salt. Ketchup also looks bad under the 100 g standards, and foods with natural, healthier, complex sugars like figs, raisins and honey get a red light because the scheme does not distinguish between different types of sugar. However, Diet Coke gets a Green Light because it is low in sugar, fat and salt.

The Guideline Daily Allowance (GDA) scheme aims to inform consumers how much of various foods they should be consuming per day. GDAs are favoured by the UK's Food and Drink Federation, by several large food manufacturers and also by some retailers, including Masterfoods, Nestlé, Tesco and Somerfield. GDAs appeal to some consumers as they are more informative than Traffic Lights, but the food industry likes them because unlike Traffic Lights nothing is labelled as explicitly 'red' or 'bad'. GDAs can be skewed by misuse of 'portion size'. For example the GDA system assumes a typical serving of cereal is 30 g but some 7-year-olds typically consume 43 g at a sitting. For Ricicles, a 30 g portion gives 13 per cent of the adult GDA for sugar, but Ricicles is more often eaten by children, for whom 30 g delivers 24 per cent of the sugar GDA. Sustain preferred Traffic Lights, saying GDAs were too complex for consumers, as did the British Heart Foundation. However, in 2010 the European Parliament voted against Traffic Lights and in favour of GDAs after lobbying by the food industry. An alternative scheme (available at www.nuval.com) uses values calculated by Yale University to give a nutrition point score from 0 (least healthy) to 100 (healthiest) for a range of common foods; broccoli scores 100 and apples 96, but milk chocolate scores 3. A similar system to Yale's is the Stars System, rating healthy foods as three and unhealthy as no stars, with one or two for those in between. The merit of Yale and Stars is that it rewards for good (more points, stars), rather than demonizing for bad (red light); people respond better to positive than to negative messages. There are also a range of visual schemes, based upon a picture of a plate divided into segments or a pyramid with the foods one should consume the most of (grains, fruit and vegetables) at the broad base and those to be eaten sparingly (sugar, sweets) at the point. These graphics include the Food Pyramid and My Plate. Some fast food restaurants have from 2011 joined a voluntary scheme to display the calorie counts of their menu items; participants include Pizza Hut, Burger King, Starbucks, Pret a Manger and Kentucky Fried Chicken. However, Pizza Express, Subway, Domino's, Nandos, Costa Coffee and Café Nero, are yet (2013) to join. However, the efficacy of this scheme may be reduced if calorie counts are displayed on the restaurant's website or on a leaflet in the seating area but not at the counter; also if the Calories are listed separately for each item, e.g. for the cheese, the burger, the bread, but not altogether for the whole order.

If labelling foods produced by some process unknown to the consumer is unreliable, an alternative might be to persuade people to grow their own food. This is the principle behind the urban agriculture or allotments movement, which is discussed in the next section.

Urban agriculture and allotments. *One man gathering firewood is pathetic. Ten thousand men gathering firewood can overthrow a city*

Farming is full of ironies. Rural agriculture gave us cities; the now-peaceful countryside was the origin of armies and wars. Another irony is that as farming has become more industrialized, factory-like, many of the urban majority of humanity feel ever more disconnected from the land. Food that nature could never have produced, visitor-hostile 'minimal-disease' farms set in huge open bleak prairie fields, and the near-vanishing of farm employment may all have contributed to this disconnect. Yet city dwellers can readily rediscover the roots of their food through urban agriculture. Ashram Acres, in the city of Birmingham, England, epitomizes many of the merits of urban agriculture. Set up in 1981 (Cressey, 1988), its aim was to utilize the agricultural expertise of local migrants from South Asia, the Caribbean and Ireland. Ashram Acres provides raised compost beds under low-cost polythene greenhouses so produce can be grown free of urban pollution. Culturally appropriate vegetables including cucumber, coriander and okra provide a low-cost alternative to shops, and any surplus can be sold, generating cash for the local economy. Livestock such as goats clear weeds, produce manure as fertilizer and give milk, and food miles are minimal. Urban greenery cools the city; it soaks up carbon dioxide from cars and people (and converts it back into food). Any city plant life is welcome in this respect, even 'green bridges' or 'green corridors' where disused railways or wide walkways over main roads are planted to resemble gardens; but why not use such space to grow food too? A similar project also in Birmingham, the Edible Eastside Café, provides land to grow fresh produce, also a community owned café and shop where fruit and vegetables can be sold, or meals made from these items served to customers. In London, UK, Spitalfields City Farm, begun in 1978 on 1.3 acres (0.5 hectares) of old railway sidings, replaced allotment land lost to developers, and also hosts educational tours for schoolchildren. The High Line, in Manhattan, New York, is a linear garden reclaimed from a disused rail track. The USA also has Community Gardens which for a rent of US$15–20 a year, including plants, tools and water, provides participants with fresh fruit and vegetables far cheaper than shop prices. In a deprived suburb of San Francisco the local community has, with the help of city government, formed SLUG (San Francisco League of Urban Gardeners) where foods such as tomatoes, red chard and string beans are grown in six foot square planter boxes; foods unobtainable in expensive local convenience stores (Cook and Rodgers, 1999: 315). Schools also often have space for vegetable growing; the benefits of this, educational and more, are discussed below.

Allotments in their modern form were pioneered in Germany in the nineteenth century, although in Britain the concept goes back to the reign of Queen Elizabeth I when tenant farmers were given plots of land to compensate for

Table 7.4 UK allotment numbers, 1909–2010

Year	*UK allotment numbers*	*Total area (hectares)*	*Average allotment size (square metres)*
1909	58,648	7,049	1,210
1914	130,526	13,566	1,039
1920	1,330,000	74,866	563
1931	608,286		
1937	589,015		
1944	1,750,000		
1970	500,000		
1978	480,000		
1997	300,000		
2010	330,000	7,425	225

Source: Author's research.

the enclosure of common land. In the 1800s urban workers rented garden plots on the edge of the newly industrializing cities; for example the Guinea Gardens of Birmingham. This arrangement of townsfolk renting peri-urban garden plots at a distance from their homes still operates today in Danish and German cities, and in St Petersburg in Russia. In 1908 the UK passed the Small Holdings and Allotments Act, producing a large increase in the number of British allotments. Trends in allotment numbers are shown in Table 7.4.

The UK's allotments came into their own at a period of artificially created food shortage, during the U-boat blockade of food imports to Britain in World War Two. During this conflict the British Minister for Agriculture, Robert Hudson, spoke on the radio about the potential to produce food from allotments, saying 'Let Dig for Victory be the matter for every man and woman capable of digging an allotment in their spare time.' Wasteland, parks, even private lawns, were given over to agriculture. Propaganda played a part; vicars were urged to extol the virtues of vegetable growing in their sermons, millions of leaflets were distributed, and prizes were organized for the best vegetables and even the best compost heap. In 1943, the US had 'Victory Gardens', and people were encouraged to grow their own food to free up distribution channels (Thone, 1943). However, by 1997, urban sprawl, driven not just by population growth but also by an increase in single person households and by the desire for houses with gardens rather than terraced yards, or flats, consumed much allotment land. However, an interest in organic food, rising food prices, and TV shows promoting home-grown food have slowed this decline, but financial pressures on allotments remain. Rents (2010) for an allotment were typically £40 a year; with discounts for the unwaged and retired. Unless allotment rents rise by a factor of 20, it is more economic to build on them. The typical annual allotment rent of £30 for 250 square metres, capitalized at an interest rate of 2 per cent, gives a value per hectare of £(30 x 1 / .02 x 10,000 / 250) or £60,000 per hectare. This compares to

UK development land prices of £1,000,000 to £3,000,000 outside London in 2011 (Valuation Office Agency, 2011). The price differential was similar for allotment versus development land prices in Lincolnshire in 2002 (Shaw, 2004: 29). Once allotment land is developed, the council receives a stream of income from the Council Tax (local UK property tax) of around £1,500 for a four-bedroom house, which can be erected (including associated garden and roads) on the land from just two allotments (annual rent £60). If interest rates rise/fall, the capital value of the allotment land then falls/rises, but likewise development land prices fall/rise, so allotment land usage is always at a financial disadvantage whatever the level of interest rates. However, if one allotment can prevent obesity in three people in a family, the health savings to the government could be £1,500 a year, and the allotment is now competitive in cost terms with development land. Planning is a crucial element; Brighton and Hove Planning Department encourages all developers to allow spaces for urban horticulture. Legal regulations may have to be amended; the US city of Chicago, in 2011, fully legalized urban agriculture, raising size limits on community gardens. This was in response to the initiative on food deserts by Michelle Obama, First Lady. In the UK, housing associations, which provide affordable rented accommodation for the less-affluent, frequently have spare land that can be utilized for allotments; little-used and neglected lawns between blocks of flats, or spare ground behind garage blocks for example. In London, UK, the East London Family Project is promoting new allotment development. However, there are social issues to be tackled, from littering to theft of plants and arranging weeding rotas.

The benefits of schemes like Ashram Acres go far beyond food and economics. Local schoolchildren can make educational visits to see how cheese, milk, honey and yoghurt are actually made. Urban agriculture provides exercise, and gardening is good therapy, both physical and mental; the Restore Project in Oxford uses gardening as a means to help those with learning difficulties. The environment benefits as food miles are reduced and urban green spaces soak up rainwater, lessening flood risks. The health of the community also benefits; allotment plots do not have fences, you garden with other people, swapping tips and community news. This contrasts with the 'green deserts' of suburban manicured lawns where neighbours tend their gardens in solitude, in competition with each other. Community gardens increase civic pride, create a feel of shared ownership in and responsibility for the area, and bond the community together, as young and old, and different ethnic communities work together. Growing allotment food may even be seen as a protest against capitalism, a lifestyle choice, a rejection of capitalist produced and retailed food (Bell and Valentine, 1997: 86).

Medical agencies. *Doctoring your food*

A range of healthy-eating promotion schemes have been initiated by health providers in parts of the UK. Doctors in Liverpool gave out vouchers, redeemable at local Co-op stores, for £6 worth of fruit and vegetables; the 2001 scheme appeared to work well as it encouraged spending on these foods of considerably more than the £6 voucher value. The NHS would recoup this cost in future reduced healthcare bills. In 2009 the Eastern and Coastal Kent Primary Care Trust tried a 'Pounds for Pounds' scheme that paid people to lose weight, with payments going up to £425; there was some initial success with one-quarter of the participants, those who stayed the course, losing an average of 25 lb (11 kg); however, two-thirds of patients failed to achieve their desired weight loss. In keeping with the discussion above concerning the negative moral hazard effects of monetizing rewards, perhaps this result was not unexpected. Britain's NHS has also attempted consumer-behaviour modifying initiatives such as the mandometer or talking plate, a £1,500 device that measures how fast food is being taken off the plate and, if too quickly, asks the diner to eat more slowly; the plate is connected to a computer screen showing actual and healthy eating rates. At a more local level the NHS hosts seminars on healthy eating, and doctors visit shops to give advice on diet. However, as with the FFV retail promotion schemes described earlier, anecdotal evidence from shopkeepers suggests at best patchy success; again more joined-up schemes with continuous standardized monitoring might reveal best practice for the future.

Educational initiatives

Nursery schools

Schools have considerable power to influence the diet of their pupils. The basic function of a school is to teach, but food and diet can be interwoven into the curriculum in many ways. Usually schools will have some spare land (it can be just a few square metres or even a window box) to grow vegetables. Some schools in the USA have stacked soil boxes up the wall to make a vertical garden or 'food wall'. Vegetables from all over the world can be cultivated. The process of seeding, growing, harvesting and even selling these vegetables can feed into lessons on art, biology, chemistry, economics, environmental studies, geography, history, languages, linguistics, marketing, mathematics, religious education, sociology, world cultures and zoology (animal nutrition and plant parasites). Cooking itself can and should be on the curriculum; simple meals, not elaborate *Masterchef* style food that makes household meal preparation seem an arcane black art, too hard to master. Critser (2003: 162) suggests getting schoolchildren to calculate (in front of the class) the nutritional benefits or disbenefits of certain foods. In 1988 the United Kingdom's new National Curriculum resulted in 'home economics' being replaced by 'food technology'; the emphasis shifted from teaching household meal preparation towards the design and technology of food and its packaging and marketing. In 1993 cooking dropped off the British school curriculum altogether (Caraher et al., 1999) as teaching focused more on core subjects such as maths and science. Schools still hosted cookery lessons, but after hours, for young single adults; the emphasis was on 'health' rather than on 'household skills'. Schools and parents can get together through the Parent–Teacher Association to continue such food initiatives in the home environment and integrate with school programmes. In 2008 cookery lessons made a (partial) comeback to British schools; 11- to 16-year-olds could earn a 'Licence to Cook' certificate, but the scheme was not compulsory for schools, did not contribute to formal qualifications, and schools could run it in school hours or as an after school activity.

Better school canteens

Besides teaching, schools are food providers. In 2006 the New Labour government in Britain did act to enforce higher nutritional standards in school canteens, a move inspired in no small way by the efforts of Jamie Oliver and his 'Ministry of Food'. Under these standards, school lunches were to include oily fish at least once a week, fried food was to be served no more than twice a week, and meals should include at least two portions of fresh fruit and/or vegetables. Junk food and sugary drinks were banned from school vending machines. In 2006 Jamie Oliver took on the task of improving the diet of schoolchildren in the less-affluent Yorkshire town of Rotherham. At Rawmarsh, in Rotherham, Jamie Oliver, who famously demonized Turkey Twizzlers (strips of processed turkey meat, with over 20 per cent fat content), ensured the canteen served healthy low-fat items; this did not gain universal approval from the children but they were forbidden from leaving the school grounds to buy food elsewhere. The parents did not entirely approve either; there were reports of them turning up at the locked school gates with supermarket trolleys containing sandwiches, fish and chips, pizzas, pies, burgers and fizzy drinks. The parents would 'take orders' during the morning break and return at lunchtime. Parental concerns included:

1. Children becoming 'picky' and changing their tastes towards (more expensive) vegetables, away from the cheap fatty sugary food they got at home. Children were no longer getting the 'bulk' (sugar and fat) at school so would demand more food at home, and costs to parents would rise.
2. If parents did try and emulate Jamie Oliver's meals at home, the ingredients would be unobtainable in local shops; if they try and grow, for example, basil in window boxes, then they would be ostracized as 'different' by neighbours, and parents might lack the skills to prepare and cook these ingredients.
3. A class issue: 'Why is this upper-middle class guy from Hampstead telling us what to eat?'

Once again, economics, affordability, is crucial. School lunches are typically priced at between £1.60 and £2.10 whereas a meal at a local takeaway can be had for £1.00, and filling up on sweets for 75p is even cheaper, with more Calories. When North Somerset Council subsidized all school meals, reducing the cost at £1.00, take-up rose sharply. Over a school year, that daily saving would add up to £190, over a week's take-home pay for some lower-wage parents. There are free school meals in the UK but not all the children of low-income parents receive them; in 2008 a million pupils from poor homes did not get these meals; whereas 25 per cent of pupils come from households below the poverty line, only 14 per cent get free school lunches. In 2013 one million children received these meals; a further 200,000 were registered to receive them but did not eat them, and 300,000 children were entitled to register for them but had not signed up. In some households, children have to alternate between who gets the school meal each day. Schools are facing financial issues including, in some areas, a rising number of pupils wanting school lunch, posing logistical problems and resulting in staggered lunch breaks, while elsewhere the emphasis on healthy lunches results in less take-up and less revenue to the school, making the canteen uneconomic. Schools may face higher kitchen staff training costs to produce this healthier food. Overall the number of pupils eating school lunches fell from 1.45 million in 2004/5 to 1.2 million in 2006/7, a drift away from the UK government's target of 1.75 million.

Providing healthy school meals is only part of the battle to get pupils to eat better; other considerations include the choice set; some canteens offer only one healthy option but a choice of less healthy meals (Jackson, 2003: 61). Peeling fruit to make it more convenient to eat, and catering for varying school subcultures where some foods are not 'in' may encourage healthier eating. In some schools the canteen is seen as smelly, dirty, busy, not relaxing (Groves, 2003: 15), so making the canteen more attractive can contribute to a healthy diet. School pupils can be encouraged to 'own' the school lunch by having a say in it, while opportunities to leave school to obtain other food should be restricted. However, initiatives such as replacing plastic plates with ceramic crockery (a more attractive eating experience) creates costs if they are broken, and they may be harder to wash, or increased weight of crockery or metal cutlery (as opposed to plastic knives and forks) creates logistical issues for canteen staff. Introducing a swipe card payment system removes the stigma of being in obvious receipt of free meals, which as noted earlier may lead to pupils eligible for such meals bringing in unhealthy lunchbox meals of crisps, biscuits, pies or similar. Swipe cards can also gather information about what a child has eaten and how healthily. Alternatively all school meals could be free; the cost would be recouped in future lower health costs. The liking for unfamiliar fruit and vegetables can be increased by having taster sessions. As little as three tastings can create liking for a fruit item; vegetables may require more exposure sessions to get children to like them (Horne et al., 2004). School canteens may provide bowls of fruit in the canteen area as well as the meals (Lakkakula et al., 2010). Some schools provide breakfast as well as lunch for their pupils, because often pupils from less affluent households go to school with no breakfast, and are then tired, irritable and disruptive all morning. Eating breakfast will reduce obesity because unhealthy mid-morning snacking is then much less likely. All this assumes that there is a school canteen; when the UK's Building Schools for the Future Programme was initiated by New Labour in 2005, some 3,500 of the UK's schools had no meal preparation facilities; many others had kitchen areas that were too small or outdated. However when the Conservative–Liberal coalition won the 2010 election, this programme was curtailed, although schools that had already signed building contracts were safe. There was also a possibility of relaxing school lunch nutritional standards, to save money in the recent recession. Vending machines in schools can be used to sell healthier food items such as sandwiches, yoghurt or fruit; however, many such machines sell sugary fizzy drinks, chocolate or crisps. The issue is one of economics; a vending machine selling unhealthy snacks from a large food producer can yield a payment of £20,000 to the school. However, removing the machine, while reducing school income, may result in fewer behavioural problems and truancy. Similarly, providing better food in another institutional environment, prison, also improves the behaviour of inmates. To deter consumption of fizzy drinks, some schools have obtained extracted teeth from dentists and put them in a glass of the drink; pupils love watching the tooth go rotten and dissolve with a week or two. While this is not exactly a dietary health message it will improve eating habits.

Pre-school, children at nurseries would benefit from legal minimum standards for meals. Some nurseries feed their charges junk food, chips, sweets and chocolate, which could be replaced by fruit and vegetable purees. As we have seen, early eating habits are crucial for healthy diet later in life. Parents who use nursery services are generally choosing to do so in order that they can work and make a financial gain. Therefore it would be harder for them to complain, as did the Rotherham parents, that their children's dietary preferences are being raised beyond their financial means. Nursery costs would rise but perhaps not significantly from their (2010) average of £31 a day; staff would require minimum cooking skills, such as boiling broccoli or carrots and peeling some fruit. School-based initiatives in other countries include the *semaine du goût* in France; a week of food tasting and cooking held annually to get children interested in food and taste. In America a facet of First Lady Michelle Obama's Let's Move initiative to tackle food deserts was the 2012 Chefs Move To Schools Project, where professional chefs were paired up with schools, and gave suggestions on canteen menu items and taught students about nutrition and cooking. Farms, too, were linked with schools in the Farm to School Program; schools source fresh produce from local farms and students learn about farming techniques and seasonal foods. California has the Edible Schoolyard Project teaching students how to grow fresh produce sustainably; the students not only get free food but also learn about nutrition and biology.

Corporate initiatives. *Healthy profits*

The private sector can also play a role in improving food access for the disadvantaged, and even find profit there. Where profits are low or absent, the principle of Corporate Social Responsibility (CSR) may apply – that business should not just exist to make money for the shareholders, but also put something back into the community, gaining a good reputation in so doing, which itself attracts more business. The Co-op chain in Britain positions itself as a Fairtrade ethical store, and gains custom this way, even though its prices are not especially low. The most direct way for the private sector to improve food access for the less affluent is to open supermarkets close to where they live, which begs the question, why are supermarkets not already in these areas? After all, poorer inner city areas are densely populated and are not exactly devoid of shops. In America as in Britain these areas have many convenience stores and large numbers of ethnic minority-oriented shops catering to a wide variety of national groups.

There are several reasons why the inner city environment is not totally suited to the business model of the large supermarkets.

- Less affluent consumers tend to buy mostly food (Engel's Law) whereas supermarkets increasingly find most profit in non-food lines. Also the poorer the consumer the fewer luxury food lines they buy; again this is where supermarket profits lie
- Less affluent consumers only buy small amounts at a time, as they can afford it. Inner city residents may live in cramped accommodation with no room for a large fridge or freezer, so they will not buy the large package sizes the supermarkets can get the best economies of scale with.
- In addition to small purchases, the less affluent have 'lumpy' food buying habits, purchasing food as and when they can afford to. When money is short, rent and utilities payments come first; hunger, or using a food bank, is preferable to eviction or having the power cut off. Wealthier outer suburbs give a smoother buying pattern, facilitating the 'just-in-time' deliveries supermarkets prefer (Gottlieb et al., 1996).
- Crime levels, including shoplifting, are higher in some less affluent areas. Crime eats up the profits from a larger amount of turnover if margins are low, as they typically are with larger supermarket chains. With vandalism such as broken windows, a small shop may simply board up the window and carry on, whereas a supermarket chain must keep up appearances for the sake of the brand; again this 'cancels' large amounts of turnover, making the branch seem more uneconomic. The Tesco Express in St Mary's, a deprived inner city part of Southampton, UK, employs a security guard, a feature not seen at wealthier branches.
- Low vehicle ownership may mean customers use the supermarket trolley to transport purchases home; the magnetic 'barrier' can be overcome by lifting the trolley's back wheels. Lost trolleys can cost a supermarket around US$100,000 annually in replacement and recovery costs.

- Lack of suitable sites. The fact that inner city areas are densely populated, with many small fragmented landholdings, makes assembling the large site needed for a supermarket with economies of scale difficult. Where older supermarkets have vacated an inner city site, as many did in the 1970s and 1980s, they may place a restrictive covenant on the site precluding future retail use by a competitor (Eckert and Shetty, 2011). As noted in Chapter 5, these sites are often too small for modern supermarkets anyway.
- Similarly, densely built congested inner city areas may hinder delivery, especially in just-in-time mode. This means retaining more stock to avoid stock-outs, raising costs and wastage.
- Small independent inner city stores, especially if run by ethnic minority proprietors, may use unpaid family labour. This undercuts supermarkets who must pay wages and other employee costs.
- Staff training may be costlier in areas where educational achievements are lower, partly because the more able teachers have left for schools in nicer areas. Other staff costs such as turnover may also be higher because once an unemployed person has a job record, they will try and get a job and a house, in a better locale.
- The ethnic diversity of many inner city areas may undermine the supermarket model by presenting a fragmented market of numerous national groups and races, each of whom has their own distinct food demands. Such a market may be better served by many small retailers.
- Especially in the USA, inner city areas abandoned by the wealthy, and with a high welfare bill, may impose higher property taxes than are faced by retailers in leafier suburban locations.

However the smaller-scale formats developed by UK chains such as Tesco have meant that inner city locations present less of a profits barrier than they once did, and these districts are gradually being penetrated by such neighbourhood supermarkets. Additionally there are less affluent parts of Britain's outer suburbs, typically the large council estates built in the 1950s and 1960s, where the problems described above have less impact; these estates have reasonable road connections, and the market is less ethnically fragmented. The Sainsbury's supermarket that opened on the deprived Castle Vale estate in Birmingham, UK, in 2000 raised the civic pride in the area considerably as well as providing much-needed jobs. In 1998 Tesco began construction of a large 9,700 square metre superstore in the deprived Seacroft area of Leeds (UK), replacing a dilapidated 1964 mall where most of the shops had closed; Tesco made efforts to employ local people. Overall consumption of FFV rose slightly from 2.88 to 2.92 portions a day among the lowest FFV consumers; the figure rose from 0.59 to 1.40 portions daily (Wrigley et al., 2002). In November 2008 the UK's Department for Health started a scheme whereby smaller grocery stores were given matching funds for any investment they made in FFV retail, for example by installing chiller cabinets or producing and distributing marketing materials. Participating stores were also invited to join other schemes such as cooking clubs at schools (*The Grocer*, 2009: 28); some stores issued Buy One Get One Free vouchers to local schoolchildren. FFV sales did rise and stores became willing to break bulk on pre-packed FFV items, benefiting people living alone such as pensioners. However, the increased demand was not maintained in some areas and the chiller cabinets now house sandwiches, packed meats, soft drinks or alcoholic beverages.

In the USA in 2011 Wal-Mart announced plans to open up to 300 stores in areas identified by the USDA as food deserts. Wal-Mart's plans were backed by Michelle Obama, and Wal-Mart, faced with flat sales performance at its existing stores, needed new markets. The food deserts initiative would gain the company CSR credibility, perhaps deflecting criticism of the way Wal-Mart squeezed costs, holding down both staff wages and prices to its suppliers. Wal-Mart, with a total payroll of 1.4 million, has been accused of depressing the payrolls of the entire US workforce, which if true would have worsened the food desert issue in the first place. Anti Wal-Mart activism delayed store openings and by May 2012 just 23 new 'food desert' stores had opened. In Chicago, Wal-Mart had promised 'dozens' of new stores; by 2012 just four had appeared in deprived areas, although a new Wal-Mart store also opened in a more affluent part of the city, already served by a Whole Foods and a Jewel-Osco supermarket. Supervalu Inc and Walgreen also pledged to open stores in deprived areas but their programme has likewise slowed. The UK chain Tesco entered the USA in late 2007 and also planned to alleviate food deserts; however, the venture never made a profit and in April 2013 Tesco announced it was pulling out of the USA.

As in the UK, US government initiatives have engaged with smaller retailers to promote FFV sales. The Food Trust loans fridges to shops to facilitate fresh produce sales, and provides advice on lighting and stock positioning (e.g. moving fresh produce to the front of the store), while the Detroit Grocery Incubator Project gives training and advice on operating grocery stores in poorer districts, helping to create jobs in those areas too. The Healthy Neighborhood Stores Alliance (HNSA) is a programme that delivers fresh organic produce to West Oakland's corner mom-and-pop liquor shops. By signing up for HNSA, businesses pay a weekly fee that ranges from $30 to $100, depending on the size of their order. In return, the store receives fresh organic fruits and vegetables, in addition to free weekly delivery and free marketing, which is done through educational tabling events held in front of the business. Where fixed retail investment is not forthcoming, mobile shops may plug the gap, as they often do in the remoter rural areas of Britain and France. The Arcadia Centre for Sustainable Food and Agriculture converted (2012) a 28 foot (8.5 metre) yellow school bus into a highly visible mobile farmers' market, while the Centre for Environmental Farming Systems encourages youths to cycle round with rickshaws laden with fresh produce, as was once done by ice cream vendors, calling them the Produce Ped'lers. Food Stamps are accepted.

Small independent stores make a valuable, but often overlooked contribution to food access; they are small and flexible enough to adapt to local needs in ways that centrally controlled chain stores cannot. In the UK, village stores may offer a local delivery service tailored to the needs of less-mobile consumers in terms of products needed, delivery times, and the type of delivery assistance required. Local shopkeepers develop a close relationship with longstanding older and perhaps less physically able customers and know exactly what brands they like and when they can be delivered. They may even act as a front-line community emergency alert if things appear wrong, the customer does not appear at her usual time or the front door is left open. Local villagers, faced with the closure of their only shop because the proprietor is about to retire and no buyer has come forward, may buy it themselves as a co-operative and run it as a non-profit organization. The schemes at Tibberton (Shropshire) and Yarpole (Herefordshire) are typical; villagers buy a £10 share each, which can raise around £10,000, enough to buy and fit out a mobile prefab building, or rent accommodation in an existing facility such as a pub or church. Labour may be provided on a voluntary basis, or paid, or be compensated in terms of shop produce; on this basis many villages have retained their local grocery store. A church or pub location enhances footfall to the shop. In a good example of environmentally and financially sustainable business synergy, the shop can sell surplus vegetables the pub has not used the previous evening in its restaurant which would otherwise have to be discarded. In Cape Town, South Africa, a dense network of 'informal' or 'spaza' retail outlets exists in poorer districts (Ligthelm, 2005); 'spaza' means 'hidden' in Zulu, referring to the location of these outlets in residential premises. Often little more than a converted shed or lean-to, these shops attempt to assist less-affluent consumers. They break bulk to smaller units than large supermarkets offer, they open longer (for customers on long or unconventional work hours), they sell low-cost lines, and significantly they offer credit. For food-insecure households, bulk buying, even if cheaper per kilo, could force the household into eating only a limited range of foods. These 'spaza' shops informally agree among themselves not to undercut each other, so they all remain in business. However, their fresh-produce offer is limited and when the lower quality of their offerings is allowed for, their prices for some branded goods are rather high. The indigenous 'spaza' sector is also under threat from Somali-owned stores which do not offer credit but are better organized to buy collectively in bulk and therefore attempt to capture market share by undercutting the indigenous retailers.

Small shops may need to diversify their property utilization to survive. Independent shops often have two floors; the upper floor may often lie unused, especially in high street settings. This space may be suitable for residential use, although access may be difficult, parking limited and there may be safety issues for children, including absence of outside play areas, traffic and delivery lorries. Property hazards may also arise, such as water from overflowing baths flooding the shop and contents below. Tenants may find the premises noisy and subject to food smells from nearby takeaways. Financially, if this lower-end accommodation is taken by people on housing benefit and the local council owns the shops, the council effectively ends up paying its own rent. However, there are a number of benefits to using space over shops, both to the retailer itself and to wider society. This space may have commercial usage, for example by a small gym, for computer classes, or even by another retailer. A police unit could be housed there to improve local security. Usage of this space may generate more income for the shop, keeping it open. There are also societal benefits. Retail areas are often deserted at night, and mixed uses keep people in the area, so it becomes self-policing, and the presence of tenants or other users generates income for other local businesses, perhaps preventing their closure too. A number of UK towns and cities now have a Living Over The Shop initiative, to promote use of vacant space to house homeless families, for example. Small grocery stores can offer additional services; their small size is a disadvantage regarding economies of scale, but an advantage in terms of business flexibility. Local village grocers may link to local artists and the shop becomes a tourist magnet; the income from arts and crafts sales subsidizes grocery sales. Many small shops act as delivery hubs for goods ordered by email, on eBay, so the recipients do not have to be home for a delivery in the middle of the day. However, food shops may have issues with hygiene, and the parcels need a secure storage area, and not present a trip hazard to customers or staff. In this way the small shops being squeezed by the supermarkets can turn the tables somewhat to their own advantage,

Other companies can benefit from promoting initiatives to improve diet. A 2012 survey, by the breakfast cereal company Weetabix, suggested that breakfast skipping cost the UK economy £300 million annually due to flagging worker productivity in mid-morning. The survey claimed that 59 per cent of British workers do not have a 'substantial' breakfast, and 56 per cent are 'too rushed' to eat any breakfast at all. There is an obvious benefit, commercially and in terms of CSR, for the breakfast cereal companies here. Londoners were the worst for missing this meal, and London Underground in 2006 had a 'Breakfast Brand' promotion (*Marketing Week*, 2006:15) with 300,000 ready to eat breakfast products being given away at tube stations. Again, London Underground had a financial interest here because breakfastless workers were prone to faint on the platform, causing long and costly delays. Large employers would benefit from promoting breakfast, even providing some at work, if the Weetabix figures are correct.

Transport schemes may provide a vital link where shops exist but some consumers cannot easily reach them. We have seen that regular bus services may be too expensive and inflexible, not going near some people's homes. This transport gap can be filled with demand-responsive services like Dial-a-Bus or community minibuses, or combining the postal transport with passenger services. One issue is that awareness of these services by those who would benefit from them can be low, because unlike scheduled buses they do not appear regularly on the same route or have fixed bus stops. Their variable timetable and route means they may not be available exactly when needed, and journey times can be lengthy and unpredictable. However, they can provide a useful missing transport link for the disabled and elderly. Many local councils also operate social car schemes; the passenger can dial anytime for a ride that costs around 35p a mile (2013), somewhat below the average fuel costs (20–25p a mile) plus other costs (around 20p a mile) of a normal car journey. Drivers are volunteers, and the scheme may be subsidized by the National Lottery or other sources. This is considerably cheaper than normal bus services or taxis, and two passengers can share the fare. Users are asked to be reasonable and not over-use the service or demand trips at awkward times. As in the UK, the US Postal Service, by its nature, reaches all areas and has collaborated with local churches to pick up and deliver food to food banks. Donors can leave food bags (non-perishable) out on a Saturday, when less post is being delivered and, like the charity bag system widely used across the UK for other good causes, these bags are delivered free by the Post as a CSR initiative.

Parental initiatives. *Eat up your greens (purples, reds, yellows ...)*

Parents may resort to bribery to get their children to eat healthy but undesired foods such as vegetables. Coercion is another form of bribery, effectively saying 'you will have a better outcome of you eat these vegetables than if you don't'; for example, 'you can only have pudding once you've eaten your main meal', or 'you can only watch TV / play computer games / have your pocket money once you've eaten your greens'. However, both bribery and coercion reinforce a negative image of these foods that lasts well into adulthood. Worse, the parent is using an obesogenic activity as a bribe, making that activity seem desirable. Telling children they cannot leave the table until the plate is clear may engender a habit of eating past the satiety point, taking in excess Calories (Davison and Campbell, 2005: 210). Deceit is another frequently used tactic, hiding the offending food item in amongst more palatable foods. Mothers have been known to hide parsnips in rhubarb crumble or put chopped carrots in fruit salad; other methods include blending leeks into mashed potato or smothering vegetables in tomato ketchup. One mother reported that, while sprouts in apple pie tasted awful to her, her child wolfed it down (*Yorkshire Post*, 2000: 9). However, deceit, like bribery, gives a negative image to healthy foods. It is better to present vegetables in a positive light, making them attractive, or raising the child's curiosity about them. Parents could grow some fruit or vegetables, involving the children in this task, and like schools, use the exercise to teach a range of subjects; involving the children in cooking these foods and in preparing fruit and vegetables. Children 'cannot learn to like foods to which they have never been exposed' (Davison and Campbell, 2005: 210), so it is helpful to make FFV accessible within the home, by storing them on the lower shelves of fridge, prepared and ready to eat. Vegetables such as cauliflower and carrots are now available in a range of colours besides the usual (despite the efforts of William of Orange), which may attract children to eating them. Fruit that might not be eaten raw can be made into 'smoothies' using a home blender. Families should eat together, as eating microwave meals in shifts will not encourage fruit and vegetable consumption.

Personal coping strategies. *Every little morsel helps*

What we put in our mouths, where and how we obtain that food, and what exercise we take, is ultimately our responsibility, although it can take an almost superhuman effort, sustained for long periods, to resist the consumption and lifestyle changes 'suggested' to us by the marketing executives. Necessity is the mother of invention and some individuals have developed ingenious coping strategies to obtain the foodstuffs they want. In Halton Moor, a deprived suburb of east Leeds, UK, the minority who owned cars drove to an FFV wholesaler 3 km away and brought back produce for unofficial car boot sales. For those who wished to buy their food by more conventional means, ingenious transport-sharing options existed, such as walking or taking the bus to the supermarket but arranging to meet with friends and share a taxi back; like local shops, local taxi drivers would help with unloading shopping for pensioners. Focusing on a positive attitude to food and diet, enjoying the food, reaching weight goals, rather than negative emotions of guilt and worry, assists in maintaining a healthy diet (Schmeichel and Inzlicht, 2013). Such positive emotions assist in 'delayed gratification', better health/lower weight later, rather than indulgence now, whereas stress leads to increased consumption of HFSS foods. Children likewise showed less self-control (as manifested by the time taken to touch a desirable but 'forbidden' toy in a controlled experiment) if the children were sad than if happy (e.g. if told their art had been rejected versus accepted for an exhibition). There are small changes that most of us could make to reduce our calorie intake. We judge the sufficiency of a portion by how much of the plate it covers (which is why restaurants often serve food on a small dish within a plate, to make the portions look more ample), so eating off smaller plates at home reduces our appetite. Delaying meals is effective because hunger is easier to bear if you know you will be eating soon, although fixed schedules for other tasks may make this strategy difficult. Drinking fills the stomach and so produces a feeling of satiety, so long as it is a low calorie drink like water or tea. Walking more, parking further from your destination (which may save on parking charges too), using the stairs rather than the lift or the escalator, or at least leaving the lift two floors below our destination, all help. And if one must watch TV, moving a little, even foot wiggling, uses more Calories than just sitting there and it all adds up over a year.

Small personal lifestyle changes, gaining a few basic cooking skills, a little social organization, can all make a big positive change to our diet and weight. The technology that has greatly increased the global food supply can be made to work for our health as well as against it. In Chapter 8 we examine on a global scale the relative contributions that technology and lifestyle changes can make to create a sustainable healthy food system for the future global 10 billion population of our planet.

8 Decelerate to sustainability

Future of food access. *Feeding the ten thousand (million)*

As we saw in Chapter 1, world population is now just over 7 billion, and projected to peak at around 10 billion in 2050 and fall slowly thereafter; the global food system must prepare to feed almost 50 per cent more people than are alive today. Physically, there should be no world food shortages. The maximum productivity of a hectare of wheat is 825,000 MJ, from 33 million MJ of annual solar energy (Spedding, 1989: 2), which allowing for a 30 per cent human efficiency conversion of food to energy (Lacey, 1991: 26) and a human energy requirement of 3,000 Calories, implies a potential to feed 5,400 people per square kilometre. If 100 million km^2 of the Earth's land area of 149 million km^2 was used for cropland the absolute theoretical maximum population the planet could support is therefore 540 billion. Of course this calculation ignores many crucial factors. There is no slack for reductions in food supply caused by disease or climate fluctuation, and these calculations allow little space for other ecosystems outside the polar regions. However, the physics alone suggests we should have no problems feeding 10 billion people or possibly several times that number, even without food from the sea and fish farms.

On the negative side, three factors are increasing the 'virtual' population beyond its actual numbers. We have discussed the issue of large developing nations like China shifting their diet towards meat, which may be only 10 per cent as efficient as vegetable production, and again in China pet ownership is increasing, adding to household meat demands. The third factor is increasing obesity. The global obesity rate is now about 7 per cent, 500 million out of 7 billion. If the world reached current US levels of obesity, 35 per cent, by 2050 we would effectively have an extra billion 'people' to feed, since adipose tissue also has energy requirements. Food wastage is the first issue we should tackle. Globally 30–50 per cent of the 4 billion tons of food produced globally is never eaten (Fox, 2013); in 2012, between 1.2 and 2 billion tons of food was wasted. In less-developed countries, food may be destroyed in wars, and considerable amounts are eaten by pests, or rot, between the farm and the retailer. Inefficient slow transport infrastructure, lack of cold storage facilities in rural areas, or insecure storage facilities prone to water and rodent penetration, are often to blame. However, in these countries the consumer is often very efficient at utilizing food; inedible scraps are fed to pigs and chickens which can themselves be eaten. In India, some 30–40 per cent of food rots between farm and retailer, compared with under 10 per cent in the USA. In the more-developed world, including the urbanized portion of many poorer countries, the picture is reversed; the supply chain from farm to retailer becomes much more efficient, but the consumer and retailer are more wasteful, as discussed below.

Reducing food waste. *Waste not, want not*

Sell-by dates are a major cause of food waste in richer countries; many consumers do not understand the difference between 'use by', 'sell by' and 'best before'. The first phrase refers to perishable foods such as dairy products and raw meat, and is an important indicator of food safety; beyond this date the food may be unsafe to consume. However, the last two phrases are used on food that may decline in quality, e.g. lose taste, if consumption is deferred, but will still be safe to eat, for example biscuits, frozen food and tinned food. Consumers routinely throw out food that is past its 'sell by' date that was perfectly edible. Sell-by dates are more helpful to the food retailer as they assist in efficient stock rotation. Even 'use by' dates can cause edible food to be discarded; ready meals have 'use by' dates that are very short, in case the purchaser leaves them in the hot boot of a car for hours after buying them, accelerating any spoilage. The law also wastes food; it is illegal in the UK to give food past its sell-by date to hostels for the homeless, which hosted an average 30,000 sleepers per night in Britain in 2011. Food packaging is another source of waste; due to geographically extended supply chains, much food in wealthier countries is excessively packaged. Not only did energy and raw materials go into that packaging, but it creates landfill, like the wasted food itself, which uses energy and scarce road space; food in landfill also produces greenhouse gases including methane and CO_2. Fifteen per cent of the UK consumer's food bill is for packaging (Gabriel and Lang, 1998: 15). A shift towards fresh foods and cooking with raw ingredients would reduce the consumption of food packaging, especially if that food was also grown locally, in back gardens, allotments and urban farms. When food is wasted, the resources used in its production and transport are also wasted: water, energy, fuel, labour, land, fertilizer and weed killers, machinery and buildings, not to mention the soil degradation and erosion associated with some farming practices. In 2012 an estimated 550 billion cubic metres of water was used to grow food that was never eaten. However, well-designed packaging can extend food life; an example is Modified Atmosphere Packaging (MAP) that delays bacterial or fungal spoilage. Going a little further, edible packaging is being developed by a UK company called Pepceuticals that could cover meat like chicken skin. Biodegradable packaging may help solve the landfill problem, although the optimal solution is still to eat local and use less packaging. Locally produced food will also have a longer home shelf-life as it reaches the consumer more quickly; remember the reason why battered fish and chips was invented (Chapter 4).

Consumer behaviour also wastes food. Misshapen but edible fruit and vegetables are binned by shops because consumers are fussy about the appearance of these items. Consumers could cut out mouldy or bruised parts of fruit and vegetables, but often throw the whole item away. Supermarkets are adept at persuading customers to buy more with BOGOFs, Buy One Get One Free. The supermarket benefits as the consumer feels they have got better value and is then liable to buy expensive luxuries, and the pre-offer price may have been manipulated so the BOGOF is not such a bargain anyway. But we love that extra free courgette anyway, and often it lies in the fridge uneaten until it has gone bad. Large fridges persuade us to buy more food; a big fridge looks emptier than a small one with the same amount of food inside, so we buy extra food, extra milk, but we do not eat it any faster and food ends up stale and is discarded. Households with children tend to waste more food, an annual average of £550 as against £430 food waste for all households (Donnelley, 2009), because mothers may want to buy healthily but at mealtimes children's preferences for sugary food often win out. Stressed parents know what their children should eat, but may be in no mood to enforce this in the home. Even simple procedures such as making a shopping list can reduce consumer food waste, but a third of supermarket shoppers do not have one.

Food waste is a considerable financial burden. In the UK in 2006 an average of £424 worth of food per household was discarded, although this had dropped to 6.7 million tons in 2009, as a result of the financial constraints of the Credit Crunch. In 2010 Britain's food waste rose again to 7.2 million tons or 250 kg per household per year, a total of 8.3 million tons. Even the 2009 figure represented £10.2 billion worth of food, 30 per cent of the food Britons bought, of which 10 per cent had not even gone bad, and a further 50 per cent was past its best but still edible. That food waste included 150 million ready meals, 5 million potatoes, 4.4 million apples, 1 million loaves of bread and 1 million slices of ham. For 2012, household food waste in the UK was estimated as £480 per household, or £12 billion in total. British retailers also bin large quantities of edible food past its sell-by date, as do restaurants, hospitals and schools. Retail food waste in the UK was estimated as 360,000 tons in 2011, and total food wasted, by households, retailers and other eateries, as 11 million tons. Food waste per household in the USA is not dissimilar to the UK; by contrast German households, much more frugal with food than the British, waste just 15 kg of food a year. A 2005 estimate put food waste in America at $587 annually. The proportion of food wasted in the USA has risen from 28 per cent of total food purchased in 1974 to 40 per cent in 2009, or 40 million tons a year. If three-quarters of all food waste could be eliminated, we would then raise the global food supply by half, and could feed a population of 10.5 billion. Some supermarket fruit and vegetables, spurned by customers because it is 'too ugly', are recycled back into the food chain as animal feed. However, because humans only capture as little as 10 per cent of the nutrition value of animal feed as meat, this recycling still wastes up to 90 per cent of the food value of those discarded items.

Consumers may have to accept that the supermarket miracle of strawberries in December is unsustainable; we need to reconnect our diet to the seasons, as far as possible, to minimize food waste and energy used in food production and transport. The word 'seasonal' in some supermarkets has lost its original meaning to become a marketing ploy to enhance impressions of freshness, so that tomatoes grown in hothouses, or chocolate, is labelled 'seasonal' (perhaps they mean chocolate eggs in April). We probably could not expect Britons to subsist totally on home-grown foods in January, and tomatoes grown in warm Spanish climes and then flown to the UK may have less energy impact than those grown in the UK in heated greenhouses, but foods like avocados would have to become scarcer and more expensive if their price reflected their full environmental impact, journey to the shop and externalities included. At the grassroots level (literally), consumers can do much to make the food system more sustainable, and enjoy cheaper healthier food as a result. Food Swap websites have sprung up across the USA, Canada, UK and other countries since the first such site was begun by Hillary Condon in San Diego, California, in 2011; unwanted household food can be sold, swapped or given to others rather than being thrown away.

More radically, we may need to rediscover the 'Dig for Victory' principles that fed Britain during World War Two, as discussed in Chapter 7, where we saw how every available scrap of land, from gardens to urban parks, was utilized for vegetable production; schemes like Ashram Acres and the East London Family Project carry on the idea today. As we saw above, it takes surprisingly little land to feed a human being. A plot of just 300 square metres can supply the calorie and protein needs for a person on a (rather spartan) vegan diet, eating mainly potatoes; a more varied diet with plenty of fruits, vegetables and legumes would require 700 square metres, and replacing a third of the Calories in this diet with Calories from milk and eggs would double the requirement, to 1,400 square metres. However 'a typical European omnivorous diet requires five times the amount of land required for a vegan diet' (The Vegan Society, 2012) and some beef cattle fed on grain may yield as little as 2.5 per cent of their gross energy input into food energy for humans. Producing meat, we need 5,000 square metres of land per person (Fox, 2013). Allowing for access roads and housing, and if sufficient inputs like water are available, we could feed ourselves at a density of 500 persons per square kilometre. The population of the UK could feed and house itself on 120,000 square kilometres, or about half the total area of the UK, not accounting for seafood inputs.

While 1.52 billion people are vegetarian, just 75 million are vegetarian by choice; 1.45 billion are vegetarian due to poverty. Rising incomes among the poor, who have the highest population growth rates, will send global meat and grain demand soaring. If Chinese annual meat consumption per capita rises from its current 60 kg to current US levels (124 kg/year), and the Chinese population levels out as predicted at around 1.4 billion, an extra 96 million tons of beef will be consumed; if this came from feedlots, a further 672 million tons of grain would be consumed (adapted from Madeley, 2002: 147). This is equivalent to almost the entire 2012 grain harvest from China (479 million tons) and the European Union (274 million tons) combined (Earth Policy Institute, 2013), and we have not even considered increasing Indian meat consumption, with its projected increase from 1.2 billion now to 1.5 billion by 2050. Although Hindus are customarily vegetarian, a trend towards secularism may erode this practice. We may need adopt the Chinese proverb 'eat food with fewer legs'. That is, eat what stands on one leg (plants, mushrooms) more than what stands on two (chickens) and more than what stands on four (animals). Since fish have no legs, probably they are good to eat too.

Cuba in 1990 showed the world how a modern version of Dig for Victory might work, in an economic, not military, war. Prior to 1990 Cuba had enjoyed considerable material support from the USSR enabling it to withstand an economic blockade by the USA, but in 1990 the USSR collapsed. Supplies of cheap Soviet food and subsidized fertilizer and weed killer dried up, and the entire island was forced to convert en masse to organic agriculture (Rosset and Cunningham, 1999: 291). Fidel Castro arranged for garden tools, seed and advice to be made available, and street markets (previously banned) were legalized. As in UK's Dig for Victory, even lawns were not sacrosanct; the front lawn of Cuba's Ministry of Agriculture was dug up by its employees for vegetable plots. It was all organic, with no artificial fertilizer or weed killer (by necessity). Life was indeed hard until trade with Venezuela picked up in 2004, but Cuba's 11 million people did not starve, until a hurricane in 2008 disrupted food supplies. Much urban waste, even human waste, could be used as fertilizer, as it is now in China. Middle-class Europeans eating rice may not wish to reflect too much on the lack of plumbed toilets in the rice fields of Southern Asia. Many Chinese cities already recycle their urban waste to the nearby *xian* or rural area, where fruit and vegetables are grown, making China's largest cities almost self-sufficient in food (Girardet, 1992: 162). Multiple cropping is another innovative way to raise food yields per hectare, as was routinely practised on pre-industrial plots in Africa and Asia before the Green Revolution and the dominance of the multinationals, the modern-day *latifundia*. Multiple cropping can raise food yields per hectare by a factor of three, and in some traditional systems up to 22 crops are grown together (Lappe et al., 1998: 80). As in World War Two, inedible household food waste can feed pigs, or poultry, creating more food, so long as it is separated from glass, bones, paper, metal and other hazardous waste. However, since the 2001 foot and mouth outbreak in the UK, food waste from catering areas or school canteens cannot be fed to pigs, forcing farmers to buy expensive feed. DEFRA stated there is no problem with retailers giving out of date fruit and vegetables to pigs, but it is cheaper for retailers just to bin it all. Urban areas would need adapting to keep pigs; the north London suburb of Tottenham was once famous for its sausages, made from pigs fed on London's recycled scraps (Steel, 2008: 280), and we may need to revive this tradition. While waste food can be processed into methane in anaerobic digesters, producing renewable energy, this is still inefficient considering the energy and other inputs that went to produce the food in the first place.

The fate of the Egyptian Zabbaleen ('garbage collectors' in Arabic) illustrates how cultural and political factors can thwart sustainable food practices, just as the legal system can. Since the early twentieth century the Zabbaleen, a Christian minority, have collected Cairo's rubbish. They took this refuse to their home village of Mokattam on the edge of Cairo and sorted it into combustible plastic and paper, recoverable metals, and food waste which they fed to pigs, a practice impermissible to Muslims. The pork was eaten by the Zabbaleen or sold to hotels catering for European tourists. Before the Zabbaleen migrated to Cairo from rural Egypt, combustible rubbish went to heat Cairo's many public baths but by the 1930s oil became the preferred heating fuel. However, in 2003 Cairo awarded the refuse-collection contract to a multinational firm, stating that the Zabbaleen's donkey carts were unsightly and a traffic hazard, even though the multinational's mechanized lorries could not access many of Cairo's narrow lanes. Cairo, expanding at a rapid rate, wanted to relocate the Zabbaleen further out, saying that Mokattam was unhygienic, lacked amenities such as sewerage, and was badly polluted by smoke from burning rubbish; since the Zabbaleen recycling system has been dismantled, rats and disease have increased. In 2009 Egypt ordered that all pigs be culled in response to the H1N1 flu virus, although no cases of this virus ever occurred in Egypt's pigs, or people. What did occur from 2009 was increasing unrest in the Arab world, as the global Credit Crunch impoverished many. This unrest was brought into sharp focus by the self-immolation of an unemployed Tunisian graduate in December 2010; unable to obtain work, he took to selling food from an unlicensed cart, until the police confiscated his stall. That event sparked the Arab Spring and the overthrow of President Mubarak by the Muslim Brotherhood in 2011, resulting in greater Islamification of Egyptian society. In 2013 the Egyptian Army seized back power from the Brotherhood, and Mubarak was released from custody, but the Zabbaleen system has gone forever. As ever, attaining a sustainable and healthy food system requires far more than simply reforming the food chains.

Technology and food. *Producing beef without cows*

An alternative to lifestyle-changing sustainable food practices is to use technology to boost our food supply, a continuation of the Green Revolution. GM crops might bring the next 'revolution', creating strains of rice and grain that can withstand both flooding and drought, if such foods ever gain general public acceptance. Another idea is to modify plants to fix nitrogen directly from the air; nature gave us nitrogen-fixing bacteria that depend on a key enzyme to do their job that is destroyed by oxygen, and photosynthesis produces oxygen. The nitrogen-fixers must therefore hide from light, only functioning at night or deep in the plant's root system; scientists aim to insert bacterial genes in plants so they can fix their own nitrogen directly (*New Scientist*, 2011b: 44). Less technophobically, precision farming has developed to where satellites can track a tractor, and soil conditions, to the nearest metre, delivering just the right amount of water and fertilizers, and the soil conditions can be mapped in 3D, allowing for the depth of plant roots. Fields of the future might be sowed and harvested by solar-powered unmanned robot tractors. Or soil can be dispensed with altogether; aquaculture and aquaponics are growing fast.

We might totally reinvent the way we produce food, completely urbanizing it. In 2012 humanity became an urban species, with 50 per cent of us living in cities, and by 2050 the UN expects this figure to rise to 70 per cent. By then much of our food could be produced in urban tower blocks, similar to the 'plantscraper', a vertical urban vegetable farm, built in Sweden (Future News Network, 2013). Effectively creating farmland out of thin air, and producing food where it is needed, minimizing transport costs, plantscrapers can be high-tech, with environments precisely manipulated to maximize productivity. Plants can be grown using only red-blue light, since green light does not contribute to photosynthesis but may overheat the crop, raising water losses through transpiration. Light can be provided for 20 hours a day; not 24 because the plants need 'rest', but an improvement on nature's 12-hour average daylight. City waste would be recycled at close range as water and fertilizer, plant nutrients enhanced by algae tanks. Energy could be gathered from solar panels, supplemented by geostationary satellites beaming down microwaves from solar panels in space. Fish and meat might be produced this way too. Aquaculture could be sited in the lower levels, and plants at the top; in the middle we would produce beef without the aid of cows. Winston Churchill, back in 1932, questioned the absurdity of growing an entire chicken, feathers and bones, just to create a chicken breast. A beef burger was created from cultured cow muscle cells in 2010, by Professor Mark Post of the University of Maastricht; it cost US$250,000 and was bland, tasteless and soggy, according to a journalist who tasted it. Meat is not just an amorphous mass of muscle cells; you need adipose cells (fat) for flavour, and real steak has structure with nerves, blood vessels and gristle. The flavour of meat is not just its cells and blood, but derives from the Maillard reaction, a partial conversion of proteins into caramelized sugars produced by cooking. An alternative 'artificial meat' is already in the supermarkets: Quorn, meat-like food derived from plant proteins. Such artificial meats could raise difficult ethical issues. Would they be suitable for vegetarians? Will the 'yuk factor' put consumers off – consumers who have never been inside a real, bloody, abattoir? The price of 'real' meat would likely soar as it became both scarce and costly to produce; is it fair that only millionaires would ever taste it? Further intractable issues would arise from the economic impacts of such a transformation in the meat industry. What would we do with all the surplus grazing land, and what would be the impact on rural employment, and village life, in both developing and developed countries? On the positive side, greenhouse gas emissions would fall sharply; cattle are a major source of methane. Converting grazing land to forest or wilderness would reduce soil erosion and lock up more CO_2, and wildlife would benefit, although conversion of grazing land to recreation areas might encourage more car travel from the cities; alternatively more land would be available for biofuels or non-food crops such as cotton. What, too, would be the fate of the world's small rural towns?

Regarding global food production, we stand not at a fork in the road but a crossroads. Ahead is business as usual, right is more technology in the food chain, artificial meat, food from urban skyscraper factories, and left is 'Dig for Victory', sustainability and local food production. Business as usual will produce ever more violent swings in food prices, with a general trend upwards, this instability boosted by food commodity speculation. Poorer countries will suffer famines as their food production is seized by the wealthy, while the economy of wealthier nations will suffer higher inflation and wage demands, and reduced consumer expenditure on non-food; house prices will fall and unemployment rise. Political instability and migrant flows will increase as will the risk of war. The right hand turn will initially appear to provide what the consumer wants, or is persuaded to want through marketing messages, without major changes in consumer lifestyles, but has a techno-fear yuk factor. This option raises the power of large corporations in the food chain, and enhances the power of developed nations over poorer ones. There may be unforeseen technical problems, leading to the need for more techno-fixes. As noted above, the right turn will eventually produce major changes in our lifestyles, especially for those now living in smaller rural communities. The left turn demands more lifestyle changes upfront, but is more sustainable in the long run. Leftwards lies a major drop in consumption, probably leading to some economic disruption and unemployment, but not nearly as great as the disruption from business as usual. The local-sustainable option might lead us to question whether we really need all the consumption we have now: cosmetics, hairdressers, beauty regimes, garden centres, fashion clothes soon discarded, rapidly obsolescent electronic goods that supplant real face-to-face social interaction. We might start to question whether we really need (and can afford, environmentally as well as economically) two or even one car per household. Do we need to fly to remote resorts rather than holiday in our home country? Do we need to work five days a week when lower consumption would free us up for a four-day weekend, albeit with one or two of those days spent in the vegetable garden? This option too might cause some global economic disruption; the economies of countries like China would need redirecting away from exports which would no longer be in demand by America and Europe.

What choices we make regarding our future food system, and who we allow to make these choices, will have impacts far beyond our dinner plates and our health, affecting almost all aspects of our lives and culture. The choices made should be fair, informed and democratic. The final chapter of this book reviews the research questions we need to answer in order to achieve a fair and healthy food system, and presents an alternative welfare-to-foodfare system that will assist our transition to a sustainable diet for all.

9 From welfare to foodfare

Food is far more than a collection of vital nutrients with a pleasant taste, smell and texture. As we saw in Chapters 3 and 4, food has deep cultural significance, it links us to our familial and national origins, to our religion and society, to our friends and locality. Food is a powerful weapon for social and political change; from the Netherlands to the USSR to Chile, food has created countries, shaped political systems and changed geography through warfare; changing food production systems have also changed the map, altering the landscape beyond recognition to our pre-industrial ancestors. Mankind's transition from hunter-gathering to farming gave us nationalism, warfare, castles, cities, luxury goods, social elites and inequalities. Food impacts significantly on our economy, from balance of trade and economic power to the looming tsunami of health costs resultant from our preferences for quick, fast, convenient, but unhealthy diet. Today we stand on the brink of further major changes in our food production system that will likely bring us equally profound changes in our society and lifestyles.

Three concepts will be crucial to shaping the foodscape of tomorrow: education, persuasion and economics. Once consumers are persuaded to eat healthily and sustainably, and can afford to do so, and know how to, the free market will tend towards a greater provision of easy access to such foods for all. Education, of all age groups, is important, and can perhaps be done cheaply, through leaflets; repeated mass distribution and targeted at key points such as doctors' surgeries and hospitals, food retailers, schools and workplaces. In 2013, leaflets can be printed *and* distributed for under 10p a household. So a campaign of four different leaflets a year, each one delivered three times, would cost just £1.00 per household, or £25 million per annum for the entire UK. Raise the cost to £35 million and leaflets in different languages could additionally be distributed in certain urban areas with large ethnic minorities, with culturally adapted dietary advice. Food has a wide range of cultural, emotional and psychological attributes which need to be taken into account in any successful healthy-eating initiative. This sum is a tiny fraction of the costs imposed by obesity-related diseases. Education should be aimed at young children under 10, and their parents, as dietary habits are set early in life. Leaflets and other messages such as TV adverts could include simple but informative dietary advice, and recipes that are cheap, appetizing and nutritious, easy to prepare, and which do not need specialist kitchen equipment like blenders. For example, a white sauce (or 'roux' for the food literati) can be prepared in five minutes with oil, butter, flour and milk, and is the basis for a wide range of sauces. Add a starch ingredient (pasta, rice, potato), a protein ingredient (tinned tuna, salmon, meat) and a vegetable (boiled broccoli, carrots, courgettes) and you have a simple meal that does not require complex herbs unobtainable in Rotherham, that costs scarcely more than £1 per person and can be made in 20 minutes, with multiple variations from the same basic set of ingredients and cooking techniques. Avoid processed manufactured puddings as much as processed savoury food; fruits can be made into crumbles, jellies, blueberries or raspberries added to ice cream; all will help to reach the 5-a-Day target in ways acceptable to children. As time goes by, the fruit element can be enhanced and the artificial sugars reduced. Dietary advice could include what foods are seasonal, how to make soups out of less attractive vegetables, even how to grow food at home, in the garden or in a window box. Dietary advice in the past has been contradictory, leading to confusion or to all dietary messages being discounted and ignored; all communication must be consistent and simple. Advice and contact numbers for starting gardening groups and community gardens might be included, together with helpful horticultural tips. Research and performance, uptake and monitoring would reveal the optimal media for these varied food and gardening messages. Not all would take up the advice immediately, but as a few took up healthier diets shops would begin to stock more fresh produce; an emphasis on communal growing might start community groups that would grow and propagate, achieving a snowball effect as people passed on information to others.

Lifestyle and exercise measures can also be simple, easy to adopt, and not life-changing; the government could achieve much by involving employers and involving the private sector in CSR initiatives, for example promoting low-intensity exercise such as short walks, walk and talk instead of email, using stairs not the lift, parking further from the office or town centre. Employers could give bonuses for stairs use (monitored perhaps by swipe cards), parking could be cheaper in car parks further out, or even on the far side of existing large car parks, companies could sponsor safe cycle routes (as they now do at roundabouts), employers could organize weekend walks and pay bonuses for attending, canteens could be awarded points for nutritious food. Companies would receive a payback in fewer sick days; the environment would benefit as many of these changes also reduce energy demand. In general, instigators have to be imaginative, and have continuous commitment, and responders need to be motivated, and rewarded, short and long term. Initiatives must be maintained, and joined up, not a muddle of fragmented disconnected plans.

As noted in Chapter 7, nudge tactics may be better than direct financial incentives. The psychology of 'nudges' is barely five years old and much research remains to be done on how to maximize the efficacy of 'nudges'.

Research is also needed on what motivates people to cook, to avoid microwave meals, to make time to prepare food; is it health concerns, or pride, or creativity, or cost or environmental considerations, or relaxation (some people do find cooking relaxing, some the opposite)? The answers to this will feed into the 'nudge' debate. Likewise further research is needed into the sociology and psychology of food – Why do we eat? A deceptively simple question, whose answer is, hopefully, not just 'to maintain nutrition'; if so we are just 'feeding as fuel', like filling the car. Remember that animals eat, but only humans dine. Nutraceuticals is another area ripe for further research, especially in the areas of diabetes and satiety-inducing foods that maintain adequate nutrition. A final disturbing but under-researched question was noted in Chapter 1 – the declining levels of micronutrients in foods, and whether this has any effect on appetite and satiety. Although organic foods are pricier per kilogram than intensively farmed foodstuffs, what are the relative costs per microgram of zinc or vitamin B, for example? We might find that what we are saving on intensively produced food is outweighed by future health costs.

The government could implement innovative fiscal measures to promote healthy eating; extending the concept of variable VAT (sales tax) rates by introducing negative rates on healthy food items. The cost would be recouped in lower healthcare bills, although only some years into the future. Since obesity and poor diet are closely linked to poverty, the welfare state could be reorganized to become the Foodfare State, to promote not just socio-economic well-being and financial equality but nutritional health and food opportunity too. In the UK in 1942 William Beveridge published his eponymous report which formed the basis for the post-war welfare state. He spoke of 'Slaying Five Giants' – Want, Disease, Squalor, Ignorance and Idleness. A similar list could apply to today's food situation – Want (poverty, unaffordability, of healthy food), Disease (obesity, diabetes), Sugar (too much in our diet), Ignorance (of cooking, nutrition) and Idleness (not cooking, not growing our own food where we possibly could). In practical terms, several measures could be taken now by central government to achieve the aims of a 'foodfare state'.

- Allow benefits claimants to sell home-grown food, allotment food, without clawback.
- Have food banks in Jobcentres.
- Dietary advice leaflets, gardening advice and recipe cards in Jobcentres.
- Since food is a major fraction of daily spending for the poor, give advice on food budgeting at Jobcentres. This would create a healthier workforce.
- Increase the food budget at schools and hospitals, and monitor for food healthiness. Rate these institutions on food as well as educational and health outcomes.
- Revisit the minimum wage and state pension to ensure these cover the costs of a healthy diet. Although a considerable 'health premium' (Chapter 6) exists now, particularly in less-affluent areas, if other measures were

implemented this premium might be expected to shrink, reducing the cost of this initiative.

- Provide guaranteed long-term funding, and advice, for setting up community gardens in communal gardens areas of blocks of flats. Disseminate best practice, and help council-rented house occupiers to pool their garden areas into vegetable gardens.
- Link with medical practitioners to provide nutritional guidance to 'at risk' patients, those with high BMIs.
- Link with schools, especially those in deprived areas, to provide dietary advice. Assist schools to retain open land for play activities and for growing food. Also link to community centres, catering for various groups (elderly, disabled, ethnic minorities, etc.) for the same purpose. For the mentally and physically disabled, gardening can be therapeutic.
- Liaise with councils to retain allotments.
- Survey urban areas for unused land that could be used for food production. Implement incentives for landowners, including utilities, etc., to allow this, and perhaps tax unused derelict land. However, subsidize the clean-up of polluted derelict land so it becomes suitable for urban farming.
- Implement a corporate tax programme that lowers the tax burden for food manufacturers and retailers producing healthier foods, and raises the tax for those producing more HFSS foods. Introduce negative VAT on healthy food as discussed above (but beware the perils of the 'fat tax').
- Discuss with all employers how to improve the diet (all three meals) of employees and introduce incentives for moderate exercise.
- Target gardens, and garden centres, to achieve a shift in emphasis from 'decoration' to food production. Use variable VAT rates to advantage food-producing goods sales (hoes, seeds) over hot tubs and herbaceous borders, or at least grow edible herbs there.
- Liaise with state-owned media channels and advertise on commercial channels to publicize these initiatives.

Food is a complex good, full of contradictions. It is a private good but also a quasi-public one, carrying as it does major cost implications for public and private health services. Food is a material good, but also incorporates many intangible factors, cultural, national and psychological. Food feeds us now but has long-term future effects on our physiology. All these factors need balancing in the food chain. Desired social change has happened, long-term and assisted by government measures, in several areas. Attitudes to smoking have changed profoundly, and car drivers now accept seat belts and far more regulation than they did 50 years ago. Changes to household waste are in the process of being modified, as we accept more recycling and become more aware of environmental considerations over the personal convenience of just discarding things. Food may be the next such arena of social change. Perhaps we can not only reduce food waste but come to see the consumption of junk food, high HFSS food, as a form of food waste; enjoyable now but, like smoking, creating costly health issues in the future.

One of the greatest legacies of the post-war generation of the 1940s and 1950s was the creation of a welfare state that ameliorated much, if not all, poverty and financial uncertainty for many. Perhaps the legacy of the post-millennium generation will be to deliver to our children a healthy and sustainable food system.

Bibliography

Abubakari, A. R., Lauder, W., Agyemang, C., Jones, M., Kirk, A. and Bhopal, R. S. (2008) 'Prevalence and time trends in obesity among adult West African populations: A meta-analysis', *Obesity Reviews*, 9(4): 297–311.

Acheson, D. (1998) *Independent Inquiry into Inequalities in Health*, London: HMSO.

Albertini, A., Tripodi, A., Fabbri, A., Mattioli, M., Cavrini, G., Cecchetti, R., Dalle Donne, E., Cortesi, C., De Girogi, S., Contarini, V., Andreotti, L., Veronesi, B., Stefanelli, I. and Di Martino, E. (2008) 'Prevalence of obesity in 6- and 9-year old children living in Central-North Italy: Analysis of determinants and indicators of risk of overweight', *Obesity Reviews*, 9(1): 4–10.

Al-Kandari, Y. Y. (2006) 'Prevalence of obesity and its relation to sociocultural variables', *Obesity Reviews*, 7(2): 147–54.

Alston, J. M., Mullally, C. C., Sumner, D. A., Townsend, M. and Vosti, S. A. (2009) 'Likely effects on obesity from proposed changes to the US Food Stamp Program', *Food Policy*, 34(2): 176–84.

Anderson, J. L. (2009) 'Lard to lean: Making the meat-type hog in post-World War II America', in W. Belasco and R. Horowitz (eds.) *Food Chains*, Philadelphia, PA: University of Pennsylvania Press.

Apparicio, P., Cloutier, M. and Shearmur, R. (2007) 'The case of Montreal's missing food deserts: Evaluation of accessibility to food supermarkets', *International Journal of Health Geographics*, 6(4), online.

Atkins, P. and Bowler, I. (2001) *Food in Society*, London: Arnold.

Australian Social Trends (2001) Australia, Australian Bureau of Statistics.

Averett, S. L., Sikora, A. and Argys, L. M. (2008) 'For better or worse: Relationship status and body mass index', *Economics and Human Biology*, 6: 330–49.

Avery, D. (1999) 'The fallacy of the organic Utopia', in J. Morris and R. Bate (eds.) *Fearing Food*, Oxford: Butterworth Heinemann.

Baines, J. (1973) *The Environment*, London: Batsford.

Ball, K., Timperio, A. and Crawford, D. (2009) 'Neighbourhood socioeconomic inequalities in food access and affordability', *Health and Place*, 15(2): 578–85.

Barthomeuf, L., Rousset, S. and Droit-Volet, S. (2009) 'Emotion and food: Do the emotions expressed on other people's faces affect the desire to eat liked and disliked food products?' *Appetite*, 52: 27–33.

Barton, H. (2000) *Sustainable Communities*, London: Earthscan Publications.

Battersby, J. (2011) 'The state of urban food insecurity in Cape Town, South Africa', *Urban Food Security* 11, Queen's University, Kingston, Ontario.

Bauman, Z. (1993) 'The sweet scent of decomposition', in C. Rojek and B. Turner (eds.) *Forget Baudrillard?*, London: Taylor & Francis.

Bauman, Z. (2011) *Collateral Damage*, Cambridge: Polity Press.

Belanger-Ducharme, F. and Tremblay, A. (2005) 'Prevalence of obesity in Canada', *Obesity Reviews*, 6: 183–6.

Belasco, W. (2008) *Food: The Key Concepts*, Oxford: Berg.

Bell, D. (2007) 'The hospitable city: Social relations in commercial spaces', *Progress in Human Geography*, 31(1): 7–22.

Bell, D. and Valentine, G. (1997) *Consuming Geographies*, London: Routledge.

Block, D. and Kouba, J. (2006) 'A comparison of the availability and affordability of a market basket in two communities in the Chicago area', *Public Health Nutrition*, 9(7): 837–45.

Blythman, J. (2006) *Bad Food Britain*, London: Fourth Estate.

Bockerman, P., Johansson, E., Jousilahti, P. and Uutela, A. (2008) 'The physical strenuousness of work is associated with an upward trend in the BMI', *Social Science and Medicine*, 66: 1346–55.

Buchanan, A. (1982) *Food Poverty and Power*, Nottingham: Spokesman.

Bugge, A. B. and Almås, R. (2006) 'Domestic dinner: Representations and practices of a proper meal among young suburban mothers', *Journal of Consumer Culture*, 2: 203–28.

Butland, B., Jebb, S., Kopelman, P., McPherson, K., Thomas, S., Mardell, J. and Parry, V. (2007) *Foresight Report, Tackling Obesities: Future Choices*, London: UK Government.

Cannon, G. (1987) *The Politics of Food*, London: Century Hutchinson.

Caraher, M., Dixon, P., Lang, T. and Carr-Hill, R. (1999) 'The state of cooking in England: The relationship of cooking skills to food choice', *British Food Journal*, 101(8): 590–609.

Carolan, M. (2012) *The Sociology of Food and Agriculture*, Abingdon: Routledge.

Carter, R. and Moodie, M. (2005) 'The cost-effectiveness of obesity prevention', in D. Crawford and R.W. Jeffery (eds.) *Obesity Prevention and Public Health*, Oxford: Oxford University Press.

Clarke, I., Hallsworth, A., Jackson, P., De Kervenoael, R., del Aguila, R. and Kirkup, M. (2006) 'Retail restructuring and consumer choice', *Environment and Planning A*, 38(1): 25–46.

Cohen, D. (2007) *Academy Sharing Knowledge*, Issue 26, Spring, http://askmagazine.nasa.gov/issues/26/26pr_interview.html, accessed 23 December 2012.

Collingham, L. (2011) *The Taste of War*, London: Penguin.

The Consumers' Association (2004) 'Ready-packed fruit and veg "lose nutrients"', *The Guardian*, 4 June: 7.

Cook, D. C. and Rodgers, J. (1999) 'Community food security: A growing movement', in D. H. Boucher (ed.) *The Paradox of Plenty*, Oakland, CA: Food First Books.

Cook, I. (2008) 'Geographies of food: Mixing', *Progress in Human Geography*, 32(6): 821–33.

Cooke, L. J. and Wardle, J. (2005) 'Age and gender differences in children's food preferences', *British Journal of Nutrition*, 93: 741–6.

Cornell Chronicle (2013) 'Organic food labels create perception of healthier fare', http://www.news.cornell.edu/stories/2011/04/organic-food-label-imparts-health-halo-study-finds, accessed 20 April 2013.

Cornish Pasty Association (2013) http://www.cornishpastyassociation.co.uk/cornish-pasty-historical-information/, accessed 15 April 2013.

Costa-Font, J. and Gil, J. (2008) 'What lies behind socio-economic inequalities in obesity in Spain? A decomposition approach', *Food Policy*, 33: 61–73.

Countryside Agency (2003) *State of the Countryside*, London: UK Government.

Coveney, J. and O'Dwyer, L. A. (2009) 'Effects of mobility and location on food access', *Health and Place*, 15: 45–55.

Crawford, M. (2005) 'The Saturday Essay', *The Grocer*, 20 August.

Cressey, G. (1988) 'Ashram Acres: Where nothing is wasted', *Town and Country Planning*, 57: 109–10.

Critser, G. (2003) *Fat Land*, London: Penguin.

Cross-Government Obesity Unit (2008) *Healthy Weight, Healthy Lives: A Cross-Government Strategy for England*, London: Cross-Government Obesity Unit.

Cummins, S. and Macintyre, S. (2002) 'A systematic study of an urban foodscape: The price and availability of food in Greater Glasgow', *Urban Studies*, 39(11): 2115–30.

Cutler, D. M., Glaeser, E. L. and Shapiro J. M. (2003) 'Why have Americans become more obese?', *Journal of Economic Perspectives*, 17(3): 93–118.

Damasio, A. R. (1996) *Descartes' Error: Emotion, Reason and the Human Brain*, Basingstoke: Macmillan.

Darmon, N., Briend, A. and Drewnowski, A. (2004) 'Energy-dense diets are associated with lower diet costs: A community study of French adults', *Public Health Nutrition*, 7(1): 21–7.

Davies, H. (2006) 'Thinking outside the box', *The Times*, 1 April: 10.

Davis, B. (1984) *Food Commodities*, London: Heinemann.

Davis, D. (1966) *A History of Shopping*, London: Routledge & Kegan Paul.

Davison, K. K. and Campbell, D. (2005) 'Opportunities to prevent obesity in children within families: An ecological approach', in D. Crawford and R. W. Jeffery (eds.) *Obesity Prevention and Public Health*, Oxford: Oxford University Press.

Dawson, J., Marshall, D, Taylor, M., Cummins, F., Sparks, L. and Anderson, A. (2008) *Accessing Healthy Foods*, report for the Food Standards Agency (Scotland), Scotland: UK Government.

DEFRA (2012) *Food Statistics Pocketbook 2012*, London: UK Government.

DETR (2000) *Our Countryside: The Future, a Fair Deal for Rural England*, London: Department for Environment, Transport and the Regions.

Donkin, A. J., Johnson, A. E. and Lilley, J. M. (1998) 'Gender and living alone as determinants of fruit and vegetable consumption among the elderly living at home in urban Nottingham', *Appetite*, 30: 39–51.

Donkin, A. J., Dowler, E. A., Stevenson, S. J. and Turner, S. A. (1999) 'Mapping access to food at a local level', *British Food Journal*, 101(7): 554–64.

Donnelley, R. R. (2009) *Recipe for Success: Scotland's National Food and Drink Policy*, Edinburgh: Scottish Government.

Dryzek, J. and Schlosberg, D. (2003) *Debating the Earth*, Oxford: Oxford University Press.

Duany, A, Plater-Zyberk, E. and Speck, J. (2000) *Suburban Nation: The Rise of Sprawl and the Decline of the American Dream*, New York: North Point Press.

Earth (2002) *The Guardian*, 1 August.

Earth Policy Institute (2013) http://www.earth-policy.org/indicators/C54, accessed 24 September 2013.

Earthwire (2013) http://www.earthwire.org/uk/?sed=2006-02-21, accessed 6 June 2013.

Eckert, J. and Shetty, S. (2011) 'Food systems, planning and quantifying access: Using GIS to plan for food retail', *Applied Geography*, 31: 1216–33.

The Economist (2003) 'Spoilt for choice: A survey of food', 13 December: 34.

The Economist (2011a) 'Lone sharks', 1 October: 62.

The Economist (2011b) 'If you build it they may not come', 9 July: 43.

The Economist (2011c) 'The struggle to eat', 16 July: 45–6.

The Economist (2012a) 'Travellers checked', 19 May: 65.

The Economist (2012b) 'The basket case', 23 June: 31.

The Economist (2012c) 'A fat chance', 17 November: 42.

The Economist (2013a) 'The British at table', 27 July: 25–6.

The Economist (2013b) 'Let's move slowly', 9 March: 53.

Ekinsmyth, C. (2002) 'Feminist cultural geography', in P. Shurmer-Smith (ed.) *Doing Cultural Geography*, London: Sage.

Ennew, C., McDonald, S., Morgan, W. and Strak, J. (1995) 'Overview of the UK food and drink industry', in J. Strak and W. Morgan (eds.) *The UK Food and Drink Industry*, Cambridge: Euro PA and Associates.

Eurofood (2007) 'McDonald's study triggers calls for tighter fast-food marketing', 8 August: 13.

Evans, L. T. (1989) *Feeding the Ten Billion*, Cambridge: Cambridge University Press.

Falk, P. (1994) *The Consuming Body*, Thousand Oaks, CA: Sage.

Feagan, R. (2007) 'The place of food: Mapping out the "local" in local food systems', *Progress in Human Geography*, 31(1): 23–42.

Ferguson, S. (1971) *Food*, London: Batsford.

Filozof, C., Gonzalez, C., Sereday. M., Mazza. C. and Braguinsky, J. (2001) 'Obesity prevalence and trends in Latin-American countries', *Obesity Reviews*, 2: 99–106.

Food (2003) *The Guardian*, 10 May.

Food Ethics Council (2010) *Food Justice: The Report of the Food and Fairness Enquiry*, Brighton: Food Ethics Council.

Food Magazine (2004a) 'How much does obesity cost?', 65: 11.

Food Magazine (2004b) 'Parents go hungry to feed their children', 66: 11.

Food Magazine (2007) 'FSA confirms link between poverty and poor diet', 78: 19.

Food Magazine (2008) 'Healthy food costs more', 80: 6.

Forbes (2013) 'The U.S. gets left behind when it comes to working women', http://www.forbes.com/sites/brycecovert/2013/01/16/the-u-s-gets-left-behind-when-it-comes-to-working-women/, accessed 20 September 2013.

Fox, M. A. (1999) *Deep Vegetarianism*, Philadelphia, PA: Temple University Press.

Fox, T. (2013) *Global Food, Waste Not Want Not*, London: Institute of Mechanical Engineers.

Francis, P., Price, J. and Yapp, K. (2000) *Never on a Sunday*, Shropshire: Scenesetters.

Fraser, D. (1980) *The Evolution of the British Welfare State*, London: Macmillan.

French, S. A., Story, M. and Jeffery, R. W. (2001) 'Environmental influences on eating and physical activity', *Annual Review of Public Health*, 22: 309–35.

Friel, S., Walsh, O. and McCarthy, D. (2004) *The Financial Cost of Eating Well*, Working Paper 04/01, Ireland: Combat Poverty Agency.

Fry, J. and Finley, W. (2005) 'The prevalence and costs of obesity in the EU', *Proceedings of the Nutritional Society*, 64: 359–62.

Future News Network (2013) http://futurenewsnetwork.com/index.php?option=com_content&view=article&id=65568%3Aplantagon-breaks-ground-on-its-first-%E2%80%98plantscraper%E2%80%99-vertical-farm-in-sweden!&catid=80%3Agreen-architecture&Itemid=169&lang=en, accessed 18 March 2013.

Gabriel, Y. and Lang, T. (1998) *The Unmanageable Consumer*, London: Sage.

Gallup (1999) *Gallup Study of Changing Food Preparation and Eating Habits*, Princeton, NJ: Gallup.

Gardner, C. (1989) *Consuming Passion*, London: Unwin.

George, S. (1999) 'Latin America: Going to extremes', in D. H. Boucher (ed.) *The Paradox of Plenty*, Oakland, CA: Food First Books.

Gerrard, C., Janssen, M., Smith, L., Hamm, U. and Padel, S. (2013) 'UK consumer reactions to organic certification logos', *British Food Journal*, 115(5): 727–42.

Girardet, H. (1992) *The Gaia Atlas of Cities*, London: Gaia Books.

Gluckman, P. and Hanson, M. (2012) *Fat, Fate, and Disease*, Oxford: Oxford University Press.

Gluckmann, M. and Nolan, J. (2007) 'New technologies and the transformations of women's labour at home and work', *Equal Opportunities International*, 26(2): 96–112.

Goffman, E. (1979) *Gender Advertisements*, New York: Harper & Row.

Goh, E. C. L. (2013) '"You must finish your dinner": Meal time dynamics between grandparents, parents and grandchildren in urban China', *British Food Journal*, 115(3): 365–76.

Gottlieb, R., Fisher, A., Dohan, M., O'Connor, L. and Parks, V. (1996) *Homeward Bound: Food-Related Strategies in Low-Income and Transit Dependent Communities*, Working Paper 336, University of California Transportation Centre.

Gould, B. W. and Villarreal, H. J. (2006) 'An assessment of the current structure of food demand in urban China', *Agricultural Economics*, 34: 1–16.

Grant, W. (1989) 'Public and political implications', in C. R. W. Spedding (ed.) *The Human Food Chain*, London: Elsevier.

Greater London Authority (2010) *Cornered Shops*, London: London Assembly.

The Grocer (2007) 'Store visit: The Polish deli', 21 July: 34.

The Grocer (2008) 'Can Indies do fresh?', 24 May: 32–4.

The Grocer (2009) 'Five a day the city C-Store way', 21 March: 46–8.

The Grocer (2011) 'Women eating less fruit and veg for the fourth year in a row', 16 April: 6.

Groves, A. (2003) *The Teenage Diet Now and in the Future*, Report for the Institute of Grocery Distribution, Watford, UK.

The Guardian (2004) 'France gives in to TV dinners', 8 October: 17.

The Guardian (2006) 'Cities in double jeopardy from Post Office closures', 4 December: 14.

The Guardian II (2011) 'The art of protest', 27 May: 12–13.

Haldrup, M., Koefoed, L. and Simonsen, K. (2006) 'Practical Orientalism: Bodies, everyday life and the construction of otherness', *Geografiska Annaler B: Human Geography*, 88(2): 173–84.

Hallam, D. and Midmore, P. (1995) 'Sugar and sweeteners', in J. Strak and W. Morgan (eds.) *The UK Food and Drink Industry*, Cambridge: Euro PA & Associates.

Hallett IV, L. F. and McDermott, D. (2011) 'Quantifying the extent and cost of food deserts in Lawrence, Kansas, USA', *Applied Geography*, 31: 1210–15.

Harcombe, Z. (2010) *The Obesity Epidemic*, Cwmbran: Columbus Publishing.

Hare, C. (2003) 'The food shopping experience: A satisfaction survey of older Scottish consumers', *International Journal of Retail and Distribution Management*, 31(5): 244–55.

Harnack, L. J. and Schmitz, K. H. (2005) 'The role of nutrition and physical activity in the obesity epidemic', in D. Crawford and R. W. Jeffery (eds.) *Obesity Prevention and Public Health*, Oxford: Oxford University Press.

Harrigan, P. (2013) 'The rite way of cooking: Food for thought', http://livingheritage.org/rite-cooking.htm, accessed 23 July 2013.

Harrington, G. (1989) 'Meat', in C. R. W. Spedding (ed.) *The Human Food Chain*, London: Elsevier.

Harrison, P. (1990) *Inside the Third World*, London: Penguin.

Health Select Committee Report (2004) *Obesity*, London: HMSO.

Heaton, S. (2001) *Organic Farming, Food Quality and Human Health*, Bristol: Soil Association.

Hendrickson, D., Smith, C. and Eikenberry, N. (2006) 'Fruit and vegetable access in four low-income food desert communities in Minnesota', *Agriculture and Human Values*, 23(3): 371–83.

Herbst, K. C. and Stanton, J. L. (2007) 'Changes in family dynamics predict purchase and consumption', *British Food Journal*, 109(8): 648–55.

HMSO (1990) *Family Expenditure Survey*, London: UK Government.

HMSO (1996) *Family Spending 1995/6*, London: UK Government.

HMSO (2003) *Family Spending: A Report on the* 2001–02 *Expenditure and Food Survey*, London: UK Government.

Horne, P. J., Tapper, K., Lowe, C. F., Hardmann, C. A., Jackson, M. C. and Woolner, J. (2004) 'Increasing children's fruit and vegetable consumption: A peer-modelling and rewards-based intervention', *European Journal of Clinical Nutrition*, 58: 1649–60.

Horton, R. (2012) 'The global burden of disease 2010', *The Lancet*, 380(9859): 2053–4.

Hulsegge, G., Susan, H., Pivavet, J., Blokstra, A., Nooyens, A., Spijkerman, A., van der Schouw, Y., Smit, H. and Vershuren, W. (2013) 'Today's adult generations are less healthy than their predecessors: Generation shifts in metabolic risk factors – the Doetinchem Cohort Study', *European Journal of Preventive Cardiology*, published online 10 April 2013, doi: 10.1177/2047487313485512.

Humphreys, J. (2001) *The Great Food Gamble*, London: Hodder & Stoughton.

The Independent (2010) 'Birthplace of "drive-thru" turns its back on fast food', 6 July: 33.

Jabs, J. and Devine, C. M. (2006) 'Time scarcity and food choices: An overview', *Appetite*, 47(2): 196–204.

Jackson, S. (2003) *A Healthy Diet – Accessible to All*, report for Dudley Health Authority and Dudley Metropolitan Borough Council, Birmingham, UK.

Jamal, A. (1998) 'Food consumption among ethnic minorities: The case of British-Pakistanis in Bradford, UK', *British Food Journal*, 100(5): 221–7.

Janke, K., Propper, C. and Shields, M. (2013) *Does Violent Crime Deter Physical Activity?*, CMPO Working Paper No. 13/312, University of Bristol, UK.

Johnstone, G. M. (1976) 'The growth of the sugar trade and refining industry', in D. J. Oddy and D. S. Miller (eds.) *The Making of the Modern British Diet*, London: Croom Helm.

Jones, P., Comfort, D. and Hillier, D. (2008) 'Moving towards sustainable food retailing', *International Journal of Retail and Distribution Management*, 36(12): 995–1001.

Joseph, M. (1991) *Sociology for Everyone*, Cambridge: Polity Press.

Juliano, B. O. (1985) 'Biochemical properties of rice', in B. O. Juliano (ed.) *Rice: Chemistry and Technology*, St Paul, MN: American Association of Cereal Chemists.

Kalof, L., Dietz, T., Stern, P. C. and Guagnano, G. A. (1999) 'Social psychological and structural influences on vegetarian beliefs', *Rural Sociology*, 64(3): 500–11.

Kim, D. M., Ahn, C. W. and Nam, S. Y. (2005) 'Prevalence of obesity in Korea', *Obesity Reviews*, 6: 117–21.

Kirchhoff, S., Smyth, H., Sanderson, J., Sultanbawa, Y. and Gething, K. (2011) 'Increasing vegetable consumption: A means–end chain approach', *British Food Journal*, 113(8): 1031–44.

Klinitzke, G., Steinig, J., Kersting. A. and Wagner, B. (2013) 'Obesity and suicide risk in adults: A systematic review', *Journal of Affective Disorders*, 145(3): 277–84.

Lacey, R. (1991) *Unfit for Human Consumption*, London: Souvenir Press.

Lagi, M., Bar-Yam, Y., Bertrand, K. Z. and Yaneer Bar-Yam, Y. (2012) 'The food crises: Predictive validation of a quantitative model of food prices including speculators and ethanol conversion', arXiv:1203.1313, 6 March.

Lake, A. (2006) 'Obesogenic environments: Exploring the built and food environments', *Journal of the Royal Society for the Promotion of Health*, 126: 262–7.

Lakkakula, A., Geaghan, J., Zanovec, M., Pierce, S. and Tuuri, G. (2010) 'Repeated taste exposure increases liking for vegetables by low-income elementary school children', *Appetite*, 55: 226–31.

Lang, T. and Heasman, M. (2004) *Food Wars*, London: Earthscan.

Langevin, M. S. and Rosset, P. (1999) 'Land reform from below: The landless worker movement in Brazil', in D. H. Boucher (ed.) *The Paradox of Plenty*, Oakland, CA: Food First Books.

Lappe, F. M., Collins, J. and Rosset, P. (1998) *World Hunger: 12 Myths*, London: Earthscan.

Lappe, F. M., Collins, J. and Rosset, P. (1999) 'Beyond guilt and fear', in D. H. Boucher (ed.) *The Paradox of Plenty*, Oakland, CA: Food First Books.

Larsen, K. and Gilliland, J. (2008) 'Mapping the evolution of "food deserts" in a Canadian city: Supermarket accessibility in London, Ontario, 1961–2005', *International Journal of Health Geographics*, 7: 1–16.

Lavik, R. and Kjørstad, I. (2005) *Kjøtt, holdninger og endring 1997 til 2004* [Meat attitude and changes 1997–2004], Report No. 5, Oslo National Institute for Consumer Research.

Lawrence, M. (2005) 'The potential of food regulation as a policy instrument for obesity prevention in developing countries', in D. Crawford and R. W. Jeffery (eds.) *Obesity Prevention and Public Health*, Oxford: Oxford University Press.

Lee, R. D. and Nieman, D. C. (2013) *Nutritional Assessment*, 6th edition, New York: McGraw-Hill.

Levitt, S. D. and Dubner, S. (2005) *Freakonomics*, London: Penguin Books.

Ligthelm, A. A. (2005) 'Informal retailing through home based micro enterprises', *Development in Southern Africa*, 22(2): 199–214.

Locke, J. (2009) 'Climate change-induced migration in the Pacific region: Sudden crisis and long-term developments', *Geographical Journal*, 175(3): 171–80.

Logemann, J. (2012) 'Beyond self-service: The limits of "Americanization" in post-war West German retailing', in R. Jessen and L. Langer (eds.) *Transformations of Retailing in Europe after 1945*, Farnham: Ashgate.

London Development Agency (2005) *Better Food for London: The Mayor's Draft Food Strategy*, London: London Development Agency.

Lorenz, K. (1977) *Behind the Mirror: A Search for a Natural History of Human Knowledge*, London: Methuen.

Low Income Project Team (1996) *Low Income, Food Nutrition, and Health: Strategies for Improvement*, report published for the Nutrition Task Force, UK Government.

Lowell, J. (2004) 'The food industry and its impact upon increasing global obesity: A case study', *British Food Journal*, 106(3): 238–48.

Madeley, J. (2002) *Food for All*, London: Zed Books.

Malik, M. and Bakir, A. (2007) 'Prevalence of overweight and obesity among children in the United Arab Emirates', *Obesity Reviews*, 8(1): 15–20.

Marketing Week (2006) 'London Underground seeks "breakfast" sampling partner', 9 February: 15.

Marshall, N. (1995) *Services and Space*, London: Longman.

Mathias, P. (1976) *The First Industrial Nation*, London: Methuen.

Merck Veterinary Manual (2012) http://www.merckvetmanual.com/mvm/index.jsp?cfile=htm/bc/206914.htm, accessed 3 August 2012.

Miljkovik, D., Ngnaje, W. and de Chastenet, H. (2008) 'Economic factors affecting the increase in obesity in the United States: Differential response to price', *Food Policy*, 33: 48–60.

Miller, D. (1998) *A Theory of Shopping*, Cambridge: Polity Press.

Mincyte, D. (2008) *Food Culture, Globalization, and Nationalism: Zeppelins in the Lithuanian Imagination*, report for the National Council for Eurasian and East European Research, published by the University of Illinois, USA.

Moisio, R., Arnould, E. J. and Price, L. L. (2004) 'Between mothers and markets', *Journal of Consumer Culture*, 4(3): 361–84.

Momtaz, N. J., Alizadeh, S. and Vaghefi, M. S. (2013) 'A new model for assessment fast food behaviour case study', *British Food Journal*, 115(4): 601–13.

Moran, J. (1996) 'Hum, ping, rip: The sounds of cooking; we talk River Café but we eat ready-made from the microwave. It's the private vice of the modern middle class', *New Statesman*, 134(4724): 12.

Morland, K. B. and Evenson, K. R. (2009) 'Obesity prevalence and the local food environment', *Health and Place*, 15: 491–5.

Morris, D., Freeland, J., Hinchcliffe, S. and Smith, S. (2003) *Changing Environments*, Chichester: Wiley.

Nasjonalforeningen for folkehelse (1998) *Slåring om fellesmåltidet* [Encircle the family meal], Oslo: Nasjonalforeningen for folkehelse.

National Obesity Observatory (2013) http://www.noo.org.uk/uploads/doc/vid_14069_noo_DB_AdultWtSocStatus3_221211.pdf, accessed 2 July 2013.

Nelson, M., Erens, B., Bates, B., Church, S. and Boshier, T. (2007) *Low Income Diet and Nutrition Survey*, report published by the Food Standards Agency, UK.

New Scientist (2010) 'Junkie food', 4 September: 38–41.

New Scientist (2011a) 'The legacy of BSE', 29 January: 3.

New Scientist (2011b) 'A blue-green revolution: Upgrading photosynthesis', 19 February: 44–5.

New Scientist (2011c) 'One minute with Robert Lustig', 24 September: 35.

NHS (2012) http://www.nhs.uk/Livewell/5ADAY/Pages/Portionsizes.aspx, accessed 12 June 2012.

Nottinghamshire County Council (2007) *Access to Healthy Food in Ashfield*, report published by Nottinghamshire County Council, UK, July.

The Observer (2004) 'Why food won't taste as good as it looks', http://www.theguardian.com/media/2004/oct/31/food.advertising, accessed 4 May 2013.

The Observer Magazine (2013) 'The demon drink', 4 August: 14–19.

Olson, C. M. and Holben, D. H. (2002) 'Position of the American Dietetic Association: Domestic food and nutrition security', *Journal of the American Dietetic Association*, 102(12): 1840–7.

O'Neill, M. (2005) *Putting Food Access on the Radar*, report published by the National Consumer Council and Staffordshire County Council, UK.

Paarlberg, R. (2010) *Food Politics*, New York: Oxford University Press.

Pain, G. (1967) *Planning and the Shopkeeper*, London: Barrie & Rockcliffe.

Pan, W. H., Lee, M. S., Chuang, S. Y., Lin, Y. C. and Fu, M. L. (2008) 'Obesity pandemic, correlated factors and guidelines to define, screen, and manage obesity in Taiwan', *Obesity Reviews*, 9(1): 22–31.

Patel, R. (2008) *Stuffed & Starved*, London: Portobello Books.

Pawson, E. (2008) 'Biotic exchange in an imperial world: Developments in the grass seed trade', in C. Stringer and R. Le Heron (eds.) *Agri-Food Commodity Chains and Globalising Networks*, Aldershot: Ashgate.

Pearce, J., Blakely, T., Witten, K. and Bartie, P. (2007) 'Neighborhood deprivation and access to fast-food retailing: A national study', *American Journal of Preventive Medicine*, 32(5): 375–82.

Pearce, J., Hiscock, R., Blakely, T. and Witten, K. (2009) 'A national study of the association between neighbourhood access to fast food outlets and the diet and weight of local residents', *Health and Place*, 15: 193–7.

Perrett, D. L., Whitehead, R. D. and Ozakinci, G. (2013) 'Eating fruit and vegetables gives your skin a healthy glow', *British Academy Review*, 21(January): 2–6.

Poggi, G. (2004) *The Development of the Modern State*, Redwood City, CA: Stanford University Press.

Pollard, S. (1963) *The Development of the British Economy 1914–50*, London: Edward Arnold.

Ponting, C. (1991) *A Green History of the World*, New York: Penguin.

Poole, J. (1996) *Coming of Age with Elephants*, Chicago: University of Chicago Press.

Poster, M. (2001) *Jean Baudrillard: Selected Writings*, Oxford: Blackwell.

Powell, L. M., Zhenxiang, Z. and Wang, Y. (2009) 'Food prices and fruit consumption amongst young American adults', *Health and Place*, 15: 1064–70.

Power, M. L. and Schulkin, J. (2009) *The Evolution of Obesity*, Baltimore, MD: Johns Hopkins University Press.

Pringle, H. and Thompson, M. (2001) *Brand Spirit*, Chichester: Wiley.

Propper, C. (2005) 'Why economics is good for your health: 2004 Royal Economic Society Public Lecture', *Health Economics*, 14: 987–97.

Raja, S., Ma, C. and Yadav, P. (2008) 'Beyond food deserts: Measuring and mapping racial disparities in neighbourhood food environments', *Journal of Planning Education and Research*, 72: 469–82.

Raynor, M. and Scarborough, P. (2005) 'The burden of food related ill health in the UK', *Journal of Epidemiology and Community Health*, 59: 1054–7.

Reisig, V. and Hobbiss, A. (2000) 'Food deserts and how to tackle them: A study of one city's approach', *Health Education Journal*, 59: 137–49.

Relph, E. (1986) *Place and Placelessness*, London: Pion.

Reynolds, J. (2004) 'Introduction to retail strategy', in J. Reynolds and C. Cuthbertson (eds.) *Retail Strategy*, Oxford: Elsevier Butterworth Heinemann.

Rguibi, M. and Belahsen, R. (2007) 'Prevalence of obesity in Morocco', *Obesity Reviews*, 8(1): 11–13.

Richardson, T. L. (1976) 'The agricultural labourer's standard of living in Kent', in D. J. Oddy and D. S. Miller (eds.) *The Making of the Modern British Diet*, London: Croom Helm.

Ritzer, G. (1996) *The McDonaldization of Society*, Thousand Oaks, CA: Pine Forge Press.

Robinson, T. M., Borzekowski, D. L. G., Matheson, D. M. and Kraemer, H. G. (2007) 'Effects of fast food branding on young childrens' tastes', *Archives of Pediatrics & Adolescent Medicine*, 161(8): 792–7.

Rose, D. and Bodor, N. (2009) *Deserts in New Orleans? Illustrations of Urban Food Access and Implications*, University of Michigan National Poverty Centre / USDA Economic Research Service.

Rosset, P. and Cunningham, S. (1999) 'The greening of Cuba: Organic farming offers hope in the midst of crisis', in D. H. Boucher (ed.) *The Paradox of Plenty*, Oakland, CA: Food First Books.

Rozin, P. and Fallon, A. E. (1987) 'A perspective on disgust', *Psychological Review*, 94(1): 23–41.

Rudawska, I. (2001) 'New trends in food consumption in Poland versus Western countries', *British Food Journal*, 103(7): 495–500.

Sassatelli, R. and Davolio, F. (2010) 'Consumption, pleasure and politics: Slow food and the politico-aesthetic problematization of food', *Journal of Consumer Culture*, 10(2): 203–32.

Schlosser, E. (2002) *Fast Food Nation*, London: Penguin.

Schmeichel, B. J. and Inzlicht, M. (2013) 'Incidental and integral effects of emotions on self-control', in M. D. Robinson, E. R. Watkins and E. Harmon-Jones (eds.) *Handbook of Cognition and Emotion*, New York: Guilford Press.

Scott, R. (1976) *The Female Consumer*, New York: John Wiley.

Seitz, J. L. and Hite, K. A. (2012) *Global Issues*, Chichester: Wiley.

Self, P. and Storing, H. J. (1971) *The State and the Farmer*, London: George Allen & Unwin.

Sellaeg, K. and Chapman, G. E. (2008) 'Masculinity and food ideals of men who live alone', *Appetite*, 51: 120–8.

Seth, A. and Randall, G. (1999) *The Grocers*, Portsmouth, NH: Kogan Page.

Seymour, J. and Girardet, H. (1986) *Far from Paradise*, London: BBC.

Shaw, H. (2004) 'The ecology of food deserts', PhD thesis, School of Geography, University of Leeds, UK.

Shaw, H. (2006) 'Food deserts: Towards the development of a classification', *Geografiska Annaler B: Human Geography*, 88(2): 231–47.

Shaw, H. (2012) 'Food access, diet and health in the UK: An empirical study of Birmingham', *British Food Journal*, 114: 598–616.

Shaw, J. J. A. (2010) 'Against myths and traditions that emasculate women: Language, literature, law and female empowerment', *Liverpool Law Review: A Journal of Contemporary Legal Issues*, 31(1): 29–49.

Shaw, J. J. A. (2012) 'The continuing relevance of *Ars Poetica* to legal scholarship and the modern lawyer', *International Journal for the Semiotics of Law*, 25(1): 71–93.

Shaw, J. J. A. and Shaw, H. (2012) 'Economic accountability, regulatory reform and ethical management: Towards a new language of largesse', in A. M. Dávila Gómez and D. E. A. Crowther (eds.) *Human Dignity and Managerial Responsibility: Diversity, Rights, and Sustainability*, Aldershot: Gower.

Simmons, I. G. (1996) *Changing the Face of the Earth*, 2nd edition, Oxford: Blackwell.

Skeggs, B. (1997) *Formations of Class and Gender*, London: Sage.

Smith, J. and Jehlika, P. (2007) 'Stories around food, politics and change in Poland and the Czech Republic', *Transactions of the Institute of British Geographers*, 32(3): 395–410.

Smith, J. L. (2009) 'Empire of ice cream: How life became sweeter in the postwar Soviet Union', in W. Belasco and R. Horowitz (eds.) *Food Chains*, Philadelphia, PA: University of Pennsylvania Press.

Smith, K., Brown, B., Yamada, I., Kowaleski-Jones, L., Zick, C. and Fan, J. (2008) 'Walkability and body mass index: Density, design and new diversity measures', *American Journal of Preventive Medicine*, 35(3): 307–26.

Smoyer-Tomic, K. E., Spence, J. E. and Amrhein, C. (2006) 'Food deserts in the prairies? Supermarket accessibility and neighborhood need in Edmonton, Canada', *The Professional Geographer*, 58(3): 307–26.

Soil Association (2013) *Organic Market Report 2013*, Bristol: Soil Association.

Spedding, C. R. W. (1989) 'The food chain: Forging the links', in C. R. W. Spedding (ed.) *The Human Food Chain*, London: Elsevier.

Spencer, E. H., Elton, L. K. and Frank, E. (2007) 'Personal and professional correlates of US medical students' vegetarianism', *Journal of the American Dietetic Association*, 107(1): 72–8.

Steel, C. (2008) *Hungry City*, London: Chatto & Windus.

Stein, R. L. and Nemeroff, C. J. (1995) 'Moral overtones of food: Judgements of others based on what they eat', *Personality and Social Psychology Bulletin*, 21(5): 480–90.

Steinfield, H., Gerber, T., Wassemaar, V., Castel, M. and Rosales, C.H, (2006) *Livestock's Long Shadow: Environmental Issues and Options*, Food and Agricultural Organization, United Nations.

Stroebele, N. and de Castro, J. M. (2004) 'Television viewing is associated with an increase in meal frequency in humans', *Appetite*, 42(1): 111–13.

Sundquist, B. (2008) http://www.civilizationsfuture.com/bsundquist/gcia.html, accessed 3 October 2012.

Tansey, G. and Worsley, T. (1997) *The Food System*, London: Earthscan.

Teed, P. (1963) *Britain 1906–1951: A Welfare State*, London: Hutchinson Educational.

Thomas, C. (1989) 'Retail change in Greater Swansea: Evolution or revolution', *Geography*, 74: 201–13.

Thone, F. (1943) 'Victory gardens', *The Science Newsletter*, 43(12): 186–8.

The Times (2005) 'The ever expanding state of the union', 25 August: 12.

The Times II (2011) 'Skip meals', 25 March: 4–5.

Townsend, J. (2003) *Research towards a Shopping and Cleaning Strategy for Older People in Leeds*, report for the Nuffield Institute for Health, University of Leeds, UK.

Trubek, A. B. (2008) *The Taste of Place*, Berkeley, CA: University of California Press.

Turrell, G., Blakely, T., Patterson, C. and Oldenburg, B. (2004) 'A multilevel analysis of socioeconomic (small area) differences in household food purchasing behaviour', *Journal of Epidemiology and Community Health*, 58: 208–15.

US Department of Labor (2013) 'American time use survey 2012 results', http://usgovinfo.about.com/gi/o.htm?zi=1/XJ&zTi=1&sdn=usgovinfo&cdn=newsissues&tm=45&f=10&tt=2&bt=3&bts=36&zu=http%3A//www.bls.gov/tus/, accessed 23 September 2013.

Vadivel, V. and Biesalski, H. K. (2013) 'Antioxidant potential and health relevant functionality of Bauhinia purpurea L seeds', *British Food Journal*, 115(7): 1025–37.

Valuation Office Agency (2011) *Property Market Report 2011*, London: UK Government.

Van de Merwe, M. T. and Pepper, M. S. (2006) 'Obesity in South Africa', *Obesity Reviews*, 7(4): 315–22.

The Vegan Society (2012) http://www.vegansociety.com/resources/environment/land.aspx, accessed 24 July 2012.

Vejrup, K., Lien, N., Knut-Inge, K. and Bere, E. (2008) 'Consumption of vegetables at dinner in a cohort of Norwegian adolescents', *Appetite*, 51: 90–6.

Villarrubia, E. (2010) 'Why do Catholics eat fish on Friday?', Catholicism.org, 16 February, http://catholicism.org/why-do-catholics-eat-fish-on-friday-2.html, accessed 19 January 2013.

Wallendorf, M. and Arnould, E. J. (1991) 'We gather together: Consumption rituals of Thanksgiving Day', *Journal of Consumer Research*, 18(1): 13–31.

West, A. (1988) *A Handbook of Retailing*, London: Gower.

West, H. G. and Domingos, N. (2012) 'Gourmandising poverty food: The Serpa Cheese Slow Food Presidium', *Journal of Agrarian Change*, 12(1): 120–43.

Whelan, A., Wrigley, N., Warm, D. and Cannings, E. (2002) 'Life in a "food desert"', *Urban Studies*, 39(11): 2083–2100.

White, M., Bunting, J., Williams, L., Raybould, S., Adamson, A. and Matyers, J. (2004) *Do 'Food Deserts' Exist? A Multi-Level Geographical Analysis of the Relationship between Retail Food Access, Socio-Economic Position and Dietary Intake*, report to the Food Standards Agency, London, UK.

Whitehead, R. D., Re, D., Xiao, D., Ozakinci, G. and Perrett, D. I. (2011) 'You are what you eat: Within-subject increases in fruit and vegetable consumption confer beneficial skin-color changes', http://www.plosone.org/article/info:doi/10.1371/journal.pone.0032988, accessed 16 January 2013.

Williams, A. (1997) 'Relief and research', in D. F. Smith (ed.) *Nutrition in Britain*, London: Routledge.

Williams, R., Bush, H., Lean, M., Anderson, A. S. and Bradby, H. (1998) 'Food choice and culture in a cosmopolitan city: South Asians, Italians, and other Glaswegians', in A. Murcott (ed.) *The Nation's Diet*, Harlow: Longman.

Wind-Cowie, M. (2010) *Civic Streets: The Big Society in Action*, London: Demos.

Winham, D. M. (2009) 'Culturally tailored foods and cardiovascular disease prevention', *American Journal of Lifestyle Medicine*, 3(1): 64–8.

Woffinden, B. (2001) 'Cover-up', *The Guardian Weekend*, 25 August: 18–24.

Wright Mills, C. (1956) *The Power Elite*, Oxford: Oxford University Press.

Wrigley, N. (2002a) '"Food deserts" in British cities: Policy context and research priorities', *Urban Studies*, 39(11): 2029–40.

Wrigley, N. and Lowe, M. (2002) *Reading Retail*, London: Arnold (Houghton).

Wrigley, N., Warm, D., Margetts, B. and Whelan, A. (2002) 'Assessing the impact of improved retail access on diet in a "food desert": A preliminary report', *Urban Studies*, 39(11): 2061–82.

Wrigley, N., Warm, D. and Margetts, B. (2003) 'Deprivation, diet, and retail food access: Findings from the Leeds "food deserts" study', *Environment and Planning A*, 35: 151–88.

Wrigley, N., Warm, D., Margetts, B. and Lowe, M. (2004) 'The Leeds "food deserts" intervention study: What the focus groups reveal', *International Journal of Retail and Distribution Management*, 32(2/3): 123–36.

Wrigley, N., Lowe, M., Guy, C., Wood, S. and Shaw, H. (2007) *Relocalising Food Shopping*, report published by the University of Southampton, UK.

Yorkshire Post (2000) 'Children's health report', 11 April: 9.

Young, B. (2012) 'State of the Nation England' *2012*, London: Diabetes UK.

YouTube (2012) http://www.youtube.com/watch?v=Z0bnXI4nTUQ, accessed 10 October 2012.

Zick, C. D., Smith, K. R., Fan, J. X., Brown, B. R., Yamada, I. and Kowaleski-Jones, L. (2009) 'Running to the store? The relationship between neighbourhood environment and the risk of obesity', *Social Science and Medicine*, 69(10): 1493–500.

Index